The Social Psychology
of Adolescence

Patrick C. L. Heaven

palgrave

First edition 1994 published as *Contemporary Adolescence*
Second edition 2001 published by
PALGRAVE
Houndmills, Basingstoke, Hampshire RG21 6XS and
175 Fifth Avenue, New York, N. Y. 10010
Companies and representatives throughout the world

PALGRAVE is the new global academic imprint of
St. Martin's Press LLC Scholarly and Reference Division and
Palgrave Publishers Ltd (formerly Macmillan Press Ltd).

ISBN 0–333–92164–X hardback
ISBN 0–333–92165–8 paperback

This book is printed on paper suitable for recycling and made from fully managed and sustained forest sources.

A catalogue record for this book is available from the British Library.

Library of Congress Cataloging-in-Publication Data
Heaven, Patrick C. L. (Patrick Charles Lionel)
   The social psychology of adolescence / Patrick C. L. Heaven.
       p.   cm.
   Includes bibliographical references and index.
   ISBN 0–333–92164–X(cloth)
     1. Adolescence.   2. Teenagers.   3. Teenagers—Social conditions.   I. Title.

HQ796 .H385 2001
305.235—dc21

2001031521

10   9   8   7   6   5   4   3   2   1
10 09 08 07 06 05 04 03 02 01

Printed in China

For Andrew, Cara, Matthew and Philip

Contents

List of Tables and Figures

Tables

Figures

Preface

Adolescence usually encompasses the second decade of life. Unlike other stages or periods of the life span, it has sometimes been referred to as a time of *transition*, as a time of *storm and stress*, and as a time of being *marginalised*. Teenagers are no longer children, yet are not quite adult. Physically, they are maturing rapidly. Emotionally and cognitively, however, their transition to adulthood appears somewhat slower. It is as though adolescents do not clearly fit into any life stage. That is what makes the adolescent years so different and why, for so many adolescents, this period of life is exciting and challenging, yet often filled with turmoil and confusion.

Being an adolescent at the start of the twenty-first century is more difficult than ever (see also Hamburg, 1990). There are several reasons for this. Firstly, adolescence is now much longer. The average age of menarche, for example, is lower than before. Moreover, many more adolescents than a generation ago undergo post-school training, thus remaining financially dependent on their parents beyond their teenage years. Compare this to the late 1800s, when adolescents were a cheap source of labour in the rapidly expanding industries of Western Europe and the USA (Grinder, 1990).

There are also other reasons why being an adolescent is now more difficult. One factor is the erosion of family and social support networks, as well as the easy access that adolescents now have to drugs, alcohol and other life-threatening substances such as weapons and vehicles (Hamburg, 1990). Thus, not only is adolescence a time of transition, but adolescents are also highly *vulnerable* to emotional maladjustment and a range of behaviours such as early sexual activity and associated health risks, depression, suicide, drug use, delinquency and dropping out of school.

RATIONALE OF THIS BOOK

This is the second edition of my book *Contemporary Adolescence: A social psychological approach* which was first published in 1994. As is the case with new editions, this version is somewhat different from the first. For a start, some chapters have changed their position in the text or had their titles amended. All have been re-drafted and updated; some material has been deleted, while new material has been added where suitable. Nearly every section has been updated in order to bring to the reader the very latest findings or developments regarding adolescent development. Those familiar with the old edition will notice that the adolescent 'Profiles' have been deleted and Research Highlights have been added into every chapter. These are close-up views of particular research studies and have been designed to emphasise a particular facet of adolescent behaviour.

The book examines the psychological principles associated with the *social* development of adolescents. This is not to suggest that the physical/biological and cognitive aspects of adolescent development are not of prime importance; they are. This book, however, will concentrate on the social aspects of development, noting implications for adjustment.

It differs from most psychological texts on adolescent development in some important respects. Firstly, it is not US-centred. Although it does cite evidence from the USA, it does also, where possible, cite evidence based on data drawn from other cultures, including Hong Kong, Russia, Australia, New Zealand, Canada, Africa, Scandinavia and elsewhere. Secondly, this book attempts an in-depth review of psychological research findings, rather than the more descriptive review of results typical of many books in this area. The book is, therefore, directed at those students, parents and professionals who are keen to read a little more deeply than usual.

OVERVIEW

Chapter 1 introduces the reader to the field of study. It reviews some of the earliest and current images of youth. How have adolescents typically been portrayed? How does this differ from current stereotypes? It is noted that the teenage years, although regarded as 'intense' and rather 'exuberant', are not necessarily a time of storm and stress. A very important part of this chapter is the review of theoretical perspectives. The chapter does not consider all possible theories, only those regarded as the most influential have been included and evaluated. The contribution of each to understanding adolescent development is considered. Theoretical points are referred to again at the end of each chapter.

In the second chapter, we consider identity formation and the search for self. Since adolescents are in the period of transition to adulthood, an important developmental task is the search for identity. The chapter will consider various identity statuses and their implications for adolescent adjustment. The chapter concludes by considering the self-concept and the development of a sex-role identity.

Chapter 3 notes the importance of family processes in adolescent development. Important are factors such as differences in parenting styles, parent–child communication and the psychological health of parents. A significant section of the chapter is devoted to adolescent reactions to parental separation and divorce, and to how adolescents cope with living in new families. It is noted that it is not the family structure as such that is important when considering adolescent adjustment, but it is the nature and quality of parenting in new families which help determine adolescent emotional stability.

The influences of friendships and peer groups are dealt with in Chapter 4. As friends are an important source of emotional support and affiliation, the chapter discusses the nature of friendships and peer groups as well as their specific functions and structure. The chapter also considers peer pressure and susceptibility to it, as well as the relative influence of parents versus peers. It concludes with reference to research on bullying at school.

The next chapter discusses the important topic of school life. There are many predictors of academic performance. The chapter discusses the importance of family life, the impact of family disruption, the role of personality factors and the role of causal attributions. It reviews school drop-outs as well as the effect of type of school on academic attainment. Two factors are important, namely, gender and state- vs. privately-funded schools. Finally, brief consideration is given to the transition from school to university.

Chapter 6 considers mental health. It notes the theoretical and empirical links between hopelessness, depression and suicide and discusses developmental trends in depression and the importance of hormonal, genetic, cognitive and other influences. With respect to suicide, incidence rates from numerous countries are recorded. The chapter concludes by noting the marked rise in suicide in rural areas and considers possible explanations for this phenomenon.

Sexuality is discussed in Chapter 7. According to the available evidence, factors such as the family, peers and hormonal factors are complexly interrelated in determining whether adolescents are likely to engage in sexual behaviour at an early age. A major section of the chapter deals with factors related to condom use and the accompanying threat of AIDS. The chapter also briefly reviews the question of sexual preference, sex offenders and adolescent prostitution.

Chapter 8 discusses the unique problems of teenagers who are also parents. It begins by discussing pregnancy resolution and the options of abortion, adoption and keeping the baby. It notes the birthing outcomes associated with teenage mothers as well as the psychosocial adjustment of children born to teenage parents. Attention is also paid to research into teenage fathers, while brief mention is made of longitudinal research into adolescent mothers. This research notes the immense variability in long-term outcomes of adolescent mothers.

Orientation to authority and delinquency are discussed in Chapter 9. There are several important theoretical perspectives on delinquency. The complex interaction between social factors (for example, delinquent groups) and biological predispositions as well as the role of personality traits in explaining delinquency is noted.

The working adolescent is discussed in Chapter 10 which notes the various developmental stages that children go through in acquiring beliefs about money, as well as a vocational identity. There are certain family and personality factors that must be considered in explaining work- and money-related beliefs. In addition, cultural differences in these beliefs have also been noted. A major section of the chapter deals with adolescents in the workplace as well as the psychological effects of unemployment. The final section deals with the importance of leisure.

PATRICK HEAVEN
Wollongong, New South Wales

Acknowledgements

The author and publishers would like to thank the following for permission to reproduce copyright material:

Table 1.1, from Roscoe and Peterson (1984), *Adolescence*, *19*, 391–6 (Libra Publishers);

Table 2.2, from Montemayor and Eisen (1977), *Developmental Psychology*, *13*, 314–19 (American Psychological Association);

Figure 2.1, from Shavelson et al. (1976), *Review of Educational Research*, *46*, 407–41 (American Educational Research Association);

Tables 8.2 and 8.3, from Correy et al. (1984), *Medical Journal of Australia*, *141*, 150–4 (Australian Medical Publishing Co. Ltd.);

Table 5.1, from Furnham and Gunter (1989), *The Anatomy of Adolescence*, London (Routledge);

Tables 5.4 and 5.5, from Graetz (1990), *Australian Journal of Education*, *34*, 174–91 (Australian Council for Educational Research Ltd.);

Table 10.1, from Furnham and Gunter (1989), *The Anatomy of Adolescence*, London (Routledge).

Every effort has been made to trace all the copyright holders but if any have been inadvertently overlooked the publishers will be pleased to make the necessary arrangements at the first opportunity.

1

General Introduction

INTRODUCTION

The scientific study of adolescence or the 'teenage years' is enjoying unprecedented attention not only from psychologists, but also other professionals. Whereas developmental psychologists previously tended to focus exclusively on the childhood years, there has, more recently, been a growing interest in the psychological study of the second decade of life. In the social sciences alone, this has resulted in an explosion of written material, the publication of journals entirely devoted to the nature of adolescence, and the establishment of professional societies and conferences dealing with its theoretical and applied problems (Petersen, 1988). Thus it would seem that the importance of sound enquiry and debate into the nature of adolescence has been established.

There are no doubt several reasons for this changing emphasis. One reason may be the higher than average levels of unemployment among young people (Winefield, 1997). Although typical of many Western nations during times of economic contraction, relatively high levels of youth unemployment are now also of growing concern in many developing countries, as they move towards market-driven economies. Whereas most youth were assured of some form of employment in the former Communist countries, this is no longer the case as unproductive factories and whole industries are either shut down or drastically restructured. Rapid technological and political changes have implications for those communities that have traditionally been reliant upon heavy industry or mining. Such change has had a major impact not only on the availability of jobs, but also on education policies, government training schemes, and so forth.

Another reason for the interest in adolescent development may lie in the relatively high levels of sexually transmitted diseases (STDs) among young people (Moore, Rosenthal and Mitchell, 1996). Consequently, behavioural scientists are expending research energy to study and hopefully understand the reasons for adolescents' risky sexual behaviours. Yet another compelling reason may be the relatively high rates of youth suicide in some countries (See Chapter 6). All of these factors have encouraged professionals to take a closer look at that period of the life span known as adolescence.

IMAGES OF YOUTH

To a large extent, perceptions of and concerns about adolescents derive from our own experiences with teenagers, as well as from available information. In this regard, the print and electronic media are powerful and influential sources of information (and mis-information), which serve to shape our perceptions, expectations, and stereotypes of youth (Furnham and Gunter, 1989).

A popular conception of adolescence is that it is a time of 'storm and stress', although some are doubtful about the amount of empirical evidence supporting this view (Petersen, 1988; Violato and Wiley, 1990; but see Arnett, 1999). Nonetheless, such a view of the teenage years has remained quite stable, over several hundred years. On the basis of a review of images of adolescence as reflected in English literature since the works of Chaucer, it was found that the adolescent years have usually been portrayed as turbulent, excessive, and filled with passion (Violato and Wiley, 1990). These authors remind us that Chaucer (1340–1400) described youth as frivolous, and as being devoted to love and silly pleasures. Shakespeare (1564–1616) saw adolescence as a time of exuberance, excess, passion, and sensuality, while Lewis Bayly (1565–1631) saw teenagers as individuals, without much character and as being rather coarse. As Bayly (cited in Violato and Wiley, 1990, 257) explained: 'What is youth but an untamed beast all whose actions are rash and rude, not capable of good council when it is given and ape like delighting in nothing but toys like babies.'

In the writings of Charles Dickens (1812–70), one theme that is developed is that of impetuosity. For instance, in *David Copperfield*, David falls on hard times, but later shows adolescent impetuosity and passion. Thus one might conclude with Violato and Wiley (1990, 262): 'Dickens uses David to depict the "storm and stress" of adolescence and the transcendent nature of the "goodness" of youth. For both David Copperfield and Oliver Twist, life was full of turbulence, excess, and passion.'

Twentieth-Century Views

In 1904, the American psychologist Stanley Hall first alerted the scientific community to the importance of adolescence as a life stage deserving formal and sound enquiry. In his attempts to lead the way, he borrowed heavily from the past, picking up on the idea of adolescence as a period of 'storm and stress' (Arnett, 1999; Dusek, 1991; Petersen, 1988; Violato and Wiley, 1990). Psychoanalytic writers, who saw teenagers as suffering from emotional turmoil (Susman, 1991), also took this point further. Perhaps as a consequence of such views, which tended to prevail until the 1960s and 1970s, problems and difficulties were thought to be quite typical of adolescence, and hence were not investigated (Petersen, 1988).

Although later writers may not have thought of adolescence as a particularly stressful period, the media continued to stereotype this life stage as, if not stressful, certainly turbulent. Nearly each decade of the twentieth century saw its peculiar representations of youth. Griffin (1993) points out the 'moral panic' that surrounded female sexuality just when women were asserting their independence with increasing vigour. During the 1950s and 1960s young African-Americans in the USA began to assert their civil rights at the same time that youth culture began to be increasingly expressed through music and film. Not surprisingly, perhaps, by the mid-1960s Adelson (1964) reported the media describing teenagers as 'moody' and suffering from 'wild enthusiasms' (1). Later, the typical youth was described as a 'symbol of renewal' and seen as a voice against injustice (Ewen, cited in Violato and Wiley, 1990).

By the end of the twentieth century many writers were questioning the notion of 'storm and stress'. In one review (Petersen, 1988), it was argued that there is little support for the idea that parents and adolescents suffer from the much-heralded 'generation gap' or that adolescent development is 'stormy'. Susman (1991) noted that, although some data suggest that adolescence may be a stressful stage of life, many findings are inconsistent. Indeed, it would appear that only a small proportion of adolescents in any group ever report feeling stressed. Although some teenagers may be maladjusted and engage in risky behaviours, most successfully meet the challenges of the adolescent years (Masten, 1991).

These views have been supported by a review of several research studies. Gecas and Seff (1990) cite a cross-cultural study conducted in ten countries that found that most of the adolescents surveyed had good relations with their families, and had a favourable attitude towards themselves. They were also relatively interested in work-related matters.

RESEARCH HIGHLIGHT 1.1
Representations of youth
Griffin, 1997

According to Griffin, the images or social representations we have of youth determine the social welfare policies we design for young people. The discourses we use when dealing with youth reflect these social representations and, ultimately, have an impact on our policies and strategies for assisting youth. Typically, the discourses centre around 'youth as trouble' or 'youth in trouble'. She suggests that 'In general, young men, especially if they are working class and/or black, are especially likely to be the focus of policies that operate with a "youth as trouble" discourse' (22). By contrast, when dealing with policies that pertain to young women, the discourse is of 'youth in trouble'.

In one of the studies, less than 10 per cent of the adolescents noted that family relationships across the teenage years had deteriorated. These findings suggest that most adolescents get on quite well with their school work, maintain satisfactory relationships with their parents, and at the same time prepare themselves for lives as adults.

Conger and Petersen share these sentiments and concluded as follows (1984, 26–7):

> While many adolescents face occasional periods of uncertainty and self-doubt, of loneliness and sadness, of anxiety and concern for the future, they are also likely to experience joy, excitement, curiosity, a sense of adventure, and a feeling of competence in mastering new challenges.

According to Arnett (1999) not all adolescents are likely to experience storm and stress although, of all the stages of the life span, the teenage years are the most volatile. Arnett's view is that, where adolescents do experience storm and stress, it is most likely to manifest itself in the following ways (319):

- conflict with parents – It is during the adolescent years that conflict with parents is at its most severe. Teenagers tend to be rebellious and to question those in authority (parents and teachers).
- mood disruptions – Adolescents are emotionally quite volatile. They can suffer extreme mood swings and frequent depressed mood.

- risky behaviours – Adolescents are more likely to engage in risky behaviours and are likely to harm either themselves or others.

DEVELOPMENTAL TASKS

The developmental tasks of a particular life stage are those skills, knowledge and functions that a person must acquire or master in order successfully to move to the following stage. Each stage of the life span has its own developmental tasks which involve motor, physical, social or emotional aspects of behaviour, and each task is normally mastered at the appropriate time. Being a unique stage in life, adolescence has its own associated problems, difficulties and developmental tasks. Children who do not successfully complete the developmental tasks of childhood will be at a disadvantage as they enter the teenage years. The same applies to adolescents moving into adulthood.

Some thirty years ago Havighurst (1972) proposed developmental tasks for various life stages and noted the following for adolescents:

- developing new relationships with peers of both sexes,
- acquiring a masculine or feminine social role,
- accepting one's physique and using the body effectively,
- becoming emotionally independent of parents and other adults,
- preparing for marriage and a family life,
- selecting and preparing for an economic career,
- acquiring values and an ethical system as a guide to behaviour,
- desiring and achieving socially responsible behaviour.

It is interesting to speculate to what extent these developmental tasks are relevant for young people in the early part of the twenty-first century. Just how important is it to 'prepare for marriage' when many young people in intimate relationships are not married? Indeed, just *how* does one 'prepare' for marriage?

Newman and Newman (1987) proposed a different set of tasks, focusing on those areas that are critical to the individual's social and psychological growth. Specifically, they concentrate on tasks they believe are relevant for modern Western society and suggest the following for those aged 12–18 years (320–51):

- physical maturation – adjust to changing body image,
- formal operations – ability to reason and think abstractly,

- emotional development – accept volatile emotions and mood swings,
- join peer groups – important for psychological development,
- heterosexual relations – opposite sex friendships become more important (also important for sexual identity).

They proposed the following tasks for those aged 18–22 years (373–92):

- autonomy from parents – regarded as a symbol of independence,
- sex role identity – adopt sex-role congruent with self-concept and body image,
- internalised morality – need to learn to exercise moral judgements and accept principles of justice,
- career choice – congruent with self-concept, attitudes, values, and ability.

There are some similarities between the tasks noted by both Havighurst and the Newmans. Some of these are:

- relationships with peers,
- emotional independence,
- preparation for career,
- sense of morality (or ethical system),
- development of a sex-role identity.

It seems that the tasks set out by the Newmans are also open to criticism. For instance, the importance of developing heterosexual relations excludes those youth who are not heterosexual. It is also quite likely that those youth in non-Western or in developing nations will have a different set of developmental tasks. Thus, developmental tasks are not fixed, do not apply equally to all youth and, to some extent, reflect the culture within which the adolescent lives (Hooker, 1991), as well as the social context of the writer.

To what extent are older adolescents *actually engaged* in developmental tasks? Are they fully preoccupied with the tasks of adolescence, or do they work on some tasks of childhood and early adulthood? This was the focus of a study of over 400 university undergraduates in the USA (Roscoe and Peterson, 1984). Most of the respondents were in their first year of study, with those who were married or parents not included in the analyses.

The students were presented with a selection of developmental tasks for middle childhood, adolescence, early adulthood and later

RESEARCH HIGHLIGHT 1.2
The developmental tasks of adolescents
Dekovic, Noom and Meeus, 1997

These authors studied the developmental tasks of the teenage years as seen by teenagers and their parents. They found that:

- adolescents had different expectations from their parents, although the views of both parents were similar;
- adolescents and parents differed on such issues as 'having a boy/girlfriend', staying alone at home, and spending a vacation without parents;
- mothers and fathers also had different views on when adolescents could take a holiday without their parents;
- parents and teenagers were agreed that tasks such as forming stable relationships should occur relatively early, while taking on responsibility for one's own family should occur later.

adulthood. Although most (93 per cent) of the respondents indicated that they regarded themselves as being in early adulthood, the results showed that they were working primarily on the developmental tasks of adolescence, with some attention being paid to the tasks of

TABLE 1.1 *Responses of students to a selection of developmental tasks of adolescence*

Developmental task	Respondents reporting engagement (%)	Respondents reporting non-engagement (%)
Achieving mature relations with age mates	94	6
Achieving emotional independence from parents	84	16
Achieving socially responsible behaviour	80	20
Acquiring a set of values	73	27
Achieving appropriate social roles	58	42
Preparing for marriage and family life	33	67

Source: Roscoe and Peterson, 1984

childhood and early adulthood. In Table 1.1 are presented the main findings with respect to the developmental tasks of adolescence. It shows that nearly all the respondents were engaged in achieving mature relations with age mates, or in achieving emotional independence from their parents. Many were concerned with achieving socially acceptable behaviour. Very few (33 per cent) were preparing for marriage and family life.

Perhaps not surprisingly, adolescents and parents set different timetables for the completion of developmental tasks. Whereas all adolescents typically expect to achieve these tasks around 14–15 years of age, parents expect them to be achieved much later (around 18–19 years of age). Moreover, girls are expected to complete their tasks before boys (Dekovic, Noom and Meeus, 1997).

THEORETICAL PERSPECTIVES ON ADOLESCENCE

There are several major theoretical perspectives that are useful when thinking about the social development of adolescents. Such perspectives or theories are quite handy, since they organise a body of knowledge so that one may make predictions about future behaviour and make sense of otherwise chaotic data or phenomena. Hollander described the utility of theories as follows (1967, 55): 'Basically, a theory consists of one or more functional statements or propositions that treat the relationship of variables so as to account for a phenomenon or set of phenomena.'

In psychology, theories of social behaviour are normally quite elaborate explanations of the causes and principles underlying that behaviour. In other words, they explain how the behaviour works. Theories break down the behaviour into parts that can be separately analysed. A useful theory sets out to explain how the different components are interrelated in determining behaviour (Williamson et al., 1982).

A detailed exposition of all of the theories of adolescence is clearly beyond the scope of this chapter. Instead, some of the main theoretical approaches to understanding adolescence will be briefly described.

From the Middle Ages to the Enlightenment

Although early Greek writers such as Plato and Aristotle formulated their philosophical ideas about the nature of the human soul many hundreds of years before the Middle Ages, these were lost to European culture during the Dark Ages after the fall of the Roman Empire.

The Middle Ages represented a neglect of the study of human development. Most people were preoccupied with survival, not only contending with wars and feudal conflicts, but also with disease. The population was generally poorly educated and the intellectuals of the time had little inclination, it seems, to consider the intricacies of human development (Hughes and Noppe, 1985).

The prevailing view was that a miniature adult (called a *homunculus*) was found within the sperm. It was thought that, once conception occurred, the small adult simply grew in size within the mother. According to this view, humans were 'preformed', giving rise to the concept of *preformation*. This doctrine dominated scientific thinking during the Middle Ages and held sway until the eighteenth century, when more scientific investigations contradicted accepted views (Crain, 1985). Writers such as Crain have suggested that, among religious leaders and moralists, preformation ideas receded as early as the sixteenth century, when the unique virtues of children began to be understood.

Preformationist views had a dominant influence on how children were viewed by adults, and depicted in art. They were treated as 'young adults' and expected to be obedient and well-behaved. In paintings, they were simply portrayed as small adults. No attention was given to the special needs or circumstances of children or adolescents. This reflected another view at the time, namely that the purpose of education was to counteract innate sin and so reveal God's laws (Hughes and Noppe, 1985).

The Renaissance heralded a re-evaluation of social thought and the value of education. The works of Plato and Aristotle were rediscovered and writers such as Descartes stimulated interest in human nature. An important thinker of the time was John Locke (1632–1704). He proposed that the mind of a child is like a blank slate, or *tabula rasa*, and that children learn behaviour according to their own unique experiences. Thus Locke laid the foundation work for later behaviourists such as Pavlov and Skinner (Crain, 1985).

According to Locke, nature forms the mind of the child. This occurs through *association, repetition, imitation, rewards* and *punishment*, concepts well-known to learning theorists (Crain 1985). For instance, a child associates a particular behaviour with punishment and quickly learns not to repeat it. For this, the child is rewarded. We also learn through repetition (or practice) and imitation (or modelling). Locke's views about the acquisition of behaviour, although seminal, were to lie dormant until the early part of the twentieth century.

The writings of Jean-Jacques Rousseau (1712–78) best reflect the mood of the Enlightenment. He strongly influenced the later work of

Gesell, Montessori and Piaget (Crain, 1985). Rousseau was not an environmentalist and, unlike Locke, did not view the mind as a blank slate waiting to be written upon. Rather, he suggested that children have their own capacities and modes of thinking, and that they should be allowed to grow and develop at their own pace, and in their own way.

Rousseau proposed the following stage theory of development (Crain, 1985):

- infancy – birth to 2 years: children learn through their senses, are inquisitive and learn quickly;
- childhood – 2–12 years: they can reason but not abstractly, and their actions represent their cognitive ability;
- late childhood – 12–15 years: not interested in social relationships, they gain physically and cognitively, but cannot think theoretically;
- adolescence – 15 years: marks the beginning of puberty, with dramatic physical, emotional, and cognitive changes.

Evaluation

The proposals of Locke and Rousseau are invaluable to contemporary views about adolescent development. Both were ahead of their time and laid the foundation for the current debate regarding the relative influences of nature and nurture. Whereas Locke emphasised external processes in the way behaviours are learned, Rousseau suggested that development is an innate process following a biological timetable. Both sets of ideas will be elaborated later.

Psychoanalytic Theory

Originally formulated by Freud, this perspective has undergone reformulation by others such as Anna Freud, Erikson, and Blos (Muuss, 1988). Erikson's approach will be dealt with in some detail in Chapter 2, in connection with identity formation.

Freud developed his theory of personality on the basis of his work with individuals suffering from mental and emotional problems. He was opposed to the structuralist tradition that emphasised the experimental approach to understanding behaviour. Rather, Freud emphasised the unconscious motives of behaviour and considered mental processes, urges, drives, passions, repressed ideas and emotions as important (Freud, 1949). Using 'physical energy' as an analogy, Freud spoke of 'psychological energy', suggesting that this is transformed into anxiety and drives (Miller, 1993). He made only passing reference to the adolescent years, believing that the first five years of life determine later development (Talwar and Lerner, 1991).

Freud suggested that human behaviour can be explained in terms of drives and noted two types, namely, *self-preservative* and *sexual* drives. The latter refer to all pleasurable activities, Freud believing that behaviour is motivated by the urge to attain pleasure. Freud later added the *aggressive* drive to explain destructive behaviour (Liebert and Spiegler, 1990). He also proposed a basic structure of personality, which was then incorporated into his psychosexual stages of development. Freud (1949) proposed two distinct but related structures of the mind. These are the:

- Unconscious
- Preconscious
- Conscious

- Id
- Ego
- Superego

The conscious refers to our awareness. Only a small proportion of one's thoughts and feelings are actually *in* consciousness. Preconscious thoughts can, however, be brought into consciousness with relative ease. Finally, there are those urges and drives of which the individual is unaware, and which play an important role in explaining behaviour. These are in the unconscious, which is regarded by Freud as dominant.

The id functions at the unconscious level and consists of drives, impulses, and basic instincts. While the ego obeys the 'reality principle' and attempts to control the wild impulses of the id, the superego reflects learned values and morals (Freud, 1949). In a sense, the superego represents social norms, values and expectations.

The psychosexual stages of development begin in infancy and progress through adolescence. They are listed in Table 1.2. During the adolescent years, the individual reaches sexual maturity, with sexual instincts being directed towards heterosexual relationships.

Three main themes pervade psychoanalytic theory (Coleman, 1992). In the first place, drives, instincts, and motives play an important part in personality development. Such drives and instincts are particularly problematic during puberty and adolescence, when a developing sexuality needs to be incorporated into the overall structure of personality. This basic drive is exacerbated by current social, moral, and religious convention, such that the id comes into conflict with the ego and superego. According to this view, the superego finds the basic instincts of the id unacceptable, while the ego seems to have little control over the id.

TABLE 1.2   *Freud's psychosexual stages of human development*

Stage	Main features
Oral	From birth until child is weaned; mouth, lips, and tongue associated with pleasure; from 8–18 months referred to as oral-biting stage
Anal	6 months– 4 years: chief pleasure is controlling bowel functions Toilet training important, since restricts child's behaviour
Phallic	4–7 or 8 years: genitals are object of erogenous interest Boys suffer from Oedipus complex (see father as competitor for mother's affection) Girls suffer from Electra complex and penis envy (they blame mother for their 'castration')
Latency	6 or 8 years–12 or 13 years: sexual drive is dormant Oedipus/Electra complexes should be resolved
Genital	Begins with puberty: individuals are sexually mature and directed toward heterosexual pleasure

Source: Phares, 1991

As a consequence, the adolescent experiences turmoil and conflict. When externalised, such turmoil may be manifest in a number of ways, including conflict between parents and teenagers.

The second theme refers to defence mechanisms (Coleman, 1992). These are strategies one develops and learns in order to resolve conflict or anguish, or to help defend oneself against the id. Such mechanisms include repression, sublimation, reaction formation, regression, displacement, rationalisation, identification and projection (see Table 1.3).

The third theme concerns the process of disengagement (Coleman, 1992). Adolescents, having successfully resolved the Oedipus or Electra complex (see Table 1.2), begin to form closer relationships first with the same-sex peer group, and then with members of the opposite sex (see Chapter 4). By this process, a gradual disengagement from the family, or a loosening of ties, begins to occur. Establishing oneself as independent from one's parents is essential, particularly in later adolescence, since this has implications for future mature emotional and sexual relationships.

Freud's daughter Anna developed her father's ideas on adolescence. She stressed the importance of Oedipal feelings within the adolescent, and suggested that many teenagers feel anxious in the presence of their parents. Thus they may resort to solitary behaviour, such as spending long periods alone in their rooms, or to running away from home. She also suggested that adolescents often become contemptuous of their parents, adopting a belligerent attitude. According to Anna Freud, many teenagers adopt defence mechanisms against a variety of feelings

TABLE 1.3   *Defence mechanisms to help defend oneself against the Id*

Mechanism	Description
Repression	Unacceptable thoughts are deliberately kept in the unconscious
Sublimation/ displacement	Drives or urges are directed towards another goal more valued by one's peers or by society
Reaction formation	One attempts to reverse an unacceptable urge or behaviour by turning it into its opposite
Regression	One reverts to satisfying behaviours characteristic of an earlier phase in the life span
Rationalisation	A form of reasoning to convince us of the merits of our action
Identification	An attempt to be just like someone else
Projection	One's desires or behaviours are believed to be characteristic of someone else.

Source: Liebert and Spiegler, 1990

and impulses. Crain (1985) mentions two: asceticism, that is, denial of pleasure (for example the following of strict diets). The second is intellectualisation, that is, the construction of elaborate theories about social and moral issues, such as love and war.

Evaluation

Freud's ideas about development and the nature of personality have made an enormous impact on psychology and psychiatry. He has, however, drawn criticism from a number of sources. Feminists have suggested that his ideas are culture-bound and sexist, and that his views of women are outdated. Others, such as Liebert and Spiegler (1990) suggest that Freud viewed the male personality as the 'prototype' on which he tried to base the female personality. Still more have questioned his views on 'penis envy'. Crain (1985, 158) echoed this argument as follows:

> Freud assumed that penis envy is based on a real biological inferiority – a view that fits well with his society's prejudice. Actually ... penis envy is much more of a culture problem, girls feel inferior to boys because girls lack the same privileges in a male dominated society ... Freud ignored women's legitimate desire for social equality.

Miller (1993) noted the following weaknesses of psychoanalytical theory:

- Freud claimed that one needs to be trained in psychoanalysis to be able to test his ideas;
- too much emphasis on childhood sexuality.

Some writers have evaluated psychoanalytic theory in terms of its scientific contribution, and found it wanting. Eysenck (1985), for instance, notes Freud's own relationship with his mother (he was her 'undisputed darling'), as well as his addiction to cocaine, suggesting that both shaped and biased his views on personality. In addition, Eysenck (1985) and others (for example, Liebert and Spiegler, 1990; Miller, 1993) have criticised the untestable nature of many of Freud's ideas, noting also that many of his concepts are poorly defined. Thus, according to Eysenck (1985, 20): 'Psychoanalysis as an art form may be acceptable; psychoanalysis as a science has always evoked protests from scientists and philosophers of science.'

Behavioural Theory

Like the psychoanalytic approach, learning theory, in its classic behavioural and social learning perspectives, has had a fundamental influence on conceptions of human development and behaviour. Learning theory derives from the ideas of Locke.

The classic behaviourist approach was first formulated by writers such as Pavlov, Hull, and Skinner. It was Pavlov who noticed that dogs salivate in anticipation of being fed. This led him to conduct a range of different experiments on the so-called *conditioning response*. He demonstrated, for example, that food could be associated with another stimulus, such as a tone, and that dogs would salivate at the sound of the tone. Thus were born the well-known concepts: unconditioned stimulus (the food), conditioned stimulus (the tone), unconditioned reflex (salivation to the food) and conditioned reflex (salivation to the tone) (Crain, 1985).

The basic principles of classical conditioning are shown in Figure 1.1. Once conditioning has occurred, it is possible to pair the conditioned stimulus (the tone) with a new stimulus (such as a light) until it elicits the desired response (salivation). This is referred to as higher order conditioning.

Further laboratory experimentation demonstrated just how short-lived conditioned stimuli are, and that it is possible for such stimuli to lose their effect (so-called extinction). Elimination of the reward reduces the likelihood that salivation will follow the tone. Moreover, it was also shown how previously extinguished stimuli can recover their effect: that is, we can re-learn behaviours that have been extinguished. Finally, Pavlov also showed experimentally that it is possible to distinguish between different stimuli. At the same time, it is also possible that similar stimuli, such as two tones, elicit the same response.

FIGURE 1.1   *The classical conditioning process*

CLASSICAL CONDITIONING

Food   →   Salivation

After food is associated with tone:

Tone   →   Salivation

HIGHER ORDER CONDITIONING

Tone is paired with light so that:

Light   →   Salivation

In an extension of these ideas, Skinner maintained that the consequences of our actions actually determine our behaviour, that is, rewards
will enhance behaviour. As Skinner explained, it is therefore possible
to *shape* behaviour (Skinner, 1953). Using this operant conditioning
method, he was able to demonstrate that we do not learn behaviours
in an all-or-nothing fashion, but that one moves *towards* the correct
response. He showed, for instance, how one can teach a pigeon to peck
at a button: the pigeon is first rewarded for facing the button. Food (the
reward) is then withheld, until the bird moves towards the button. Next
it is rewarded for pecking closer and closer to the button. Finally, it is
rewarded for executing the desired action or behaviour.

Central to all forms of learning theory is reinforcement. Classical
theorists demonstrated the link between removal of reward and extinction of responses. Skinner (1953) distinguished between positive and
negative reinforcement and punishment. Whereas in the former a stimulus is presented after the correct behaviour, in negative reinforcement

a stimulus is removed following correct behaviour. For example, the threat of punishment is withdrawn once a child performs acceptable behaviour. Both positive and negative reinforcement increase the likelihood of acceptable behaviour occurring. Punishment, on the other hand, reduces the likelihood of unacceptable behaviour (see Table 1.4 for a summary).

Fundamental to learning or behavioural theory, therefore, is the fact that one is rewarded for acceptable behaviour. Individuals (including adolescents) are much more likely to execute certain behaviours if they gain from doing so. If, in order to gain acceptance by the peer group (highly rewarding), a teenager needs to behave in a certain way, or dress in a certain style, then it is highly likely that he or she will do so. If certain ways of behaviour need to be avoided to gain approval by the group, then again it is highly likely that this will occur. Thus, a reward for correct behaviour fixes in the mind of the individual the close association between a stimulus and a particular response. Likewise, punishment indicates that certain behaviours or attitudes are inappropriate.

Evaluation

Behaviourists such as Pavlov and Skinner do not discuss internal states. Rather, they focus on external events such as stimulus and response. For the classic behaviourist, personality is simply the sum of all previously learned responses, while cognitive input is not given much credence. For some developmentalists, an adolescent's feelings and thoughts, likes and dislikes, are intimately tied up with behaviour. Skinnerians would argue, however, that behaviour is constantly shaped and determined by the environment (Crain, 1985).

TABLE 1.4   *Principles of operant conditioning*

Positive reinforcement
Example: Praise
Presented after the desired behaviour; increases its rate

Negative reinforcement
Example: Scolding
Removed after correct behaviour; increases the rate of behaviour

Punishment
Example: Cancellation of pocket money
Presented after incorrect behaviour; suppresses behaviour

Source: Skinner, 1953

Some (for example, Liebert and Spiegler, 1990) have suggested that the radical behaviourist approach is dehumanising, as well as being rather simplistic. It is argued that human behaviour and development is much more complex than what is reflected in learning theory, and that behaviour cannot be reduced to simple stimulus and response categories. By so doing, behaviourists ignore the complexity of behaviour as well as individual differences, cultural influences and free will.

Social Cognitive Theory

Dollard and Miller were the first to use the term social learning theory (Liebert and Spiegler, 1990). They elaborated some of the principles of behavioural theory, suggesting that human behaviour is also deter-mined by factors such as drives and cues (Dollard and Miller, 1950). Thus, there are internal stimuli or drives (for example, hunger) that cause us to look for food (a response). Just where or when we eat, how-ever, is dependent upon certain cues (for example, 'I'll eat when I see the pizza sign' or 'I'll eat when I have completed this task'). In this way, correct (or acceptable) behaviour is appropriately rewarded. According to Dollard and Miller, human behaviour is learned through drive reduction, attaching responses to new stimuli, reinforcing or rewarding new responses, and creating secondary motives.

Dollard and Miller (1950) acknowledged the importance of *social models*, or modelling cues. Unlike more recent social learning theorists, they overlooked the possibility that one can learn simply by observation rather than through direct experience.

Rotter and Bandura later expanded these ideas, yet it is Bandura (1973) who is synonymous with social learning or social cognitive theory. Although he acknowledged the importance of classical and operant conditioning, he also emphasised the importance of observational learning, modelling, imitation, and identification in human development. Together with his colleagues, Bandura demonstrated empirically that young children can learn aggressive behaviour, for example, simply by watching violent films, and that such observational learning is not merely confined to young children.

Bandura (1973) was of the opinion that adolescents and adults also learn a variety of behaviours by observing the actions of others. Teenagers will emulate the behaviour or dress of their idols through observation and imitation; identification therefore facilitates learning. Likewise, the role of the peer group should not be underestimated. Adolescents are highly likely to smoke or engage in early sexual intercourse, for example, if some of their closest friends are already doing so (Kandel, 1990). As will be noted in Chapter 4, the peer group sets the cultural norms or 'rituals' for acceptable behaviour.

Because it is possible to learn behaviour simply by observing the actions of others, Bandura (1973) pointed out that social learning also involves a cognitive element. We have inner representations of behaviour which allow the observer to perform a new behaviour. Moreover, Bandura stresses the importance of *vicarious reinforcement*. This refers to expectations about reinforcement or reward without actually performing the behaviour. In other words, we have the capacity to think about the likely consequences of our actions before performing them. If we *expect* to be rewarded, then we are likely to perform an action. An expectation of very little reward reduces the likelihood of action.

There are four fundamental components of observational learning (Huston, 1983). They are:

- attentional processes,
- retention processes,
- motor reproduction processes,
- reinforcement and motivational processes.

In order to perform a behaviour we first need to pay attention to the model performing the action. Thus, we watch a television character or pay attention to the behaviour of others in our environment. Implicit is an understanding of the observed behaviour, itself a cognitive process. Having observed and understood behaviour, we also need to remember what we have seen so that we can later recall and reproduce the actions. We also need to be physically mature enough to execute what is required. Finally, behaviours are strengthened through rewards and reinforcement.

Social cognitive learning is a three-stage process. The first two stages, namely, exposure and acquisition, have been discussed. The third stage is referred to as acceptance. It has been defined as follows (Liebert and Spiegler, 1990, 452): 'Acceptance refers to whether or not the observer uses (accepts) the modelling cues as a guide for her or his own actions.'

No doubt, there are many factors that determine whether the observer finds others' behaviour acceptable. They may include the status of the person being observed, the personality of the observer, the observer's own values and attitudes, the desirability of the observed behaviour, and so forth.

Evaluation

Some (for example, Crain, 1985) are of the view that theorists such as Bandura have greatly enhanced our understanding of social learning. He showed the extent to which the environment is connected to individual behaviour (Miller, 1993). Although the theoretical principles are well founded in laboratory experiments, it is not clear whether all human behaviour can be explained as a function of observation and imitation. Indeed, some have argued that this approach is far too dependent on laboratory experimentation (Liebert and Spiegler, 1990). Nonetheless, Bandura demonstrated that much learning does occur in the presence of others, rather than alone through trial and error (Miller, 1993).

There are those who would argue that social learning theorists over-emphasise the importance of the environment on the acquisition of new behaviour. At the same time, social learning theorists appear to undervalue the role of internal processes such as human values and beliefs, and a range of personality factors.

Cognitive-developmental Theory

One cannot consider the impact of cognitive change on human development without considering the work of Jean Piaget. Piaget was a gifted thinker, writing his first scientific paper while still a teenager, and earning his doctorate at the age of twenty-one at which time he had already published 20 papers (Miller, 1993). Working first on intelligence tests for children, he later became interested in childrens' patterns of reasoning (Crain, 1985).

Piaget proposed a stage theory of intellectual development, although in his later work this received less emphasis, Piaget referring instead to 'steps' (Miller, 1993). Although he did not see a formal link between a stage and the age of the child, he firmly believed that each of us progresses through the stages in the same order. Each stage represents a more complex way of thinking, as explained in Table 1.5.

It is possible to characterise Piaget's stage theory as follows (Miller, 1993):

- each stage is an integrated entity in a state of balance;
- stages are interconnected; they are based on the preceding one and form the basis for the next one;
- stages follow in a set sequence;

TABLE 1.5   *Piaget's stages of cognitive development*

Stage	Main features
Sensori-motor intelligence	Birth to 2 years: knows environment through senses and motor activity. Constructs schemes. Later responds to interesting events outside body. Will later look for objects that have disappeared. Also develops object permanence and recognises self.
Pre-operational stage	2 years to 7 years: toddlers capable of mental representations. Are able to imitate behaviour.
Concrete operations	7 years to 11 years: can reason about concrete events. Can deal with concepts of classes, relations, and quantity. Has developed conservation of number, quantity, mass, volume, etc. Capable of cognitive conceit.
Formal operations	12 years to adulthood: begins to reason abstractly. Develops hypothetico-deductive reasoning, combinatorial analysis, contrary-to-fact reasoning.

Source: Crain, 1985; Hughes and Noppe, 1985

- children everywhere progress through the same stages in the same order;
- each stage comprises a preparation phase and an achievement phase.

The adolescent years coincide with the advent of formal operations. This means that teenagers are not constrained by having to function only at the non-abstract level, but are increasingly able to think about imaginary and hypothetical events: that is, they are able to reason abstractly. Adolescents are not only able to understand relationships between actual events, but also understand relationships between actual and possible events. This appears to be much more marked in the physical field (for instance, dealing with chemical relationships) than in the social field (Boyle, 1969). Typically, adolescents tend to be egocentric and, in terms of emotional and interpersonal relationships, far less able to distinguish the possible from the actual. They attain formal operational thought, therefore, in some areas before doing so in others.

Egocentrism during adolescence can be manifest in a number of different ways. It is well known, for example, that many teenagers are overly concerned with their appearance. They appear to be convinced that they are the centre of attention. Consequently, they play to what Elkind (1967) referred to as an 'imaginary audience'. Adolescents construct a 'personal fable' (Elkind 1967) thinking of themselves as quite special people who experience events in a very intense way. They believe that no one can feel as passionately about something as they do.

The teenage years mark a significant qualitative change in reasoning ability. With formal operational thinking comes the ability to begin to deal with a range of complex issues. Of course, not every dilemma they face will be successfully resolved. However, given that they are now able to combine the possible with the actual, their capacity to deal with the many challenges (biological, social, emotional, and educational) they will confront increases enormously.

Although many adolescents may attain the stage of formal operational thought, they are still en route to becoming adults. Very often, they are unable to view a problem or dilemma from the more experienced viewpoint of their elders. Only with increasing maturity are they able to think more realistically.

One may ask how an individual progresses through the various Piagetian stages. According to Piaget, one acquires new knowledge through the processes of assimilation, accommodation and organisation. Assimilation refers to the ability to absorb or take in new information. Once such information has been assimilated, it needs to be accommodated in pre-existing or newly constructed mental categories. An adolescent, for example, could accommodate negative information about a good friend in a variety of ways, such as changing her views about the friend or questioning the motives of the person providing the information. This process restores equilibrium. Thirdly, teenagers must organise their information into coherent theories or views about phenomena.

Evaluation

Piaget made a profound contribution to our understanding of cognitive development – and not just during the adolescent years. Indeed, no discussion of such development is complete without reference to his work. According to Crain (1985), an enormous amount of research has been generated by Piaget's ideas, most of it supporting the stage sequence.

According to some critics, it is doubtful whether all teenagers and adults employ formal operational thought. It has even been suggested that most adults in their everyday lives function at the concrete operational level. Only periodically is it necessary to function at the highest level of reasoning.

Biological Theory

An early exponent of this approach was Gesell (1928). Although he believed that the environment plays some role in the development of young children, internal biological and genetic processes were thought to be the primary factors accounting for human development. Gesell is well known for the construction of his behaviour norms, although it is to physical development that he devoted most of his attention.

Gesell (1928) argued that much of human development is biologically predetermined. A child crawls before it can walk, and walks before it can run. Likewise, development of the foetus and embryo follow specific patterns. For example, the development of the brain begins before that of the arms and legs. Thus, there appears to be a genetic principle or schedule governing one's development. Although we may not all begin to walk at the same age, we all follow the same sequence of development. Like Rousseau, Gesell firmly believed that children perform certain actions (for instance, walking) when they are biologically ready, driven by 'intrinsic maturational forces' (Crain, 1985).

The physical and biological changes occurring during puberty and adolescence have been well documented. Nearly all adolescents are subject to what has been described as the 'growth spurt'. Boys seem to have a greater growth spurt than girls. In one report (Tanner and Davies, 1985), it was suggested that the average boy grows about 10 cm per year in the fastest year of the growth spurt, about twice as fast as the previous year.

Tanner (1991) has documented the composition of some aspects of the growth spurt. He noted that all skeletal and muscle parts undergo change, while the peak weight spurt occurs about six to nine months after the height peak. Importantly, in Gesell's terms, is the fact that growth peaks follow a particular sequence. Tanner (1991, 422) explains this as follows:

> There is a regular order to the peaks; leg length as a rule reaches its peak... first, with trunk length... about a year later. In between occur the peaks of shoulder and hip breadths. The muscles' peak coincides with that of trunk length, and so follows after the height peak.

The development of secondary sex characteristics also follows a specific pattern. In girls, breast budding is followed by the appearance of pubic hair, followed by menarche. In boys, testicular growth occurs before spermarche, which can occur together with early pubic hair growth (Paikoff and Brooks-Gunn, 1991).

An integral part of biological and physical change during adolescence is the changing nature of the endocrine system. During this time, it changes into its adult form, resulting in a significant increase in hormonal levels. This is noteworthy, since hormonal increases have been linked to behavioural change (Offer and Church, 1991; Susman and

Dorn, 1991). The actual mechanisms explaining the effect of hormones on behaviour are, however, not clear (Susman and Dorn, 1991).

During late childhood and early adolescence, the levels of three types of hormones rapidly increase (Susman and Dorn, 1991). These hormones are:

- gonadotropins: luteinising hormone (LH)
  follicle stimulating hormone (FSH)

These have a stimulating effect on the testes and ovaries.

- gonadal steroids: testosterone (T)
  oestrogen (E)

These steroid hormones initiate and maintain masculine body changes in males and females; produced by the testis and ovary (Rabin and Chrousos, 1991a).

- adrenal androgens: dehydroepiandosterone (DHEA)
  dehydroepiandosterone sulphate (DHEAS)

These are secreted by the adrenal cortex and cause masculine-like changes in the male or female body. Excess production of this hormone may result in ambiguous development of the sex organs in the female foetus as well as heightened sexual activity in adolescents (Rabin and Chrousos, 1991b).

It is beyond the scope of this chapter to explain in any detail the functions of these hormones and their relationship with observable behaviour. Suffice to say that the link between some hormones and behaviour has been well recorded. For example, research has demonstrated a relationship between certain hormones and aggressive and 'acting out' behaviour among boys, but not girls (Susman and Dorn, 1991). A link has also been demonstrated between hormone levels and sexual motivation, although the effects appear to be different for boys than girls. (This point will be taken up again in Chapter 7.)

Some evidence suggests a link between hormonal changes and depressive affect, particularly among girls (Paikoff and Brooks-Gunn, 1990; see also Chapter 6), although findings are less clear with respect to hormones and mood lability. Hormonal changes have also been implicated in changes in the parent–child relationship through their effect on secondary sex characteristics (Paikoff and Brooks-Gunn, 1991). Teenagers react differently to these changes, which have an impact upon social and familial relationships and child–parent communication (see also Chapter 3).

Evaluation

Since the early work of Gesell, modern technology has enabled us to make great strides in our ability to detect hormonal levels (some quite small) and to link these with changes in adolescent behaviour. This link remains correlational, and more sophisticated research is required in order to detect any cause–effect relationships.

The view that behaviour can be explained in terms of biological and/ or physiological processes is a contentious one that has, at times, taken on ideological overtones. Objective analysis, however, would reveal that human development, rather than being influenced by only one factor, reflects the interaction between the forces of heredity and genetic endowment on the one hand, and the influences of the environment on the other. Thus, this viewpoint recognises that behaviour is multidimensional and is influenced by a range of different factors.

Each of the theories presented in this chapter emphasises different sides of the nature–nurture debate. Freud, for example, emphasised inner sexual urges and drives, at the same time recognising the importance of parent–child relationships by referring to such issues as identification with the parent. Most psychologists today would argue that both one's inherited biological make-up and the environment determine behaviour. As Miller (1993, 25) notes: 'The way that heredity is expressed depends on the specific environment in which this expression occurs. In other words, a given hereditary influence can have different behavioral effects in different environments.'

SUMMARY

The importance of the adolescent period as worthy of academic study is firmly established in psychology. This chapter has noted traditional images of youth as well as recognised developmental tasks. It was suggested that, with regard to images of youth, an enduring stereotype is one of turbulence, exuberance and passion. Certainly, adolescents tend to live life 'intensely' as they play to imaginary audiences and create personal fables (Elkind, 1967). However, the view that this period is one of 'storm and stress' is increasingly being questioned (Arnett, 1999). With respect to noted developmental tasks, some of these (for instance, preparation for marriage) can be questioned in the light of changing cultural norms and expectations.

This chapter briefly reviewed several important theories of adolescent development. Theories serve a useful function since they direct our thinking and help us to understand our observations of adolescent behaviour and interpretations of research data. What is quite clear is that each theory highlights unique or selected aspects of development. Some are based on extensive laboratory research, while others are grounded in observation and subjective interpretation. No theory, however, is absolutely comprehensive, nor is it able fully to explain adolescent development in all its richness and diversity. It is suggested that each contains elements that aid us in understanding adolescence.

In the following chapters we shall consider some important aspects of adolescents' social development. The necessity for considering each topic will be noted, followed by a careful consideration of available research evidence. Each chapter will conclude by considering the fit between theory and available research data. We begin by considering adolescents' attempts to understand the self and achieve a personal identity.

ADDITIONAL READING

Crain, W. (1985) *Theories of Development: Concepts and Applications*. Engle-wood Cliffs, NJ: Prentice-Hall.
Miller, P. (1993) *Theories of Developmental Psychology* (3rd edn). New York: WH Freeman and Co.
Muuss, R. (1988) *Theories of Adolescence* (5th edn) New York: Random House.
Petersen, A. (1988) 'Adolescent Development', *Annual Review of Psychology* 39: 583–607.

EXERCISES

1   Which theory do you find most helpful when thinking about adolescent development? Explain why you find this particular theory appealing. what are its strengths/weaknesses compared with others?
2   Compile a list of developmental tasks for teenagers in the early twenty-first century. How does your list differ from those proposed by earlier writers? How do the tasks you have identified compare with those identified by other students in your class?

2

Identity and the Self

INTRODUCTION

As the individual progresses from infancy and childhood into adolescence, an important developmental task is the awareness and acceptance of self and the development of an identity. This means that as teenagers mature, they come to the realisation that they differ from others in important and fundamental ways. It is desirable to come to terms with one's self as a unique individual and to reach acceptance of what one is: someone of value and worth. A crucial aspect of development during these years is attaining a sense of psychological well-being, a sense of knowing where one is going (Erikson, 1968, 165).

Fundamental to identity formation is the merging of one's past with future aspirations, while at the same time recognising one's present talents, limitations and characteristics (Newman and Newman, 1988). Not only is this an important aspect of identity formation, it is also a relatively difficult task and requires of the adolescent a fine sense of judgement and level-headedness. Once the task is complete, the person can expect to experience increased awareness of self-worth and importance, as well as a sense of self-assurance.

The processes of identity formation and self-conceptualisation have their roots in infancy, a process characterised by the emergence of self-recognition. We know that at a very young age (by about 12–18 months), the child is aware of others as quite separate and distinct from the self. Identity formation and the development of self-awareness continue throughout adolescence and beyond. An important development during adolescence is the coincidence of developing an identity (an understanding of who I am) and self-concept (the collection of beliefs about myself). Thus, the teenager has the challenging task of integrating his or her physical, sexual, and psychological identities.

In this chapter, we shall examine the nature and development of adolescent identity. We shall also examine the concept of self and the formation of a sex-role identity. Although these themes are closely connected, the respective literatures have developed quite separately. We begin with identity formation.

IDENTITY FORMATION

Identity formation and development are synonymous with the work of Erik Erikson (1968) who was recognised by the American Psychological Association for his theoretical contributions to psychology. In 1955 he was elected a Fellow of the Division of Developmental Psychology. Many of his ideas were adopted by the White House Conference on Children, and in 1960 he was offered a professorship at Harvard University (Crain, 1985; Sprinthall and Collins, 1988).

Strongly influenced by the work of Sigmund and Anna Freud, Erikson proposed psychosocial stages of development. Seen as an expansion of Freud's psychosexual stages of development (see Chapter 1), Erikson's proposals emphasise the importance of the social context and social forces in the life of the individual.

Unlike Freud, Erikson's stage theory encompasses the whole of the life span. It does not concentrate on sexual drives and instincts, but rather focuses on social drives and the impact of social experience. A further essential feature is that each stage is characterised by two opposing poles, reflecting crises, or choice to be made across the lifespan. One pole or possible response option ensures positive emotional development, while the other hinders such growth (Erikson, 1968). Throughout development, therefore, the individual faces many choices, the outcomes of which often determine future behaviour. Although a certain amount of tension may exist between any two given poles, one should not assume that all teenagers will experience turmoil (Douvan and Adelson, 1966; Noller and Patton, 1990). Generally, successful resolution of one stage facilitates the successful resolution of the following one (Erikson, 1968).

According to Erikson there are eight stages across the life span. They are:

- trust vs. mistrust   birth to 1 year
- autonomy vs. shame and doubt   1 to 3 years
- initiative vs. guilt   3 to 5 years
- industry vs. inferiority   5 to 12 years
- identity vs. identity confusion   adolescence

- intimacy vs. isolation   young adulthood
- generativity vs. stagnation   middle adulthood
- integrity vs. despair   late adulthood to death

A healthy or vital personality weathers each of these psychosocial stages to emerge with an enhanced sense of what Erikson calls inner unity (Erikson, 1968). Progressing through each stage, the individual faces a potential crisis or turning point. Erikson sees each phase as a crucial period during which the individual strives to successfully resolve the issues at hand. Unsuccessful resolution has negative implications for the subsequent stage, while successful resolution facilitates positive emotional and social adjustment. It is not possible here to discuss each of Erikson's life stages. Rather, attention will be devoted to identity vs. identity confusion, which is salient during the adolescent years.

ADOLESCENT IDENTITY

Adolescents find themselves caught between childhood and adulthood. They must deal with physiological maturity and the impending demands and roles of an adult life. It is not surprising, suggests Erikson (1968), that teenagers, living in a 'no-man's-land' become pre-occupied with their own subculture and initial identity formation. In this regard, the influence of the peer group assumes a growing importance (see also Chapter 4). As the adolescent explores an awakening socio-emotional, sexual and physical identity, the peer group will play a prominent role in providing acceptable role models, and will set the boundaries for behaviour (Meeus and Dekovic, 1995). The growing importance of this group will totally engage the teenager. It is possible to explain this process in the following terms (Muuss, 1988, 6l): 'Conforming to the expectations of peers helps adolescents find out how certain roles fit them. The peer group, the clique . . . aid the individual in the search for a personal identity, since they provide both a role model and a specific social feedback.'

A fundamental task for the adolescent is the integration of biological and cognitive change, own free choice, and the pressures of parents and peers. Very often, adolescents feel impelled by their friends to engage in new behaviour (Newman and Newman, 1988; Emler and Reicher, 1995). At the same time, teenagers must confront the expectations of their parents, whose values often contradict those of the peer group. Thus the adolescent walks a fine line in balancing others' demands and personal needs. To save face and avoid embarrassment, it is important that decisions reached are seen to be those of the teenager.

Implicit in identity formation is role experimentation (Newman and Newman, 1988). Whereas younger children are more narrowly socialised into what is acceptable behaviour, teenagers are aware of a variety of behaviours, roles, values and life styles. In this respect, social modelling is important, with adolescents learning from external agents such as friends, magazines, and television. Within the limitations set by the family, and with encouragement from friends, adolescents are likely to experiment with a range of behaviours and roles as they set out to achieve their identity. In experimenting with different modes of conduct, they may challenge family norms which can lead to parent–adolescent misunderstanding and conflict.

Heterosexual relations during the adolescent years form an integral part of self-exploration and identity formation. These friendships, as well as the more serious instances of 'being in love,' are also a form of role experimentation and assist teenagers in uncovering their underlying socio-emotional and sexual identities. Moreover, such close and more intimate friendships act as a sounding board (see Chapter 4) and reflect one's own values, attitudes and emotions. As such, they are an invaluable part of self-growth and identity formation. As Erikson (1968, 132) put it: 'To a considerable extent adolescent love is an attempt to arrive at a definition of one's identity by projecting one's diffused self-image on another and by seeing it thus reflected and gradually clarified.'

In this wider search for meaning, it is important that adolescents avoid identity confusion. Unless they successfully resolve their identity and move beyond their childhood identifications, the adolescent process will remain incomplete (Erikson, 1968). As we have been reminded (Muuss, 1988), personal identity does not necessarily come with age, as does physical maturity. Teenagers need actively to seek out and uncover their identity and come to terms with their own shortcomings and inadequacies. In some individuals, this process is still underway during early adulthood.

Since it is natural for adolescents to experiment with a wide variety of behaviours roles and friendships, it follows that adolescents are particularly susceptible to role diffusion. Most of these activities and behaviours, argues Erikson, are simply experimentation in 'fantasy and introspection' (164) and serve, ultimately, to clarify personal identity.

The search for one's true identity is not a stress-free exercise. It is fraught with challenges to one's attitudes, values and behaviours. As Kidwell and colleagues explain (Kidwell et al., 1995, 789–90):

> adolescents who are actively involved in the exploration process are more likely than their low-exploring peers to manifest inner confusion, agitation, dissatisfaction, unhappiness, periodic episodes of depression, a vacillation between poor self-concept and grandiosity, and disturbed thinking ....

Closely linked with the development of a personal identity are vocational identity and a personal philosophy (Muuss, 1988). The development of the former is one way by which the adolescent loosens what are normally close parental ties. Acquiring paid employment or embarking on post-school training signals a new-found identity and independence from the family. By developing a vocational identity, the individual lets it be known that he or she has skills and qualities others do not have. Thus, vocational identity reinforces personal identity.

The inability of some teenagers to develop a vocational identity or to acquire paid employment, has detrimental effects on identity formation and self-esteem. Many authors share this view. In one study, for example, the researchers (Winefield and Winefield, 1992) conducted a longitudinal study of Australian youth. They were interested in the effects of employment, post-school education at university and unemployment on the mental health of school leavers. The respondents' psychological health was assessed in various ways: self-esteem, locus of control, depressive affect and negative mood. The results showed that the employed group as well as the students had greater psychological well-being on all measures than the unemployed group. Thus a vocational identity, or just being employed, reinforces, for the young teenager, a sense of identity, leading to overall psychological health.

Gender and cultural differences have been noted in the extent to which youth are engaged in identity exploration of future vocational and family commitments. In a comparative study of Finnish and Australian youth from rural and urban areas, the following trends were observed (Nurmi, Poole and Kalakoski, 1996):

- Older urbanised youth in Australia showed higher levels of exploration of future educational issues than did younger youth. This pattern was reversed in rural areas, however. The same applies to exploration of vocational issues.

- Older Finnish youth in rural areas showed higher levels of exploration of future educational issues than did younger youth. This pattern was reversed in urban areas.
- Girls showed higher levels of exploration regarding future education and vocation than did boys.
- Australian youth showed higher commitment than Finnish youth to vocational exploration.
- Finnish girls showed a higher degree of future family exploration than did Australian girls.
- Rural adolescents showed greater exploration regarding their future family commitments than did urban adolescents.

The authors acknowledge that the lack of city/rural differences in the Finnish sample may simply reflect the fact that the rural students were drawn from a relatively affluent rural community, which was not the case among the Australian respondents. Another possible explanation for the cross-cultural differences found may be due to the fact that Australian students complete their schooling before Finnish students, the Australians therefore showing higher levels of commitment at an earlier age.

Not all adolescents accomplish identity formation adequately. Many difficulties and challenges remain unresolved beyond the teenage years and may only be accomplished in early adulthood, or later. The death of a loved one or the breaking off of a close relationship can plunge the adolescent into a new crisis that can take some time to resolve. Identity, therefore, is established at different times for different people, although it is desirable that the adolescent makes some progress toward identity formation. Perhaps the best one may hope for is that, upon leaving adolescence, teenagers will have grown in maturity, independence and have acquired some sense of psychological well-being and personal accomplishment.

Identity Statuses

Marcia (1966; 1980) has elaborated Erikson's (1968) model by suggesting that adolescents can resolve their identities in one of several ways. Central to identity formation are crisis (or exploration) and commitment. Crisis refers to teenagers selecting various behavioural and attitudinal options or alternatives. Commitment refers to the extent to which teenagers make a personal investment in attitudes and behaviours. As some have noted (Newman and Newman, 1988, 552): 'Essential to identity achievement is that commitments be made following a period of experimentation or crisis and that these commitments are perceived as an expression of personal choice.'

Crisis and commitment vary from individual to individual, giving rise to the following four identity statuses:

- identity diffusion
- identity foreclosure
- identity moratorium
- identity achievement

Identity diffusion

These teenagers have not yet made a personal commitment to a set of beliefs or an occupation and have not yet felt compelled to make choices from a range of available options. In other words, they have not yet experienced an identity crisis (Muuss, 1988). It is quite natural that teenagers in early adolescence may have diffused identities as they may not yet have faced crises regarding attitudes, values or behaviour and are therefore unlikely to have made a personal commitment. Should identity diffusion persist into late adolescence or adulthood, however, this would be cause for some concern.

Identity-diffused adolescents appear to have lower self-esteem scores than those in other status groups. They also appear more willing than other groups of teenagers to accept incorrect personality descriptions about themselves, and are prone to change their own opinion (Muuss, 1988). These findings therefore underscore just how little these individuals know about their true identities.

It would seem that the identity diffusion category is not uniform (Marcia, 1966). Some identity-diffused individuals, according to Marcia, may suffer extreme adjustment problems. Among university students, for example, diffused individuals may manifest as a 'playboy' type, while among other samples extreme diffusion may manifest as schizoid.

Identity foreclosure

These adolescents have made a personal commitment to certain values, beliefs, acceptable behaviours and an occupation or course of study. However, they have not experienced a crisis, nor have they had to struggle and consider different alternatives. Most often, these teenagers simply adopt the beliefs and wishes of their parents. Foreclosure teenagers have been strongly socialised by their parents or peer group.

Muuss (1988) notes that they have not been sufficiently challenged to make their own decisions and have adopted a set of 'preprogrammed' (70) values and beliefs. Marcia (1966) found that these individuals were highly likely to endorse authoritarian values, obedience, strong leadership and respect for authority. They were also found to have unrealistic responses to failure which tended to exacerbate the situation.

Identity moratorium

Adolescents in this phase may be experiencing a crisis, but have not yet made choices or a personal commitment. They are engaged in a personal struggle and are busily evaluating alternatives. It is quite likely during this phase that teenagers experiment with different roles and behaviours. They may follow peer group pressure one moment and then abandon that for something else. Contact may be lost with friends, while new friendships are made. Although parents may find this rather tedious, the adolescent is fully engaged in identity formation. Moratorium, therefore, is essential for identity achievement (Marcia, 1980).

Identity achievement

This stage is synonymous with maturity and, ultimately, identity formation. It marks the completion of adolescence, and signals that identity crises have been successfully resolved. Having experienced a crisis (or crises), the individual has now made a commitment. This is an important accomplishment because achievement of identity helps to link, in the mind of the adolescent, future aspirations with the past, thus creating a sense of personal continuity (Muuss, 1988). Marcia (1966) found that these individuals scored best on a measure of stressful concept attainment, that is, they tended to persevere longer on problems and were also more realistic regarding their aspirations.

Evaluation

Kerpelman, Pittman and Lamke (1997) have recently noted some concerns about this approach to identity statuses. In the first place it seems more preoccupied with the *outcomes* of exploration rather than the *process* itself. This approach also seems to ignore the fact that exploration involves several choices and changes during identity development and not a 'single, terminal decision' (327).

It has also been suggested that identity achievement as originally formulated is male oriented in that it espouses the values associated with white middle-class males, while under-valuing female virtues, such as warmth and understanding (McKinney and Vogel, 1987; Wearing, 1984). It is doubtful whether Erikson's (1968) view's on identity achievement can be applied to working-class youth. It has been noted (Wearing 1984, 18) that:

> Research which has applied Erikson's identity statuses to employed working-class youth...indicates that for these youth the route to identity is more concrete and direct than for their middle-class counterparts. They do not have the luxury of the extended moratorium associated with tertiary education.

It would appear from these arguments that middle-class youth (particularly those at university or college) have a distinct advantage over their working-class counterparts. Middle-class youth have an opportunity while at university to engage in leisurely identity exploration, particularly of a vocational nature. As far as Marcia's (1980) elaboration of Erikson's stages is concerned, some authors have questioned whether statuses can be referred to as stages or not. Some have also noted that the developmental sequence of the identity statuses remains unclear (McKinney and Vogel 1987; see also Meeus et al., 1999).

Meeus and colleagues (1999) reviewed several studies into identity statuses and arrived at the following conclusions:

- There does seem to be a developmental sequence to identity statuses. Thus, for instance, there is an increase in achievement and a decrease in diffusion.
- There appears to be greater movement to achievement in university than among school students which suggests that achievement may be age related.
- The moratorium phase has the lowest ranking with respect to psychological health suggesting that 'low commitment is not conducive to psychological well-being' (429).

It has been argued that, rather than adolescents having to acquire stable identities, it might be more desirable that they acquire flexible ones (Wearing, 1984). Societal values and norms are in a state of constant flux. Some adolescents live amid radical social and political change that may require that they re-evaluate any commitments they may already have made, particularly of an ideological nature. In some countries, teenagers have to cope with relatively high levels of youth unemployment (Winefield, 1997), and changing views about such

RESEARCH HIGHLIGHT 2.1
The effects of parental separation on identity
achievement of males and females
Imbimbo, 1995

How does parental separation influence identity exploration in young men and women? Imbimbo studied college students whose parents had been separated for 4 years or more and who were living with their mothers. She found that female respondents were more identity achieved or in moratorium with respect to occupation than were males. Females were also more likely to be identity achieved with respect to premarital sex than males. It was concluded that 'divorce may be particularly disruptive to late adolescent males as they go about the task of making occupational commitments ... Males ... did not have the benefit of a same-sex parent living at home ... sons receive valuable information from fathers related to the world of work, and the lack of guidance and role modeling from a resident father may leave these young men at a disadvantage relative to females in the same situation' (755).

matters as abortion, drugs and gender roles. It is therefore increasingly unrealistic to expect a teenager to adopt belief systems believing that these will remain largely unchanged throughout life.

IDENTITY STATUSES: RESEARCH EVIDENCE

Development of Identity

Not all teenagers who move into early adulthood will have accomplished complete identity achievement. Indeed, one would expect developmental shifts to occur throughout adolescence with such shifts or changes taking several forms (Waterman, 1982). For example, it is possible for someone to be in the moratorium phase for most of adolescence before seriously contemplating making firm commitments.

Research has shown that younger teenagers are more likely to be in the identity diffusion and foreclosure stages. One may therefore expect progressive identity formation as adolescents move through the teenage years (Waterman, 1982). This is manifest in a number of ways, such as stability of attitudes, values and personality traits.

It could be argued that the greatest advances in identity formation and achievement usually occur at university, due to a diversity of social and intellectual stimuli. A university education certainly appears to facilitate the development of vocational identity, although it has a negative effect upon the development of religious beliefs (Waterman, 1982). For most youth, however, older adolescents show the greatest progress toward psychosocial maturity and the resolution of an identity. This was confirmed by Zuschlag and Whitbourne (1994). They studied three cohorts of college students in 1969, 1977 and 1988. An important implication of their data is that the progress older adolescents make toward identity resolution is not dependent upon changing social attitudes and norms or other social pressures.

Meeus and Dekovic (1995) studied the development of identity across different domains in a large Dutch sample and concluded as follows:

- Relational identity: commitment and exploration become steadily stronger over the teenage years;
- School identity: commitment stabilises around age 15 years, but exploration continues to grow albeit less consistently;
- Occupational identity: commitment and exploration do not grow steadily and consistently over the teenage years.

Family Relations and Identity

Several research studies have examined family functioning and identity status among adolescents. The expectation is that adolescent competence and adjustment are related to the quality of family relations (Papini, Sebby and Clark, 1989; Waterman, 1982). Specifically, it is suggested that supportive and communicative families are likely to create a climate within which the adolescent is able to resolve crises and progress toward identity achievement. Parental rejection, on the other hand, has been found to be associated with a lack of identity crises thus hindering the adolescent's progression toward identity achievement (Papini et al., 1989). Table 2.1 summarises some of the family antecedents of identity statuses.

It is possible for identity exploration to occur during adolescence notwithstanding disagreements between parents and adolescents. This is just the opposite of what happens among foreclosure adolescents, who adopt (without dissension, it seems) parental belief systems. It has

TABLE 2.1   *Family antecedents of identity statuses*

Identity diffusion	Adolescents report distance from their families
	Parents viewed as indifferent, inactive, detached, not understanding and rejecting
	18 to 21-year-old males likely to come from broken homes
Identity foreclosure	Adolescents view family as being child-centred
	Fathers possessive and intrusive to sons
	Fathers supportive and encouraging of daughters
	Adolescents involve the family in important decisions
Identity moratorium	Adolescents likely to be in conflict with parents
	Sons tend to make decisions on their own
Identity achievement	Adolescents likely to be in conflict with parents
	Sons tend to make decisions on their own
	Two-thirds of females in one study from broken homes, or had experienced death of one parent

Source: Waterman, 1982

been noted that greater emotional distance between an adolescent and parents (but not parental rejection) tends to be associated with an increased exploration of the self among teenagers, a prerequisite for identity achievement (Papini et al., 1989). It is suggested, nonetheless, that communicative families have the necessary skills to facilitate the resolution of crises, thus enhancing adolescent identity formation.

Writers such as Campbell, Adams and Dobson (1984) have recognised the role of the family in facilitating identity achievement. They argue that adolescents need to develop independence from their family, yet at the same time maintain a degree of connectedness, thereby enhancing identity formation. As Bartle-Haring (1997) recently put it, adolescents need to 'balance' separateness and connectedness in family life and that the correct balance will facilitate identity exploration and, ultimately, adjustment. On the other hand, poor family communication, weak affectionate bonding with parents, and psychological withdrawal from family members, often lead to feelings of insecurity and inadequate identity formation among youth.

A principal ingredient of successful identity exploration is the degree of separation or independence from parents, while also maintaining emotional warmth with the family. Diffused youth, it would seem, lack a secure family base from which to engage in identity-seeking behaviour. Foreclosed youth, while having a strong emotional attachment to their parents, lack independence. Thus one may conclude as follows

RESEARCH HIGHLIGHT 2.2
'More similar than different'? Family influences on identity
among American and Turkish adolescents
Taylor and Oskay, 1995

Traditionally, it has been possible to distinguish American and Turkish families in terms of the extent to which they encourage their teenagers to become autonomous and independent. Whereas American families pride themselves on their promotion of individualism and independence of thought and action, Turkish families have tended to be more controlling emphasising obedience and respect for authorities (although this would now seem to be slowly changing). Taylor and Oskay studied the impact of these different family approaches on identity exploration among American and Turkish students.

In terms of ideological and interpersonal exploration, it was found that American students were higher on the moratorium and identity achievement stages, respectively. Unexpectedly, American students were higher on foreclosure in the ideological domain. For American respondents, authoritarian parenting and parent–adolescent conflict correlated with identity diffusion on the ideological and interpersonal domains. Among Turkish students, however, parent–adolescent conflict predicted moratorium status on the interpersonal domain. For both groups, authoritarian parenting and parent–adolescent conflict were related to low self-esteem.

(Campbell et al., 1984, 512): 'a moderate degree of connectedness, reflected through shared affection and an acceptance of individuality, provides the psychological foundation and security to begin the searching process for self-defined commitments'.

Another key factor in understanding family relationships and identity is pubertal change. These dramatic physical changes signal that the adolescent is about to leave childhood and assume new roles. It is not surprising, therefore, that these changes have a significant impact on the quality of family relations (see also Chapter 3). This combination of physical maturation and a change in family relations is an important impetus for identity achievement (Papini et al., 1989).

Personality Traits and Identity

Identity status is related to certain personality traits, it having been found that identity-achieved teenagers are more self-assured and not self-conscious (Adams, Abraham and Markstrom 1987). By engaging in identity exploration, it would seem that teenagers develop a satisfying sense of self (Cramer, 1997) and are also unlikely to be anxious or embarrassed should they be the focus of attention.

Muus (1988) has noted that those in the foreclosure stage are conventional and more authoritarian than are those in other stages. Moratorium teenagers are more questioning of authority and more anxious than other groups, which may be due to the fact that they are experiencing a crisis and are insecure. Identity-achieved and moratorium teenagers seem to have the highest self-esteem. Further evidence has demonstrated links between identity status and empathic concern for others (Erlanger, 1998) such that higher levels of ego identity status were associated with greater empathic concern. Moreover, those who reported a past or present crisis were also likely to manifest cognitive empathy, that is, they were more likely to take the perspective of another individual. Identity crisis has also been linked to the use of defense mechanisms (Cramer, 1997) and shyness (Hamer and Bruch, 1994).

THE DEVELOPING SELF-SYSTEM

As identity formation and achievement imply a discovery of the self, it follows that they cannot easily be divorced from such concepts as self-understanding, self-concept, and self-esteem.

Early writers, such as William James suggested that there are two crucial or fundamental aspects of the self (William James, 1892, cited in Harter, 1983). These are the self as actor (the 'I') and the self as the object of evaluation (the 'Me'). The I observes the Me; the Me characterises the individual as a unique being, while the I interprets experience (Damon and Hart, 1982).

Self-concept: The Development of I and Me

As noted earlier, the journey of self-discovery begins in infancy. Young children of about eighteen months of age are aware of others as distinct from the self. It is around this time that children recognise their reflected image. When viewing themselves in a mirror, they may smile, chatter to themselves or even reach out to their reflection (Brooks-Gunn and Lewis, 1984).

During childhood, the young individual is busily formulating a 'personal theory' or self-concept. As the child matures, this takes on different forms, first being rather rudimentary and ill-defined. The young child is aware of being 'a boy' or 'a girl'. This is referred to as the categorical self (Berk, 1989).

As the child develops cognitively, the view of the self undergoes some change. The pre-schooler becomes aware of an inner self, that is, thoughts that no one else has access to, and is also likely to describe oneself in concrete and observable terms (Harter, 1996). Later, a psychological self emerges which continuously changes in nature throughout adolescence (Harter, 1990). One study (Montemayor and Eisen, 1977) demonstrated that, as children grow, their self-concept becomes more abstract. This move towards more abstract and subjective descriptions is illustrated in Table 2.2, which sets out the self-descriptions of a seventeen-year-old adolescent and two younger children.

TABLE 2.2   *Self-descriptions of three individuals*

9-year-old boy
My name is Bruce C. I have brown eyes. I have brown hair. I have brown eyebrows. I'm nine years old. I LOVE! Sports. I have seven people in my family. I have great! eye site. I have lots! of friends. I live on 1923 Pinecrest Dr. I'm going on 10 in September. I'm a boy. I have an uncle that is almost 7 feet tall. My school is Pinecrest. My teacher is Mrs V. I play Hockey! I am almost the smartest boy in the class. I LOVE! food. I love fresh air. I LOVE School.

11½-year-old girl
My name is A. I'm a human being. I'm a girl. I'm a truthful person. I'm not pretty. I do so-so in my studies. I'm a very good cellist. I'm a very good pianist. I'm a little bit tall for my age. I like several boys. I like several girls. I'm old-fashioned. I play tennis. I am a very good swimmer. I try to be helpful. I'm always ready to be friends with anybody. Mostly I'm good, but I lose my temper. I'm not well-liked by some girls and boys. I don't know if I'm liked by boys or not.

17-year-old girl
I am a human being. I am a girl. I am an individual. I don't know who I am. I am a Pisces. I am a moody person. I am an indecisive person. I am an ambitious person. I am a very curious person. I am not an individual. I am a loner. I am an American (God help me). I am a Democrat. I am a liberal person. I am a radical. I am a conservative. I am a pseudoliberal. I am an atheist. I am not a classifiable person (i.e. I don't want to be).

Source: Montemayor and Eisen, 1977

What this shows is that the self-descriptions of older adolescents are more tortuous and evaluative and more likely to include personality descriptions. Whereas the descriptions of younger children can be described as 'unreflective self-acceptance', those of the older adolescent are more searching (Harter, 1983) and often contradictory, as adolescents agonise over who they think they are (Harter, 1998). Thus, it is clear that the self-concept changes as the individual matures cognitively.

Based on a review of the literature, Damon and Hart (1982) have suggested that the development of an understanding of 'Me' proceeds through four phases. These are the:

- physical self,
- active self,
- social self,
- psychological self.

The social self becomes important in early adolescence, and by late adolescence, there is the realisation that personality traits form the basis of many actions of the self. At the same time, older adolescents are capable of using qualifiers (for example, 'I run *very* fast') and are able to modify their behaviour to suit a quite different range of circumstances (Damon, 1990). The psychological self is fully developed by late adolescence, when belief systems characterise the active self. This congruency between belief systems and true self is one of the hallmarks of identity achievement.

Burns (1979) has remarked that 'Me' is indistinguishable from self-concept or one's judgement of self. This includes what one believes to be the perceptions of others as well as one's ideal self. These perceptions are the result of everyday experiences and interactions with others. As the understanding of 'Me' evolves, so too a gradual emerging of the 'I' takes place, involving the following (Damon and Hart, 1982):

- continuity – an unchanging physical self;
- distinctiveness – no one experiences things as I do, I am a unique individual;
- volition – mind can deceive others, can manipulate self's experience, I can make decisions;
- self-recognition – recognition of conscious and unconscious processes.

Self-evaluation

A constituent part of the self-concept is self-evaluation (Burns, 1979, 55). In evaluating the self, one is making: 'a conscious judgement regarding the significance, and importance of oneself or of facts of oneself'.

One therefore makes a judgement about one's behaviour and abilities, personality and physical attributes. Self-evaluation comprises three important facets (Burns, 1979). In the first instance, one has an ideal self, or a view of how one would like to be. One sets out to attain the ideal and to achieve self-actualisation which means that we strive to be self-sufficient and autonomous individuals. Self-actualisation fosters personal growth (Liebert and Spiegler, 1990) and gives rise to the fulfilment of one's potential (Cloninger, 1996). Adjustment problems arise when large discrepancies exist between the ideal self and the real or actual one. If the ideal self appears out of reach or unattainable, low self-esteem could result.

The second important facet relates to our beliefs about how others view us. It was early writers such as Charles Cooley and George Mead in the early part of the twentieth century who alerted us to the fact that part of the answer to the question 'Who am I?' is found in the appraisals of others. Thus, our perceptions of ourselves are based, in part, on our social interactions. Cooley used his own children as experimental subjects and observed that they closely monitored others and then drew the connection between their own acts and the responses of others. This led to Cooley's use of the term 'looking glass self' (Franklin, 1982).

An important process in the development of a psychological self is the ability to accurately perceive what others think of us. Such an ability is more evident with older and more cognitively mature adolescents. Mead (cited in Berk, 1989) referred to this as perspective-taking skills, a characteristic indicative of a healthy psychological self. Should one consistently perceive others' evaluations of us as negative, this is likely to lower an individual's self-esteem. Naturally, this process also works in reverse: One may deliberately misinterpret a negative experience in order to maintain positive self-esteem. This is referred to as perceptual distortion (Liebert and Spiegler, 1990).

It is therefore not surprising that significant others (such as parents, teachers and friends) play an important role in how adolescents evaluate themselves. Not surprisingly, researchers have found that younger children and adolescents tend to be more influenced by the beliefs of parents and teachers, whereas older adolescents are more likely to be sensitive to the opinions of peers (see Lackovic-Grgin and Dekovic, 1990).

Multidimensionality of the Self-concept

In addition to making an overall evaluation about oneself (for example, 'I am liked by most people'), it is also possible to evaluate various aspects of the self (for example, 'Most people are better than I am at mathematics, although I am quite good at marathon running'). The self-concept is therefore a multidimensional or many-sided construct and evaluations may include academic and physical ability as well as one's relationships with significant others (see also Addeo, Greene and Geisser, 1994; Harter, 1990; Watkins et al., 1998). Young people are well aware of their strong and weak points.

Shavelson and colleagues (1976) have also proposed that the self-concept is hierarchically ordered. Individual experiences of a particular nature (for instance, not getting on with one's mathematics teacher and consequently not doing as well as one could) have implications for academic self-evaluations ('Perhaps I am not good at mathematics after all' or 'I am not good at school-work'). Such evaluations may, ultimately, have consequences for one's general self-esteem. In this sense, then, self-concept has a hierarchical structure. This is illustrated in Figure 2.1.

One empirical study (Marsh, Relich and Smith, 1983) found support for the multidimensional nature of the self-concept among young adolescents. The various facets of self-concept showed predictable correlations with academic achievement and attributions for success

FIGURE 2.1 *The structure of self-concept*

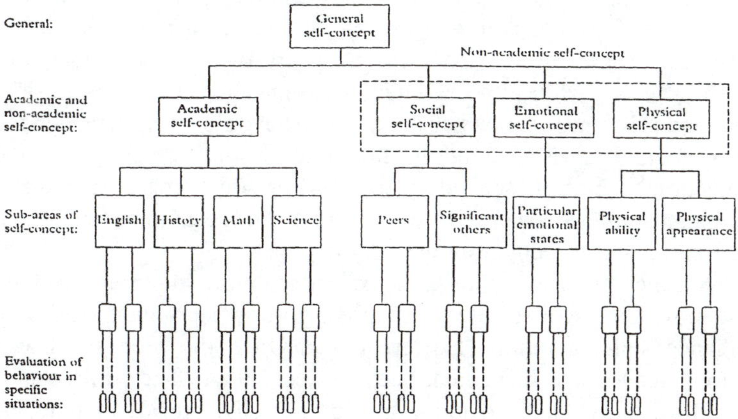

Source: Shavelson et al., 1976

and failure. It was noted that adolescents who explained personal success in terms of their own effort and ability were most likely to have elevated levels of self-esteem. Not surprisingly, academic performance was closely related to academic self-concept. Other factors such as achievement motivation and the expectation of succeeding, are also important factors in this regard, and will be discussed in more detail in Chapter 5.

The Stability of Self-esteem

Several important empirical studies have demonstrated the relative stability of self-evaluation, not only during the childhood years (Verschueren, Marcoen and Buyck, 1998), but also during the adolescent years. A longitudinal study conducted in the USA (Savin-Williams and Demo 1984) examined changes to the experienced self (that is, the self as evaluated by the individual), the presented self (that is, the self which we reveal to the world) and self-feelings (those more diverse and differentiated feelings about the self). It was found that there are no dramatic changes in various aspects of self-evaluation. Any changes that do occur, the authors argued, tend to be associated with normal adolescent development rather than a turbulent adolescence. It was concluded that, for most adolescents, the self-esteem is quite stable, showing only gradual increase.

Other studies (for example, O'Malley and Bachman, 1983) have demonstrated that self-esteem scores show moderate rises between the ages of 13 and 23 years. These researchers based their conclusion on the results of a large longitudinal study conducted in the USA. Such a rise in self-esteem is not surprising, according to the authors. For instance, after the age of about thirteen years, the adolescent increases in physical size, while also beginning to assume adult roles, responsibilities and privileges all of which are likely to have a positive effect on the self-esteem. It is also around this time that most adolescents make the transition to high or secondary school. For some, this is a stressful period, resulting in lower self-esteem. This would seem to be temporary, whereafter self-esteem levels usually increase.

With increasing age, teenagers experience more autonomy and are also more likely to associate with support groups, peers and friends who enhance self-evaluation (Harter, 1990). Once the teenager leaves school, academic achievement becomes less salient. The adolescent is therefore more likely to judge him or herself in terms of personal happiness and life satisfaction, rather than academic performance.

Sex Differences in Self-esteem

The question as to whether there are sex differences in regard to various psychological traits is an important issue in contemporary psychology, generating much research and debate (for example, Wilgenbusch and Merrell, 1999). Much has been written on this topic, including the now classic volume by Maccoby and Jacklin (1974). Their review of the literature concerning sex differences in self-esteem yielded equivocal findings. Only a small number of studies showed that males have higher general self-esteem than females and, in fact, many of the studies reviewed found no significant sex differences at all.

Some evidence suggests that boys have significantly higher self-esteem in physical ability and mathematics, although girls have higher self-esteem in reading (Marsh et al., 1983). Sex differences are accentuated in the state co-educational schools, thus maintaining traditional stereotypes. Although sex differences are also observed among the private school students, the effects appear smaller.

A meta-analysis of studies of sex differences in multidimensional self-concept among school students yielded the following conclusions (Wilgenbusch and Merrell, 1999):

- Boys had higher self-esteem on a global index as well as on mathematical ability, musical/job competence, physical appearance, physical coordination, emotional/affect and anxiety.
- Females had higher self-esteem on the following dimensions: verbal, close friendships, same-sex peer relationships, honesty and religion.

One's satisfaction with different aspects of the self is not only affected by gender, but also by culture. Watkins and his colleagues were able to demonstrate this phenomenon in a study of over 3000 students of both sexes from 15 different cultures differing in their degree of collectivism versus individualism (Watkins et al., 1998). Students were asked to rate the importance of and satisfaction with 20 areas of the self. Factor analysis of these ratings reduced the data to the following dimensions:

- being cultured vs. physical appearance,
- family values vs. personal success,
- intelligence vs. group morality,
- social relationships vs. physical abilities.

Some of the major findings can be summarised as follows: Respondents from collectivist cultures ranked 'being cultured' quite highly. Males from individualistic cultures ranked personal appearance and personal success high, while females from individualistic cultures ranked social relationships as high. They were also most satisfied with family relationships rather than personal success. Males from individualistic cultures were most satisfied with their intelligence (Watkins et al., 1998).

SEX-ROLE IDENTITY

The extent to which we adopt typical 'male' or 'female' behaviours has, with the advent of the women's movement, given rise to considerable research and theorising in psychology (Huston, 1983). This section will explore the development of a sex-role identity.

Theories of Sex-role Identity Formation

There are a number of influential theoretical perspectives which are useful in explaining the formation of sex-role identities (Archer, 1992; Huston, 1983). Each will be briefly described.

Social learning theories

We noted in the previous chapter that one can learn behaviour through imitation and observation. We learn gender-appropriate behaviours in very much the same way. Traditionally, gender-appropriate behaviours have been reinforced, while unacceptable behaviours have been frowned upon. A young boy playing with his sister's dolls, for example, is unlikely to receive much encouragement and reinforcement from his father who, in turn, is likely to regard this as gender-inappropriate play (Langlois and Downs, 1980).

The previous chapter explained that social learning is distinguishable from more classic forms of learning, in that it highlights the importance of observation. Therefore, the girl who notices that it is only mother who keeps house, may come to believe that it is inappropriate for males to do such chores.

Cognitive developmental theory

According to this perspective, teenagers' *understanding* of masculinity and femininity is important, rather than their actual behaviour. Teenagers look for consistency between understanding and behaviour, and it is the former which seems to determine the latter (Archer, 1992). Naturally, the understanding of concepts such as gender is age-related. As a consequence, therefore, one progresses through various stages of sex-role identity formation with increasing age (Archer, 1992; Huston, 1983).

One exponent of this view of sex-role identity formation is Kohlberg (1966). In the first stage, according to Kohlberg, young children of two to four years recognise that they are a 'boy' or a 'girl'. They learn from their parents or siblings about acceptable and gender-appropriate behaviours. Children interpret their daily experiences in accordance with their understanding of 'boyness' or 'girlness'. They also derive pleasure from gender-appropriate behaviour. In middle childhood, individuals are aware that they possess gender constancy, that is, that they will one day grow up to be either male or female. At this age, children adhere rigidly to rules about being a member of a gender group and cross-sex behaviour is unacceptable.

During adolescence, individuals are asking the question 'Who am I?' Not only is the teenager confronting the psychological self, but also the sexual self, brought on by rapid physical and biological maturation (Hughes and Noppe, 1985). Whereas early adolescents have quite fixed ideas about appropriate behaviours for the sexes, they become more flexible in their views as they get older. In late adolescence, it is believed that teenagers are much more willing to adopt either 'masculine' or 'feminine' traits in accordance with their own evolving personal identity. It is during the latter part of this psychological orientation period (Hughes and Noppe, 1985, 48) that: 'Sex-stereotyped traits are not assumed to be crucial aspects of personal identity. Principles of equality and freedom are proposed as standards for behavior, and are used to define an ideal model of personal and interpersonal functioning.'

An important element of the cognitive developmental perspective is the adolescent's understanding of being male or female. Gender schema theories have extended this view by arguing that sex-role stereotypes set the framework within which much of our thinking about gender-related matters is conducted. Thus, we develop schema or cognitive frameworks that help organise our information and help us interpret and process stimuli. Schema are especially useful in new and unusual situations in that we draw on previous experience in helping us deal with current events. Schema, moreover, may be culturally driven or learned from parents, role models or friends.

Like most frames of reference, schema can bias our interpretation of information. It has been found that individuals who tend to adhere to sex-role stereotypes are much more likely to distort or to reconstruct information to match their world view or schema. Archer (1992) was able to demonstrate how those holding traditional sex-role views reconstructed non-traditional pictures (for example, a female doctor) into more traditional ones (for example, a male doctor).

In summary, although schemas are useful in helping us process information quickly and deal with novel situations, they over-simplify our social world and are sometimes based on incorrect information.

Sex-role identity and adjustment

Is there a relationship between sex-role identity and psychological adjustment? There are three models that make quite different predictions about the relationship between sex-role identity and adjustment. The first is referred to as the *congruence* model (Whitley, 1983). It assumes that masculinity and femininity are opposite poles of a single continuum. According to this model, masculinity and femininity are mutually exclusive and incompatible. The model predicts that high self-esteem is dependent upon one's sex-role orientation being congruent with one's gender. In its slightly reformulated version, the model predicts that high masculinity and low femininity in men, and high femininity and low masculinity in women are related to high self-esteem.

The *androgyny* model suggests that individuals can incorporate both masculine and feminine traits to varying degree. This two-dimensional model (shown in Figure 2.2) gives rise to four sex-role types: androgynous, undifferentiated, masculine and feminine. It is therefore possible to fit into any one of the quadrants, irrespective of one's gender. The model predicts an association between androgyny and psychological well-being (Whitley, 1983).

Finally, the *masculinity* model predicts that psychological well-being depends upon the masculinity component of androgyny (Whitley, 1983). In other words, the femininity component makes only a very small contribution to overall well-being, suggesting that so-called masculine traits (for instance, dominance, assertiveness, etc.) are influential in explaining psychological adjustment in both sexes.

Support for these models varies, and is largely dependent upon the samples studied and the measures used. Generally, most support has

FIGURE 2.2   *Two-dimensional model of sex-role identity*

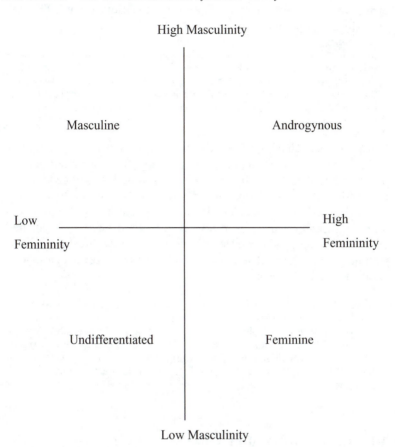

been found for the androgyny and masculinity models. In an early study (Massad, 1981) it was found that, among adolescent females, both masculinity and femininity were related to positive self-esteem. Among adolescent males, high masculinity was associated with high self-esteem. It was also observed that androgynous and sex-typed males had higher self-esteem than cross-typed males. Androgynous females had higher self-esteem than either sex-typed or cross-typed females. Thus, the results of this study suggest that adolescent females may be under more pressure than their male counterparts to adopt non-traditional sex-role traits.

Research among university students has found support for the androgyny and masculinity models. The authors (Orlofsky and O'Heron, 1987, 1041) concluded that:

> masculine qualities appear to have broadly positive implications for self-esteem and adjustment...Feminine qualities do not relate to self-esteem and adjustment indices as strongly or consistently as do masculine qualities...they do play a central role in more communal aspects of self-esteem while also contributing somewhat to more general aspects of adjustment.

Recent research has qualified the links that exist between masculinity and positive self-esteem among young girls approaching puberty (Lobel, Slone and Winch, 1997). In addition to assessing levels of gender-role orientation, the authors categorised respondents as either high or low on a measure of tomboyishness. It was found that girls high on masculinity and tomboyishness were less liked by their peers, less satisfied with their gender, and low on social self-esteem and self-esteem related to home and parents. The authors explained these results as follows (Lobel et al., 1997, 406):

> It would appear that society attributes respect to a girl who is assertive, dominant and ambitious under the condition that she does not show exclusive male interests and does not prefer to play solely masculine games. Similarly, although peers and parents may extend greater latitude to girls who behave in a masculine way...there may exist the expectation that this will be complemented by some feminine traits such as sensitivity and gentleness.

THEORETICAL CONSIDERATIONS

There can be no doubt that Erikson's (1968) views on identity formation have had an enormous impact on our thinking about the nature of adolescent identity and the search for self-meaning. His psychosocial stage theory (and the subsequent reformulations by others such as Marcia) have generated empirical research which has largely served to support its validity. Erikson broadened psychoanalytic theory to a considerable extent, and eloquently explained just how important social factors are in human development (Crain, 1985).

Identity development is closely associated with knowledge about and evaluation of the self. The identity and self perspectives have evolved quite independently of each other, yet are closely connected. Acceptance of one's identity is important for the development of a positive self-esteem.

SUMMARY

The development of one's identity is a crucial task for the adolescent. Of course, this process is not necessarily completed by the end of the teenage years. Indeed, some individuals continue with this task well into adulthood. Fortunately for many adolescents, by the time they leave school they have a fair idea of their sexual orientation and likely occupation. They have a fair sense of knowing just 'who I am' and 'where I am going'.

A vitally important aspect of identity formation is the development of a sexual identity. Thus by late adolescence most teenagers are able to identify themselves as either heterosexual or gay/lesbian. This stage of the life span can be difficult as teenagers confront their sexuality and rapidly changing body. It is also quite clearly a time of excitement for many, as they contemplate life as an adult.

The development of a vocational identity is also seen as an integral part of the process of identity formation. For many teenagers, this is a difficult process. Thus, governments and communities have an enormous responsibility to harness the talents of these teenagers and to assist, as best they can, those who are at risk of long-term unemployment and its side-effects, such as depression and feelings of hopelessness.

As adolescents embark on identity formation, they are greatly influenced by their family and friends. Both act as sources of emotional support and psychological well-being. Both help mould teenagers' behaviour by setting the boundaries of what is acceptable. Sometimes these boundaries are contradictory. Most teenagers will accept them and experiment with a range of behaviours and roles. This is a natural part of growing up and helps define the self.

Another important influence on adolescent development and emotional adjustment is the family. It is to this important topic that we now turn.

ADDITIONAL READING

Erikson, E. (1968) *Identity: Youth and Crisis*. New York: W.W. Norton and Co.

Marcia, J. (1966) 'Development and Validation of Ego-identity Status', *Journal of Personality and Social Psychology* 3: 551–8.

EXERCISES

1   To what extent are the development of a vocational and sexual identity during adolescence related to overall identity development? Can these develop in isolation from one another?
2   Conduct a study in which you survey the self-esteem of men and women in your university/college. Are there sex differences across different domains of the self (for example, spatial ability, verbal ability, and so on)? Are sex differences a function of particular courses of study? Are sex differences a function of social class, age, or other factors?

3

Family Influences

INTRODUCTION

The young individual's first awareness and experience of other humans occurs in the context of the family. The family is a powerful socialising agent and many empirical studies have demonstrated quite conclusively that the quality of the attachment and bonding processes between parent and infant in the first few months and years of life are important for the later emotional health of the individual. The family is an important arena in which much learning about the world occurs. Research has shown that family relationships during adolescence have important flow-on effects for a number of domains, such as the autonomy and later independence of the individual (Coleman and Hendry, 1990), adolescent personality (Chiariello and Orvaschel, 1995; Heaven, 1997; Rosenberg and Kaplan, 1982), individual pathology (Scott and Scott, 1987), and problem behaviour (Peiser and Heaven, 1996; Pettit, Bates and Dodge, 1997; Shaw and Scott, 1991), to mention just a few.

The family is regarded as an important support system available to the child and adolescent. Consequently, any disturbance of this support system through factors such as changes within the adolescent, parental separation or a particularly negative parenting style, have implications for adolescent functioning, adjustment and identity achievement. Indeed, the quality of the parent-adolescent bond is a central research theme and of major interest to developmental psychology (Collins, 1990). This is not to suggest that other factors such as peer influences are not important, but certainly the role of the family is a pivotal one.

In this chapter, several aspects of the parent–adolescent relationship will be examined. Central to this discussion will be the extent to which family factors influence adolescent development. Of concern are the effects of parenting styles and control, and those of divorce and parental separation on adolescents' emotional adjustment. Attention will also be briefly paid to parent–adolescent communication, as well as the challenges teenagers face when they move into new families.

THEORETICAL PERSPECTIVES

In an attempt to better understand family interactions, various theories of the family have been proposed. The following have been listed as particularly influential (Callan and Noller, 1987): symbolic interactionism, social exchange theory and family systems theory.

Briefly, symbolic interactionism refers to attempts to view the world through the eyes of the adolescent. Key concepts (or symbols) include roles, categories, positions and definitions of situations. According to this view of the family, teenagers organise their behaviour and interact with others in terms of their perceptions of these symbols (Callan and Noller, 1987). Adolescents and their parents fulfil quite different roles in the family and their interactions depend, to a large extent, on their definition of these roles. When adolescents respond to the actions of their parents, their response incorporates an interpretation of the parental action. According to this perspective, then, behaviour must be viewed in terms of perceptions and expectations of other family members.

Maximising rewards and minimising punishments is central to social exchange theory. Thus, an adolescent may engage in some behaviours and not others in the hope that this might have some beneficial effect on someone else (for instance, smiling to gain approval). Such two way exchanges occur in all person-to-person interactions.

Other writers have argued that the family should be viewed from a systems oriented perspective in which the family is viewed as an integrated network of individuals and relationships. An underlying principle of this approach is that, not only are all members of a system interconnected, but each has links outside it. Each element, therefore, has the potential to have an effect on any other within the system and its immediate environment. According to Schneewind (1990), this perspective emphasises the organisation of the family in terms of relationships. Callan and Noller (1987, 33) have argued that: 'To see the family as a system, operating by system rules, with each part affecting the others in systematic ways is very different from seeing the family as a collection of individuals who happen to live in the same house.'

According to the systems perspective, the family is regarded as an intricate arrangement of interconnecting relationships. Many family units consist of harmonious relationships, while others experience conflict. Although not all are characterised by conflict (Noller and Patton, 1990; Paikoff and Brooks Gunn, 1991), there appears to be no doubt that the nature of the parent–child relationship undergoes change as the child approaches early adolescence. This is almost certain as the child faces, and parents witness, biological, cognitive and emotional change.

Pubertal change also has the ability to determine the nature of the family climate (Paikoff and Brooks Gunn, 1991). Firstly, hormonal changes occurring within the child are likely to have an effect on his or her emotional lability, thus affecting interactions with parents. This has led some researchers to focus on such factors as depression and moodiness in adolescents, boys' increasing levels of aggression, and so forth. Secondly, it is possible that the timing or rate of development of secondary sex characteristics in teenagers may influence the nature of parent–child relationships. This may occur by influencing individual perceptions. In one study, for instance, it was found that parents attached more importance to pubertal changes than did adolescents (Savin-Williams and Small, 1986). No doubt, physical changes in the adolescent are a dramatic reminder to parents that their children are growing up and will soon take on new roles in society. Physical changes in the young adolescent symbolise the approach of adulthood and, according to Paikoff and Brooks Gunn (1991, 51): 'are salient to both adolescent and parent, and they signal the incipient reproductive and social maturity of the child, an event laden with meaning'.

Thirdly, pubertal changes interact with a number of other important factors to influence parent–adolescent relationships. Such factors may include social and cognitive changes in the child, particular individual and familial characteristics such as parenting styles and parent–child communication, perceptions of physical change by the adolescent and parents, and changes to the self-identity of the parent and child (Paikoff and Brooks Gunn, 1991).

Models of Family Functioning

There are several different, although related, models of family functioning (Callan and Noller, 1987; Walsh, 1982). It is beyond the scope of this chapter to review these in detail. Suffice to say that some writers have proposed an integrative model of family functioning which combines elements and constructs of each of the major models. Accordingly, eight dimensions of healthy family functioning have been identified (Walsh, 1982). These are:

- individuation vs. enmeshment,
- mutuality vs. isolation,

- flexibility vs. rigidity,
- stability vs. disorganisation,
- clear vs. distorted perceptions,
- clear vs. role conflict,
- role reciprocity vs. conflictual roles,
- clear vs. diffuse generation boundaries.

Healthy family functioning requires a balance between the poles of each of these dimensions. Families with psychologically healthy adolescents demonstrate a balance between enmeshment and emotional connectedness on the one hand and encouragement of adolescent independence on the other. Walsh (1982) stresses that the factors mentioned above characterise normal family functioning and that an improvement in one is likely to lead to an improvement in others. It is also important to bear in mind that 'normal' functioning is not the sole prerogative of the traditional family unit.

Although the nature of the parent–child relationship in nearly all families will undergo some change across time, certain familial characteristics have been identified as crucial in predicting the psychological adjustment of adolescents. Some of these will be discussed below. Before we do that let us first consider adolescents' views of the 'ideal' family.

THE 'IDEAL' FAMILY

Research in this area has been surprisingly limited especially when one considers that most adolescents have quite positive and favourable attitudes towards their families (Noller and Patton, 1990; Payne and Furnham, 1990). Young people identify a number of components as characteristic of the 'ideal' family (see Table 3.1).

Research among adolescents in Barbados found that girls, more than boys, considered family openness, expressiveness and cooperation to be the hallmarks of the ideal family. Girls, but not boys, appeared more concerned about getting various household chores completed and considered these chores to play an important part in the day-to-day functioning of the ideal family – which may reflect their socialisation experiences. Adolescents who rated their family environment as 'open' with 'constructive communication' were more likely to be satisfied with their families (Payne and Furnham, 1990).

TABLE 3.1   *Adolescents' dimensions of the ideal family*

Dimensions of ideal family	Example of questionnaire item
Age and status	Older persons should have more privileges than younger ones
Authority structure/division of labour	All family members should share in doing chores
Cooperational togetherness	Every member of the family should help each other
Emotional expressiveness	Children should be open and honest with parents
Extra-familial activity	Boys should have more privileges than girls
Individual rights	Every family member has a right to keep certain thoughts and feelings private
Positive/open relationships	Adults should be able to admit their mistakes to their children
Problem-solving/decision-making	A family should get problems solved right away

Source: Payne and Furnham, 1990

PARENT–ADOLESCENT INFLUENCES

The family plays an important role in shaping child and adolescent behaviour (Bahr, 1991; Chiariello and Orvaschel, 1995; Heaven, 1997; Jaccard and Dittus, 1991; Noller and Callan, 1991; R. Scott and W. Scott, 1998). This is not to say that factors such as social experience or peer groups are not important. Rather, it is suggested that the influence of the family is a pivotal one.

Parents influence their teenagers in several ways (Jaccard and Dittus, 1991). In the first place, parents serve as role models, and teenagers learn by observation and imitation. Secondly, parenting styles and child rearing patterns have an important influence on teenagers' social and emotional development. Thirdly, parents transmit their values and morals to their children and this may include beliefs about what constitutes acceptable behaviour. Finally, parents are an important source of information on a range of topics. Communication between parents and teenagers is therefore vital (see p. 64).

Psychological research into parent–adolescent influences has tended to concentrate on a few quite specific domains. Some of the more salient ones will be discussed below. What will become clear is that most (but not all) of the studies deal with *adolescent perceptions* of their family. Although such perceptions may be inaccurate, they remain 'real' for the child and therefore have important implications for subsequent behaviours, attitudes, and personal constructs (Bruner and Tagiuri, 1954).

Parenting Styles

Notwithstanding the sex, social background or other characteristics of the adolescent, all teenagers confront major developmental tasks. As was noted in Chapter 1, some of these are adjustment to physical changes, establishing effective social and working relationships, coming to terms with one's sexuality, and establishing an identity or preparation for a career. It has been argued that a crucial factor in assisting one attain these goals is the family (Conger and Petersen, 1984).

In a now classic study, Schaefer (1959) proposed his well-known two-dimensional scheme of parental behaviour patterns, namely, autonomy–control vs. hostility–love. He argued that parents in the hostility–control quadrant are likely to be demanding and authoritarian in their relationships with their children, while those in the autonomy–love quadrant are more likely to act in a democratic and cooperative way. Various theorists have proposed several schemes and, although the labels theorists use are to some extent different, two dimensions appear quite consistent. These have been referred to as emotional support and parental control (Amato, 1990). Most parental behaviours vis-à-vis the child can be classified under these two groupings. Perhaps of greater importance, however, is that each of these styles has been shown to relate to adolescent adjustment to varying degrees.

Research evidence has found that, if parents are supportive and tend to use low levels of coercion, their adolescent offspring are more likely to be socially competent (Noller and Patton, 1990). On the other hand, coercion combined with lack of support is likely to result in behavioural problems among adolescents. These parental qualities can act in isolation, or in combination, in determining psychological adjustment (Conger and Petersen, 1984).

Acknowledging that parenting qualities such as emotional support and control are useful devices for thinking about family interactions, one may question whether they coincide with adolescents' perceptions of family relationships. In other words, just how valid are these dimensions? In order to determine this, Amato (1990) interviewed 402 pairs of Australian children, including adolescents, and their parents. Respondents were asked a range of general questions about family processes. For instance, they were questioned about their perceptions of parental closeness and support, decision-making, punishment, family cohesion and how their parents reacted to misbehaviours. It was found that adolescents do indeed perceive two dimensions, namely, support and control leading Amato (1990, 618) to conclude that: 'the dimensions researchers have used to guide their observations and analyses are very similar to the dimensions children use in cognitively organizing family events and relationships'.

Not all children emphasise the same dimensions when thinking about their family. Adolescents tend to emphasise the control dimension, rather than the support one. By contrast, younger children are more likely to emphasise parental support, which may simply reflect the child's developmental stage (Amato, 1990). Adolescents are more likely to view control and independence from parents as important issues since they tend to have support outside the family (for example, peers). Thus, not all forms of parental behaviours may be suited to all children within one family.

The Parent–adolescent Bond

Researchers have developed measures of the perceptions of parents' rearing behaviours. Perhaps the most widely used measures are the Parental Bonding Instrument (PBI; Parker, Tupling and Brown, 1979) and the Egna Minnen Betraffande Uppfostran (EMBU; Perris, Jacobsson, Lindstrom, Von Knorring and Perris, 1980). Both the PBI and the EMBU (the latter means 'memories of my upbringing') are multidimensional measures and comprise quite similar facets as shown in Table 3.2 although, as is shown, there is some dispute about the exact nature of the PBI domains. In fact, a recent French adaptation of the PBI suggests three dimensions, namely, Care, Denial of psychological autonomy, and Encouragement of behavioural freedom (Mohr et al., 1999). It has also recently been shown that there is considerable overlap between Emotional warmth (EMBU) and Care (PBI) while Rejection (EMBU) correlates highly negatively with Care (PBI) (Arrindell et al., 1998).

Perhaps of more immediate interest is the fact that both the EMBU and PBI are useful in predicting a wide range of psychopathologies. For example, low parental care combined with overprotection (PBI) is referred to as affectionless control and has been found to be predictive of schizophrenia, borderline personality, anxiety, depression, bulimia, and drug addiction in young people (Biggam and Power, 1998; Mohr et al., 1999; see also Research Highlight 3.1).

TABLE 3.2   *Facets of the EMBU and the PBI*

EMBU (Perris et al., 1980)	PBI (Parker et al., 1979)	PBI (Mohr et al., 1999)
Emotional warmth	Care	Care
Rejection	Overprotection	Denial of psychological autonomy
Protection		Encouragement of behavioural freedom

Note: EMBU: Egna Minnen Betraffaude Uppfostran (*memories of my upbringing*)
PBI: Parental Bonding Instrument

In one study, the PBI and other measures were administered to 125 incarcerated young Scottish offenders aged 16–21 years (Biggam and Power, 1998). Although respondents revealed their perceptions of maternal care to be significantly higher than that of a normative sample, respondents scored significantly lower on all of the other domains for mothers and fathers. In addition, overprotection was found to sig-

RESEARCH HIGHLIGHT 3.1
Perceptions of parental bonding and adolescent adjustment
in Britain
Shams and Williams, 1995

Cross-cultural research by Shams and Williams examined the influence of parental bonding on psychological distress levels in two groups of British adolescents aged 14–15 years. Respondents were British Asians (mainly from the Indian subcontinent) and non-Asians (mainly Scottish). British Asian teenagers reported receiving less care and more protection than their non-Asian counterparts. British Asian girls were more likely to report that their parents were 'cold' towards them, were non-praising, and did not understand their problems. British Asian adolescents (boys and girls) thought their parents too controlling and too protective. Finally, among both cultural groups adequate parental care was significantly related to low anxiety, low depression, and low psychological distress as measured by the General Health Questionnaire. Just the opposite was obtained with respect to overprotectiveness.

nificantly predict anxiety, depression and hopelessness for this sample. It was also found that those likely to be classified as manifesting clinical levels of anxiety, hopelessness or depression, were more likely to report weak bonding (low care and low protection) and affectionless control (low care and high protection).

Types of Parental Control

The effect of parental discipline on adolescent developmental outcome has received much attention in the research literature. Empirical studies have shown that teenagers who rate their parents as authoritative are likely to score higher on measures of competence, social development, self esteem and mental health than those who rate their parents as permissive or authoritarian (Lamborn et al., 1991; Shucksmith, Hendry and Glendinning, 1995).

Following the earlier suggestion by Maccoby and Martin (1983), it has become customary to differentiate between authoritative and authoritarian forms of control, as well as indulgent and neglectful permissiveness. Indulgent permissiveness refers to low parental control coupled with trust and a democratic attitude. Neglectful, by contrast, refers to low parental control coupled with disengagement from the responsibilities of child-rearing (Lamborn et al., 1991).

It has been empirically demonstrated that each of these styles has unique adolescent outcomes (see Tables 3.3 and 3.4). The greatest differences have been observed between teenagers from authoritative and neglectful homes. The differences in outcome between authoritarian and indulgent homes tend to favour teenagers from authoritarian homes, although the differences are not always significant. Table 3.3 shows that adolescent outcomes are most favourable for those from authoritative homes. Teenagers from such homes appear to be better adjusted and more competent and are also usually more confident about their abilities. Children from authoritarian homes conform and are obedient, yet are lacking in self-confidence. Although indulged teenagers are likely to engage in some deviant behaviours, these are not particularly serious. In addition, such youngsters are also likely to score quite high on measures of social competence (Lamborn et al., 1991).

The main thrust of these ideas was later replicated in a major Scottish study of 10 000 adolescents (Shucksmith et al., 1995). According to the respondents, families in the sample can be grouped as follows:

- permissive – 37.8%

TABLE 3.3   *Effects of parental control on adolescent outcomes*

Parental control	Adolescent outcomes
Authoritative homes	High competence High adjustment High academic competence High psychosocial development Low problem behaviour Fewer psychological and somatic problems than neglected youth
Neglectful homes	Lower on psychosocial development, but not significantly different from authoritarian homes on self-reliance, perceived social competence, and perceived academic competence High on internalised distress High on problem behaviour
Authoritarian and indulgent homes	Teenagers tend to perform between above two groups. Youth from authoritarian homes rate lower on school misconduct, drug use and somatic symptoms. Have positive orientation to school. Youth from indulgent homes score higher on social competence and self-confidence. Also higher on less serious deviant behaviours.

Source: Lamborn et al., 1991

- problem parent–adolescent relationships – 16.8%
- authoritative – 23.7%
- authoritarian – 15.3%

Table 3.4 shows the specific outcomes and characteristics associated with each type of family. The information presented here differs from that in Table 3.3 in that demographic data that characterise these families are also presented. It is clear that, not only do adolescents from authoritative families have fewer emotional problems, but that those families also tend to have parents with higher levels of formal education and are described as 'middle class'. In conclusion, the data highlight the extent to which family types influence adolescent adjustment and Shucksmith and colleagues (1995, 268) concluded as follows:

> it would appear therefore that relational difficulties within the family are indicative of multiple problems for young people with regard to psychosocial development at this stage of adolescence, and also that parenting which combines high levels of acceptance with appropriate levels of control

TABLE 3.4   *Descriptions and distinguishing characteristics of Scottish families*

Description	Characteristics
Permissive families	Both parents tend to work
Families with problem relationships	Single parent/blended families
	Both parents tend to work
	They have less formal education
	Tend to be socio-economically disadvantaged
	Children disaffected with school
	High levels of psychological distress
Authoritative families	Higher levels of formal education
	Middle-class parents
	Children have positive attitudes to school
	Low levels of psychological distress
Authoritarian	These families tended to attain 'middling' scores on most of the measures used

Source: Shucksmith et al., 1995

is perhaps the most 'effective' family environment in early and middle adolescence.

Does discipline style matter?

Following the theorising of Hoffman (1963), measures of parental discipline style have been constructed and validated (Shaw and Scott, 1991). The dimensions are as follows:

- punitive discipline style – the parent asserts power such that the child fears detection and punishment of 'bad' behaviours;
- inductive discipline style – here the parent seeks to explain to the child the consequences for and the effects on others of the child's behaviour;
- love-withdrawal style – the child is anxious about losing the love of the parent and so seeks to restore the relationship by ceasing unacceptable behaviours.

Evidence has shown quite clearly that these discipline styles are consistently and logically related to adolescent adjustment, in particular self-reported delinquency (Shaw and Scott, 1991; Peiser and Heaven, 1996). Inductiveness, for instance, is related to lower levels of delinquency. This point will be taken up again in more detail in Chapter 9.

Family Communication

Implicit in parenting styles is the nature of communication between parents and adolescents. It is quite reasonable to assume that a warm, empathic, and caring parenting style will result in communication with a teenager that is qualitatively different from that resulting from an autocratic and coercive parenting style. In line with this view, it is maintained that family communication is a prerequisite for the healthy functioning of the family and its individual members (for example, Barnes and Olson, 1985; Heaven, 1997; Noller and Callan, 1991). Healthy communication is likely to have beneficial effects on the adolescent's level of independence and self-esteem. Families with high levels of communication show more cohesion, adaptability and satisfaction (Barnes and Olson, 1985). Positive communication in families is related to lower levels of (Eysenckian) psychoticism (or toughmindedness) in adolescents. Among males, perceptions of negative family communication in families has direct effects on levels of interpersonal violence (Heaven, 1994).

Adolescent males and females differ with respect to their perceptions of communication within the family. Females report talking more often with their mothers than with their fathers, while males report talking more often to fathers about sexual issues and general problems. Females report disclosing more to mothers than to fathers, although males report equal disclosure to both parents. Generally, mothers are seen by adolescents as more willing to listen and initiate conversations, while fathers are seen as more judgemental. Moreover, what adolescents actually disclose to their parents seems determined in part by the sex of both the adolescent and the parent (Noller and Callan, 1990).

THE PSYCHOLOGICAL HEALTH OF PARENTS

In addition to the importance of factors such as discipline style and parental bonding on adolescent adjustment, there is much evidence demonstrating significant links between the psychological health of parents and that of their adolescent children. An examination of the results of several longitudinal studies has found links between pathological behaviours in parents and serious disorders (for example, schizophrenia and depression) in their children several years later (Downey and Coyne, 1990; Goldstein, 1988).

W. Scott and R. Scott (1987) assessed the linkages between what they referred to as family and individual pathology in 724 members of 'normal range' families (including adolescents). They were interested in the extent to which manifestations of family pathology, that is, inter-member conflict, low solidarity and member dissatisfaction, were related to individual symptoms, namely, neurosis, self-esteem and dissatisfaction with life circumstances.

The results indicated that the various manifestations of family pathology tended to be interrelated. For example, within-family conflict tended to be associated with low family solidarity. Moreover, most members of pathological families tended to perform their roles rather poorly, while parent-reported family pathology was predictive of children's individual pathology. Thus, evidence was found to support the view that the family acts as a strong socialisation agent, and that parental attitudes, values and behavioural manifestations are often reflected in the behaviour of the children (W. Scott and R. Scott, 1987; see also R. Scott and W. Scott, 1998).

One research team documented the familial links with respect to psychopathology (Goodyer et al., 1993). It was found that girls with major depressive disorder were much more likely to have mothers with depression (in 68 per cent of cases) than were girls diagnosed with a partial syndrome of depression (35 per cent of cases) or girls in a control sample (30 per cent). Similar trends were observed among fathers. In another study, the incidence of ADHD (attention deficit hyperactivity disorder) was found to be greater in those families with evidence of parental psychopathology (particularly among mothers) and parental conflict (Biederman et al., 1995).

Robertson and Simons (1989) observed that parental rejection, rather than factors such as family conflict, perceived parental control or perceived family religiosity were crucial in determining adolescent depression. Indeed, parental rejection seemed to *interact* with adolescent self-esteem in a quite specific way. Parental rejection was important in predicting adolescent depression, *especially* in those homes where parents failed to nurture adolescents' self-esteem by providing love, understanding, or support. Thus, parental rejection was found to have an indirect effect on depression through adolescent self-esteem. Other factors (such as family religiosity and family conflict) tended to become less important in understanding adolescent depression as parental rejection *increased*.

TABLE 3.5   *Changes in family composition in Australia, 1986–96*

Description	1986 %	1996 %
Children living in a registered marriage	80.1	72.1
Children living in de facto marriages	3.0	6.1
Children in single mother households	9.8	14.4
Children in single father households	1.3	1.8

Source: Australian Bureau of Statistics, 1999

PARENTAL SEPARATION AND DIVORCE

Parental separation and divorce will affect an ever-increasing number of children and adolescents. According to some estimates, between 30 to 50 per cent of school-age children will experience the break-up of their family in the United Kingdom, Canada, and the USA (Pagani et al., 1997). In Australia the divorce rate has risen from 10.7 per 1000 married males in 1986 to 12.9 in 1997 (Australian Bureau of Statistics, 1998). The number of children living in de facto marriages and single-parent families has been steadily increasing at the expense of children living with their parents in registered marriages. Table 3.5 shows that between 1986 and 1996 children living in single-mother households increased from 9.8 to 14.1 per cent, while the number of children in de facto marriages rose from 3.0 to 6.1 per cent (Australian Bureau of Statistics, 1999). As these rates have increased, so too has interest in the consequent psychological adjustment of former spouses and their offspring.

How do children and adolescents respond to divorce, separation, and remarriage? They may react with anger, resentment, anxiety, depression or aggression. They may be confused and apprehensive about the future and the changing relationships around them. This very often has negative consequences for scholastic performance. So-called 'easy' children, however, are likely to cope better with divorce and remarriage, while a support network for the child (understanding teachers, grandparents, etc.) is likely to ameliorate stress levels (Hetherington, Stanley-Hagan and Anderson, 1989).

It is generally believed that parental separation and divorce is stressful for most adolescents, not least because of the disruption to daily routine, the structure of the new family and the associated financial, emotional, and social costs that are involved (Hetherington et al., 1989;

TABLE 3.6   *Parental separation and its impact on the child's family system*

- Likely increase in parental conflict. May result in heightened stress for the child and disturbed parent–child relationship.
- Disturbed parent–parent relationships may lead to disturbed parent–child relationships.
- Children experience structural changes (for example, are split between two homes). This may lead to diminished parent–child relationship.
- Children may be less likely to learn healthy interpersonal skills, leading to unsatisfactory interpersonal relationships in the future.

Source: Tucker et al., 1997

Westman, 1983). Westman estimates that up to one third of adolescents and parents do not adjust to divorce. Others (see Fine, Moreland and Schwebel, 1983) have noted the sometimes negative effects of divorce on adolescents' relationships with their parents, as well as a reduction of trust in, and increasing anger at, their parents. Yet others have reported on the adverse effects of divorce on adolescents' coping strategies (Irion, Coon and Blanchard-Fields, 1988) and self-esteem (Harper and Ryder, 1986).

An important consequence of parental separation is disruption of the family network and support system, acknowledged to be detrimental to children and adolescents. Tucker and colleagues (Tucker et al., 1997) noted the varied ways by which the family system can become impaired. Their views are summarised in Table 3.6 where it is suggested that parental separation is likely to affect various domains of the child's family system. These include interpersonal skills and disturbed parent–child relationships.

The Role of Cognition

It is perhaps not surprising that older children are cognitively better equipped than younger ones to cope with the effects of family disruption. Of course, this does not reduce the pain and anger they feel (Hetherington et al., 1989). Why might older children cope better with family disruption? One explanation may lie in the different abilities of the age groups to decipher the often subtle messages about divorce contained in day-to-day communication between parent–parent and parent–child (Neale, 1983). What is important, but largely unanswered by these reports, are the long-term emotional effects, if any, of divorce on adolescents.

Psychological and Physical Health of Adolescents

There have been numerous studies into the effects of divorce on adolescent adjustment. Some evidence suggests that boys from divorced homes tend to have higher self-esteem than girls (Frost and Pakiz, 1990). Others (see Wallerstein, 1984) have intimated that boys from such families are at greater risk from delinquency and drug use, while it has also been found that teenagers from divorced families are more likely than others to endorse defensive and less mature coping strategies (Irion et al., 1988).

Further evidence of a heightened risk of delinquency among males comes from a Canadian longitudinal study (Pagani et al., 1998). It was found that boys aged 12–15 years whose parents were about to be remarried showed the greatest risk of delinquency with a peak around 14 years. These boys were most susceptible to engaging in physical violence and theft.

At the same time it must be acknowledged that several large-scale studies have begun to question the view that divorce always has negative effects on the emotional well-being of children. Some evidence suggests that such risks are substantially reduced when childrens' pre-divorce behaviour is taken into account. Thus, in one study Amato and Booth (1996) found evidence of problematic parent–child relationships 8–12 years *prior* to divorce. Parents who divorced, compared with those who did not, indicated dissatisfaction with their partners' relationship with their offspring up to 12 years prior to the divorce.

By contrast, Pagani and colleagues (Pagani et al., 1997) were able to predict childrens' negative behaviours after divorce even after accounting for pre-divorce behaviour. The behaviour of children was assessed at age 6 years and then again at 8, 10, and 12 years as they were entering adolescence. It was noted that children whose parents separated before they were six years old were most negatively affected by this experience in the long-term even after controlling for earlier behaviour. Thus, there were negative effects of divorce on hyperactivity at age 8 and 12, although re-marriage reduced this effect by age 12 years. Parental separation also had negative effects on childrens' oppositional behaviour and anxiety.

Time since Divorce

Another important factor when considering adolescent adjustment is elapsed time since the divorce. One research team (Frost and Pakiz, 1990) followed a group of adolescents over a ten-year period, until they

RESEARCH HIGHLIGHT 3.2
The effects of parental divorce on offsprings' later
adult relationships
Burns and Dunlop, 1998

Burns and Dunlop conducted a longitudinal study into the effects of parental divorce on the quality of relationships formed by the children in such families. The study was conducted with the assistance of the Family Court of Australia. Young adolescents and their parents were interviewed at the time of divorce (Time 1), and re-interviewed 3 (Time 2) and 10 (Time 3) years after the divorce when the offspring were aged 23–27 years. At all the interview times, mothers were rated as more caring than fathers, while the overprotectiveness ratings of parents declined after Time 1. Divorced fathers were seen as less caring than married fathers. Perceptions of father and mother care at Time 3 were significantly positively related to offsprings' ratings of relationship intimacy and satisfaction and negatively related to offsprings' ratings of their wariness and disagreement. Thus, many years after teenagers had experienced the divorce of their parents, their perceptions of their parents' care and protectiveness were significantly related to the adequacy of their own personal relationships.

were about 15 years of age. It was found that adolescents who in the preceding five years had experienced marital separation, were more likely to suffer adjustment difficulties than were adolescents whose parents separated before they were six years old, or adolescents whose parents separated while they were six to nine years old (but see Pagani et al., 1997 above). They found that girls from recently separated families were more likely to skip school and to be depressed. In addition, girls whose parents separated when they were young were more likely to engage in alcohol and drug use.

Satisfactory adjustment in children (including adolescents) is more likely to occur in those families where the restructuring took place when the child was quite young. Such children are more likely to regard the step-parent as 'real', although by the time they reach adolescence, children are more likely to become 'curious' about their biological parent (Ochiltree, 1990).

There can be no doubt that, irrespective of the time family restructuring takes place, it is the quality and style of parenting that has an important effect on adolescent adaptation and functioning. A warm, cohesive, and emotionally supportive family, irrespective of its structure, is important for the psychological health of the adolescent.

Family Conflict

Not all writers emphasise the negative consequences of parental separation. Some (see Barber and Eccles, 1992) have cogently argued the benefits of children living in conflict-free environments, suggesting that adolescents adjust better in serene one-parent families than in conflict-ridden intact ones. Several studies support this view. In one, for example, 64 adolescents were questioned about their views regarding the separation or divorce of their parents. Based on their findings, the writers concluded that divorce may in fact be of some benefit to particular children and that it does not necessarily impede children's psychological adjustment. Adolescents appear to prefer one-parent families to conflict-ridden intact ones. Provided that parents keep their children informed about their intentions pertaining to possible divorce, and remain friendly towards each other after the event, adolescents will adjust quite well to the disintegration of their family (McLouglin and Whitfield, 1984).

More recently, it has been demonstrated that parental separation can have beneficial consequences for children and adolescents, especially in those families characterised by high parental conflict (Amato, Spencer-Loomis and Booth, 1995; Jekielek, 1998). Jekielek (1998) found that children in such families showed an improvement (that is, reduction) in anxiety and depression after parental separation. This effect was even more marked for the children of parents who had been separated for a longer period.

Relationships have also been found between adolescent personality traits and the level of conflict in the home. Results show that continuing parental conflict in intact *and* divorced families had a deleterious effect on adolescents' anxiety, self-esteem and feelings of personal control (Slater and Haber, 1984). These findings suggest that adjustment is not necessarily negatively affected by divorce, but rather by the amount of inter-parental conflict the adolescent experiences.

Positive self-esteem among adolescents is related to the perceived happiness of their biological parents. One study found that the self-esteem of girls in intact happy homes was higher than that of those from unhappy intact homes and those whose parents had separated (Long, 1986). These findings lend added support to the view that actual family structure is less important than whether the family is conflict-ridden or not. It is now clear that inter-parental conflict increases stress in adolescents which negatively affects their adjustment and academic performance. Jekielek (1998, 931) concluded as follows:

> These results altogether suggest that children benefit emotionally from marital disruptions which remove them from high conflict family situations...[the] findings are in accord with the possibility that parental divorce, following high conflict, may actually *improve* the well-being of children.

Another important aspect of inter-parental conflict influencing adolescent adjustment is the extent to which adolescents feel 'caught between parents'. Such adolescents, it is suggested, are likely to adjust poorly to divorce and parental separation (Buchanan, Maccoby and Dornbusch, 1991). The strongest predictor of feeling 'caught' is the continuing nature of the relationship between mother and father. Specifically, conflict, high discord and poor and uncooperative communication between parents *after* separation are more likely to result in poor adjustment by the adolescent. There do appear to be some exceptions, however. For instance, when parents who are in conflict refrain from quizzing their adolescent about the other parent, adolescents are less likely to feel caught and therefore adjust better to the disintegration of their family (Buchanan et al., 1991).

Summary

Important reviews (Amato and Keith, 1991; Barber and Eccles, 1992) of the literature on adjustment following divorce have noted inconsistencies in many of the findings. This may be due, they suggest, either to methodological variations or to the characteristics of the children studied (for example, social class differences). Amato and Keith conducted a review of almost 100 research reports in this area and concluded that children from divorced families were more likely to report lower levels of psychological well-being than were children from intact families. Although they found the differences between the groups of children to be significant, they were, in fact, not large.

It has therefore been suggested that emotional adjustment in children and adolescents following divorce is a 'short-term' consideration. Although longitudinal studies are now appearing more frequently in the literature, some have been conducted on rather small samples (for example, Burns and Dunlop, 1998). What is needed are longitudinal studies with larger samples in which children are traced into adulthood. By so doing, it will be possible to examine the long-term quality of life outcomes of these children as adults (Amato and Keith, 1991). Barber and Eccles (1992) add that we must dispense with the outmoded view of adopting a 'negative crisis orientation' when thinking about family transitions. Rather, we should consider the *quality* of parenting in all types of families.

ADOLESCENTS IN NEW FAMILIES

There has been such a marked increase in marital separation and divorce over the last few decades that one might be tempted to view new families (that is, step-parent families, one-parent families, blended families, and so on) as the norm (Visher and Visher, 1982). Nonetheless, much research evidence would suggest that adolescents find it difficult, at least in the short term, to adjust to the new family structure, particularly one with 'new' siblings (Hetherington et al., 1989). Although divorce or separation may end years of bitter inter-parental dispute and conflict, a new family with changed norms and expectations poses a variety of emotional and social challenges for the adolescent.

Not all new families are dysfunctional (Coleman and Ganong, 1997; Visher and Visher, 1982) and an unhealthy family environment is not a necessary consequence of divorce and separation. Although members of divorcing families may indeed experience some stress, for many the break-up of the family unit presents those concerned with new opportunities for personal growth (Barber and Eccles, 1992). It has been suggested that, sociologically, the new family takes on the same roles and responsibilities as the former, although tasks may now be assigned to different members (Goldsmith, 1982). The new family (including the adolescent) is presented with its own set of unique developmental tasks (Visher and Visher, 1982), successful completion of which will launch the family and individual members along the path to psychological adjustment.

New families face unique developmental tasks. These are (Visher and Visher, 1982):

- mourning of losses – new families involve change; to a certain extent, all members mourn the loss of the familiar;

TABLE 3.7   *Adolescent evaluations of being in a blended family*

Positive experiences:
Pleased my step-parent cares about me
My horizons have broadened
Step-parents can be used as consultants
Step-fathers provide financial security

Negative experiences:
Teenagers experience a conflict of loyalty between step- and biological parent
Dislike discipline provided by step-parent
Adolescents feel that they have no control over family changes
Material goods provided by step-parent are seen as a bribe

Source: Coleman and Ganong, 1997

- negotiation and development of new family traditions;
- formation of new alliances and preserving those that are still regarded as important;
- step-family integration – it may take up to two years for step-parents to form a friendly relationship with stepchildren.

For many teenagers being in a new and blended family can be a positive experience; for others the experience is less than ideal. Coleman and Ganong (1997) interviewed several teenagers in new families documenting their positive and negative perceptions of family life. The major positive and negative perceptions have been summarised in Table 3.7

Problem-oriented vs. Normative-adoptive Frameworks

Two general frameworks or paradigms have guided past research on children in new families, namely, the problem-oriented and the normative-adaptive (Barber and Eccles, 1992; Coleman and Ganong, 1990). Most studies seem to fit the first, although research adopting the second approach is becoming more common (Coleman and Ganong, 1990).

Table 3.8 contrasts the two approaches. The problem-oriented perspective assumes, for example, that adolescents in new families are likely to be deficient in certain attributes compared with adolescents in intact families and this view may be a reflection of society's stereotypes of the step-family (Coleman and Ganong, 1990).

The stress hypothesis emphasises that family restructuring is stressful and, accordingly, has negative influences on the social psychological adjustment and development of the adolescent. Thus these adolescents

TABLE 3.8   *Two perspectives on research into children in new families*

Problem-oriented	Normative-adaptive
Deficit-comparison	Parent–child relationships
Stress-hypothesis	Step-parent–child relationships
Self-esteem	
Problem behaviour	
Cognitive functioning	
Parent–child relationships	
Socialisation hypothesis	
Biological discrimination	
Incomplete-institution hypothesis	

Source: Coleman and Ganong, 1990

suffer from lowered self-esteem and particular behavioural problems such as depression, anxiety, school-related problems, and alcoholism (Coleman and Ganong, 1990). There are also some inconsistencies: according to the first perspective children in new families are likely to perform below expectations at school. Yet, a British study that high-lighted the importance of controlling for social class found no differences in academic performance between children in new and intact families.

Research following the normative-adaptive approach tends to focus on the nature and quality of the parent–child relationship. Some studies report few differences in terms of level of support and conflict between new and intact families (Coleman and Ganong, 1990). Most research studies focus on structural differences between families rather than on stressful family transitions (see also Goldsmith, 1982). Thus, intact families have their own stressors (for instance, financial considerations, unemployment, parental pathology) affecting the adjustment of adolescents. The first perspective also suggests inadequate family socialisation experiences for children in new families, compared with others. It is suggested that family disintegration limits the child's exposure to adequate role models. It is further assumed that inadequacies in step-parent–adolescent relations may also be due to the fact that biological or genetic ties are absent. Moreover, it is argued that new families lack guidance regarding their roles and how problems should be dealt with, the so-called incomplete-institution hypothesis (Coleman and Ganong, 1990).

According to the normative-adaptive perspective, parental separation or divorce and the resultant creation of a new family, whether it be blended or single-parent, is not an unusual phenomenon in most industrialised nations (Barber and Eccles, 1992; Coleman and Ganong, 1990;

Demo, 1992; Goldsmith, 1982). Researchers adopting this perspective have ceased to focus on assumed 'pathological' behaviours, and begun to study *family process* (Coleman and Ganong, 1990). Research interest is therefore focused on parent–child and step-parent–child relationships. The quality of parent–child relationships varies depending on the children involved, changes in parent–child contact over a number of years, custody/residence arrangements and so forth. Although relationships between step-parent and child have the potential to be less close than parent–child relationships, they need not necessarily be characterised by stress and conflict. Should the biological parent be absent, step-parent–child relationships have the potential to be rewarding (Coleman and Ganong, 1990; 1997). According to Barber and Eccles (1992, 113): 'Divorce research must now go beyond the narrow conceptualisation of a family transition as a crisis-potentiating event. New frameworks must be constructed that describe normal development in single-parent families.'

THEORETICAL CONSIDERATIONS

The research findings reviewed here have implications for theories of the family as well as theories of adolescence. The research results appear to lend support to the view that the family is an integrated system and that change in one element has consequences for other elements of the system. Thus, parenting style has implications for adolescent adjustment, while the nature of parent–adolescent communication is an important predictor of teenagers' behaviour and psychological health. Likewise, restructuring the family is important in understanding changes in adolescent behaviour.

With respect to theories of adolescence, elements of several of them appear to be germane here. Adaptation to parental separation appears to be related to level of cognitive development. Perhaps not surprisingly, evidence suggests that older children have the cognitive capacity better to understand and adjust to family disruption. They are able to reason abstractly and consider the likely consequences of remaining in what is usually an unhappy family. Certain parenting styles and family communication patterns facilitate adolescent adjustment. Both, no doubt, have implications for adolescent identity formation. Finally, biological changes in puberty and beyond have been shown to be related to changes in parent–child relationships and, consequently, to psychological adjustment.

SUMMARY

This chapter has examined family influences on the psychological adjustment of adolescents. A number of crucial factors were identified, each important in shaping adolescents' emotional health. These were parenting styles, communication, parental pathology, parental discipline style, separation or divorce, family conflict, as well as the reactions of adolescents who find themselves in new families. The research evidence at our disposal suggests that particular parenting styles (such as lack of emotional support) are less conducive than others to healthy psychological adjustment among adolescents. Moreover, parenting styles interact with particular characteristics of adolescents such as self-esteem to determine emotional adjustment in teenagers.

Perhaps one of the most crucial factors influencing the emotional health of adolescents is family pathology. Research evidence is quite clear on this. Parents manifesting personality and behavioural disorders can expect their adolescents to be emotionally and behaviourally maladjusted. What is not quite clear from the evidence is just how much family pathology an adolescent can tolerate. For example, are everyday mood swings in a parent as influential a factor in determining adolescent adjustment as major affective disorder in the parent? If not, what is the critical threshold, if any?

It is interesting that, whereas many studies suggest negative emotional consequences of divorce for adolescents, a meta-analysis of research suggests otherwise. Adolescents in new families may be disadvantaged in terms of their emotional health and development, but the effects are not large. This is an important finding and worthy of consideration by psychologists, other professionals and parents. Perhaps of far greater importance, as Amato and Keith (1991) have suggested, are the long-term effects of divorce on the emotional health of the individual. What are needed, therefore, are more longitudinal studies with large samples of adolescents over several years in which their adjustment as adults is examined. Of further importance is the finding that being in a new family per se is not a necessary precursor to maladjustment. More important is the quality of family life; adolescents prefer a happy new family to an unhappy intact one.

What does appear to be beyond dispute is the fact that divorce or parental separation is a complex event. Not only is there the splintering of relationships, but also the challenges of forming new ones. Intertwined are the personality characteristics of all concerned, as well as other social and economic pressures. It is difficult to disentangle all of the possible causes from their many effects. Careful attention to methodological detail and design should be a priority for future research.

ADDITIONAL READING

Amato, P. and Keith, B. (1991) 'Parental Divorce and the Well-being of Children: A Meta-analysis', *Psychological Bulletin*, 110: 26–46.
Barber, B. and Eccles, J. (1992) 'Long-term Influence of Divorce and Single Parenting on Adolescent Family- and Work-related Values, Behaviors, and Aspirations', *Psychological Bulletin*, 111: 108–26.
Jekielek, S. M. (1998) 'Parental Conflict, Marital Disruption and Children's Emotional Well-being', *Social Forces*, 76: 905–35.
Pagani, L., Boulerice, B., Tremblay, R. E. and Vitaro, F. (1997) 'Behavioural Development of Children of Divorce and Remarriage', *Journal of Child Psychology and Psychiatry*, 38: 769–81.

EXERCISES

1 Plan a study to investigate the effects of parental separation on adolescent adjustment. Operationalise your dependent and independent variables and give details of your research design.
2 Describe how you would construct a measure to assess adolescents' perceptions of their family. Provide details about your reliability and validity checks.

4

Friendships and Peer Groups

INTRODUCTION

In addition to the family, close friends and the wider peer group have a significant influence on the teenager's social development. As individuals move from late childhood into adolescence and beyond, peer influences and the social network begin to play an increasingly important role in the life of the teenager. The adolescent is undergoing rapid cognitive and biological development, and it is reasonable to assume that these are a major impetus for change to his or her self-concept as well as changes to family and social relationships (Cole and Cole, 1989; Paikoff and Brooks-Gunn, 1991). It is the peer group that forms a vital and often useful avenue by which the adolescent makes the transition from the family to the wider world (Dunphy, 1963).

Research has shown quite clearly that as children move into early adolescence, an increasing amount of time is spent with other members of peer groups, while the amount of time spent with the family decreases (Larson and Richards, 1991). We find ourselves in social relationships with others at every stage of the life span. Indeed, even infants and toddlers are aware of the presence of others of different ages. Infants express interest in one another and react differently to other infants than to adults (Parke and Asher, 1983). They are also capable of differentiating social contexts in which a mother might be present or absent. Likewise, during the teenage years peer interaction forms an integral part of everyday social relationships and is an important part of social and emotional development as well as the development of social competence (Ary et al., 1999; O'Koon, 1997; Parke and Asher, 1983; Parker and Asher, 1987). The view that peers are an essential part of adolescent development is echoed by Johnson (cited in Parker and Asher, 1987) who noted that (357): 'Experiences with peers are not superficial luxuries to be enjoyed by some students and not by others. Student–student relationships are an absolute necessity for healthy cognitive and social development and socialization.'

Belonging to a peer group and its associated youth culture is important in the transition from childhood to adulthood. Such a group is an important vehicle by which the teenager achieves a sense of identity and independence. Close identification with the youth culture is temporary, however, and is abandoned once full autonomy is acquired (Fasick, 1984).

Forming satisfying relationships with close friends and one's peer group is an important developmental task of adolescence (see Chapter 1), which also has implications for the successful completion of one's life tasks (Manaster, 1989) and one's emotional adjustment (Hartup and Stevens, 1999). The successful completion of this task will have significant implications for general tasks relating to friends and the general community, as well as one's sense of self and the ability to get on with others.

We turn now to particular aspects of friendships and peer groups. We begin by considering the nature of friendships.

THE NATURE OF FRIENDSHIPS

Having well-liked and close friends is not a new experience for teenagers; friendships are formed early in primary school. In addition to a network of somewhat closer friends, the adolescent may also have several companions drawn from school, sporting teams and clubs. As adolescents undergo cognitive, social and emotional development, the nature and quality of friendships also change. New interests are developed, and ideas about the self change. In addition, adolescents' views about a range of issues are being challenged and altered in many different ways. Not surprisingly, some friendships may lose their appeal, while new ones will be formed, particularly during early adolescence.

The Formation of Friendships

The formation of friendships in childhood and adolescence proceeds through various developmental stages (Hartup, 1983):

- One of the earliest and clearly identifiable stages is the *reward–cost* stage. This occurs around the second or third grade in school and is characterised by the sharing of common activities and similar expectations.

- The second stage, referred to as the *normative* stage, develops during the fourth or fifth grade. Its main feature is a commitment to sharing.
- The *empathic* stage occurs in early adolescence. It is characterised by understanding, self-disclosure and shared interests.

Friendships in adolescence appear to be qualitatively different from childhood ones (Hartup, 1983). They are formed on the basis of inter-personal relations, physical attributes and achievement. Various age groups regard interpersonal relationships as an important basis for friendships, although this appears to be more important for older than younger adolescents.

The development of friendships in late adolescence is like a gradual unfolding process. Longitudinal studies (see Hays, 1985) have found that friends first tend to share jokes or discuss local events. As the friendship becomes more intense and meaningful, individuals are more likely to discuss personal problems, exchange gifts and visit relatives. Thus, as friendships develop they undergo qualitative change so that, ultimately, they are characterised by self-disclosure, closeness and mutual assistance (Shulman et al., 1997). Some writers have noted exceptions to this *general–penetration* approach to friendship forma-tion. Adolescents at boarding school who share the same dormitory, for example, are much more likely to progress through the stages of friend-ship at a quicker pace.

Close friendships are theoretically grounded on two core themes, namely, closeness and individuality (Shulman et al., 1997). Whereas closeness refers to aspects of security and love, individuality refers to maintaining distinct identities. These themes are further elaborated in Table 4.1.

The basis for friendship formation among boys is the sharing of common activities. They are more likely to go camping or form a rock band and an essential feature is the sharing of attitudes and 'having fun' together (Richey and Richey, 1980). Boys' friendships are likely to be less intimate and more guarded than girls' who, by contrast, are likely to form friendships on the basis of verbal communication about them-selves. They, too, 'have fun', but the nature and essential features of their activities are slightly different. Girls are more likely to self-disclose and characterise their friendships as mutually intimate and understand-ing. Boys tend to de-emphasise affection; instead, they stress the instru-mental aspects of friendship, such as being supportive (Sharabany, Gershoni and Hofman, 1981). Friendship bonds appear to be equally

TABLE 4.1   *The nature of closeness and individuality in close friendships*

Closeness	Individuality
Empathy	Developing a distinct identity
Security	Free to express one's own views in a climate of mutual respect
Conformity to pressure which borders on control of the other	Creating a 'personal' style
Love	
Self-disclosure	

Source: Derived from Shulman et al., 1997

strong for both sexes, although males and females have different ways of expressing their friendship (Hays, 1985).

Same-sex and opposite-sex friendships exhibit different developmental patterns. It has been shown that girl–girl relationships are more intimate (in terms of aspects such as self-disclosure) than boy–boy friendships. Opposite-sex friendships, as viewed from the girl's perspective, rapidly increase in intimacy over time, compared with boys' perceptions of such friendships. However, by the time adolescents leave school, major differences between same-sex and opposite-sex friendships have diminished (Sharabany et al., 1981).

Same-sex friendships change over time in some fundamental respects. Characteristics such as trust remain relatively stable, while others tend to increase (Sharabany et al., 1981). These changes are listed in Table 4.2.

Finally, adolescents are able to differentiate between friendships and romantic relationships (Hays, 1988). Late adolescents view same-sex friendships as having fewer fluctuations than romantic relationships. Same-sex friendships are also perceived to level off at a lower magnitude than romantic relationships. Moreover, adolescents view the

TABLE 4.2   *Developmental changes in aspects of same-sex friendships*

Stable over time	Increasing over time
Trusting the friend	Knowing and being sensitive towards the friend
Preferring to do things with the friend	Conveying one's own thoughts and feelings frankly and spontaneously
Feeling free to take from, or impose on, friend	Ability to know others' point of view

Source: Sharabany et al., 1981

intensity of friendships to increase more gradually than romantic relationships (Hays, 1988).

Functions of Friendships

Friendships, even in adolescence, serve an important socio-emotional function. It is now well established (Hays, 1988) that friendships are intrinsically satisfying since they provide companionship, stimulation, a sense of belonging and emotional support. Not having friends can be an important source of stress and low self-esteem. There is an increased need for emotional intimacy during early adolescence and close friends help satisfy that need. Should the need not be met, loneliness, psycho-social disturbance and alienation may result (Buhrmester, 1990).

A characteristic feature of a close friendship is involvement, reciprocity and commitment (Hartup, 1989; Hartup and Stevens, 1999) as well as trust and loyalty (Dusek, 1991). During adolescence, friendships will evolve around leisure activities and the sharing of beliefs, values, and information about books, movies and who is dating whom. Very often, adolescents will offer advice to their close friends on a range of topics. In short, close adolescent friends are confidants (Richey and Richey, 1980).

Friends are reliable and act as allies. Good friends are 'social capital' (Hartup and Stevens, 1999) and give moral support in times of emotional crisis. Friendships embody trust, loyalty, equality, consideration, mutual understanding and intimacy. Friendships encourage spontaneity as well as open and honest exchanges of feelings and ideas (Mannarino, 1978). If friends argue, their friendship forces them to show some self-restraint, while also encouraging them towards quick reconciliation (Richey and Richey, 1980).

Shulman and colleagues (1997) have summarised the functions of close friendships as providing the following:

- mutual trust and loyalty,
- exclusivity,
- emotional and material support,
- the right environment to discuss secrets and to exchange and share views.

Hartup and Stevens (1999, 76) put it this way: 'Friends may or may not share likes and dislikes, but there is always the sense that one supports and sustains one's friends and receives support in return.'

Although they are all likely to share private information, girls are perhaps more likely than boys to disclose intimate information (Hays, 1988). Not only do friends share attitudes, values, and information, but also behaviours. In this regard, Kandel (1990) has suggested that behaviours such as illicit drug use are often shared by close friends. She found that when best friends did not use marijuana, only 15 per cent of adolescent respondents reported smoking it. However, when best friends reported using marijuana once or twice, 50 per cent of adolescent respondents reported using it. These findings suggest, therefore, that close friends can play an important role in shaping each other's behaviour. They are important in initiating a range of behaviours and in helping to form attitudes.

Friends are also important in determining adolescents' emotional adjustment (for example, Giordano, et al., 1998; Hartup and Stevens, 1999). Numerous research reports have indicated the strong relationships that exist between having a good friend and psychological health. Having a close friend predicts higher self-esteem, feelings of being relaxed and being 'myself', and psychological maturity (see Research Highlight 4.1).

The relationship between having a close friend or 'chum' and pre-adolescents' self-esteem was examined in one study (Mannarino, 1978).

RESEARCH HIGHLIGHT 4.1
The role of friendships in teenagers' emotional adjustment
Hartup and Stevens, 1999

Hartup and Stevens recently summarised the important ways friendships shape a teenager's behaviour and emotional adjustment. They suggest the following:

- well-adjusted friends help the kids of divorced parents to better cope with their situation;
- levels of anti-social behaviour will increase if young people associate with anti-social friends;
- anti-social friends are poor role models because these kids tend to have poor social skills;
- behaviour problems will increase if one's friends engage in problem behaviours.

Boys in the sixth grade were asked to nominate other children in their class whom they would like to play with, and with whom they would participate in group activities. From these nominations, the author compiled a 'chum checklist,' and divided the sample into those boys who had a close friend and those who did not. Results showed that having a best friend was positively related to higher self-esteem.

These results emphasise the importance of close friendships for psychological health. Friends act as a support network, raising one's feelings of self-worth, and acting as a buffer against daily stressors. As Mannarino (1978, 108–9) explained: 'As two youngsters communicate openly, the preadolescent realizes that he shares certain ideas and feelings with his chum and begins, perhaps for the first time in his life, to appreciate the common humanity of people.'

PEER GROUPS

We have so far seen that friendships provide a sense of belonging and emotional support in that friends feel comfortable sharing private information. Friends generate feelings of trust and well-being. Peer groups, on the other hand, have as their members individuals of the same age who may be known to the adolescent, but who might not necessarily be a close friend. Peer groups, comprising companions and other acquaintances, embody the wider cultural norms and values that are important to the adolescent. Strict normative codes often exist, with those who deviate from these norms being rejected by other members of the group (Gavin and Furman, 1989). Peer groups dictate the *rituals* that members should perform (Coleman and Hendry, 1990). Rituals refer to a variety of activities, including modes of dress, codes of conduct, hairstyles and general attitudes.

Not surprisingly, there is much pressure to conform to group norms. Group conformity is strongest during middle adolescence (Costanzo and Shaw, 1966), although others dispute this by suggesting that conformity pressures increase linearly over the adolescent years (Gavin and Furman, 1989). What is beyond dispute is that the adolescent comes under pressure to experiment with new roles and behaviour. This forms a natural part of the identity formation process (see Chapter 2) and teenagers look to the peer group not only for guidance about such things as fashion, but also for acceptance. Thus, the adolescent expends much energy in making friends and winning a place in a group (Tedesco and Gaier, 1988).

Functions of Peer Groups

Peer groups serve several important functions. They provide a context for sociable behaviour, the exploration of personal relationships and a sense of belonging (Emler and Reicher, 1995; Hopkins, 1994). Furthermore, they foster learning and a concern with the integrity of the self (Zarbatany, Hartmann and Rankin, 1990). The peer group is a source of self-esteem and helps build one's reputation. It facilitates the achievement of identity and is also a source of companionship, since it helps avoid loneliness and generates various social activities (Brown, Clasen and Eicher, 1986; Emler and Reicher, 1995). Peer groups also serve an important function for those adolescents who have been rejected by their parents. In these instances, the group provides valued support and friendship. Peer groups, then, form a major context in which the adolescent learns social skills and strategies, serving very often as an emotional anchor (Tedesco and Gaier, 1988). Coleman and Hendry (1990, 107) argue that during adolescence 'Peer groups become more important in determining interest and influencing the behaviour and the personality of the individual.'

Gavin and Furman (1989, 827) explain it this way: 'Without being connected to the peer group, one may be left without an important source of support during a period of physical, emotional, and social upheaval.'

Schools play a vital role in the formation of peer groups, and facilitate affiliative behaviour in a number of important ways. Firstly, schools are age-graded which results in concentrated numbers of adolescents at similar levels of cognitive development who are easily able to share ideas and values. Secondly, they are at similar levels of biological development sharing similar physical experiences. Spending large amounts of time in the presence of others, teenagers are increasingly reliant on one another (Kandel, 1990).

Another important function of the peer group is to provide the teenager with a sense of status, which can be either *earned* or *derived* (Ausubel, Montemayor and Svajian, 1977). Because the relationship with parents is slowly changing, and the adolescent is not yet fully a member of adult society, he or she experiences a loss of status. By filling this important gap, peer groups can provide adolescents with earned status in the group. A close relationship with the peer group, based on group interests and approval, enhances the teenager's self-esteem thereby providing derived status (Emler and Reicher, 1995). As the adolescent moves beyond the familiar realms of childhood, the peer group provides a welcome frame of reference. This provides the adolescent with security (Emler and Reicher, 1995) as well as a sense of being liberated from the constraints of the family circle.

Peer groups help protect the individual from adult authority by acting as a pressure group (Ausubel et al., 1977). In other words, parents are very often likely to find themselves negotiating acceptable attitudes and behaviour with the close friends of their teenager. Parents therefore need to develop the skill to have their opinion considered without alienating their adolescent. The peer group can also be viewed as a socialising agent, transmitting those norms and values not usually transmitted by parents (Emler and Reicher, 1995). Finally, peer groups act as a stabilising force during a transition period, when the adolescent is undergoing fundamental social, emotional, and physical change.

In summary, it is apparent that peer groups reduce the dependence of the adolescent on the family by facilitating the development of new social skills (for instance, dating) and the restructuring of teenagers' values and attitudes (Dunphy, 1990).

The Structure of Peer Groups

Peer groups can be categorised as cliques, crowds or gangs (Dunphy, 1963; 1990). A clique consists of a relatively small number (from five to nine) of same-sex teenagers. They are usually close friends and share many leisure activities. They quite probably attend the same school, and are of a similar age. In most urban centres, cliques also share residential proximity (Dunphy, 1990).

Cliques serve important functions (Dunphy, 1963). Their main function (like that of close friends) is to talk and share information, as well as to plan social activities. A clique is cohesive and closely-knit and, given its small size, it is very often difficult for a stranger to gain access. Cliques have leaders and followers, and it is the leaders who are more likely to date sooner and more frequently than the followers. Dusek (1991, 310–11) suggests that leaders 'tend, by their example, to push the other members toward more advanced levels of development'.

Crowds are larger, contain members of both sexes, and may comprise several cliques, although not all cliques need necessarily be represented in a crowd. All individual members of crowds are also members of cliques, while it is possible for a clique member not to be a member of a crowd (Dunphy, 1963). Crowds tend to be less intimate than cliques (Dusek, 1991). Crowds are characteristic of middle adolescence and are born of a need to make heterosexual contact; as such, they facilitate the transition from single-sex to heterosexual interactions (Dunphy,

1963). According to Dunphy, boys tend to be slightly older than girls in a crowd, with most socialising occurring over weekends. Crowds provide the adolescent with an opportunity to meet others with different attitudes and values, and are therefore an important source of social comparison.

Crowds can form quite spontaneously. Opposite-sex class mates for example, who happen to be neighbours and on good terms with each other might introduce the members of their respective cliques, thus forging heterosexual contact. As Dunphy (1990, 174) has indicated, a clique is a prerequisite for crowd formation and serves as the 'pivotal point in the change in the adolescent's association structure from unisexual to heterosexual groupings and is the structural base for the development of a new heterosexual role'.

Dunphy (1963; 1990) has proposed an elaborate theory of group development from early to late adolescence. According to his model, there are five stages of group development. These can be summarised as follows:

- stage 1 – this is the primary stage of development consisting of same-sex isolated cliques;
- stage 2 – same-sex cliques engage in tentative heterosexual interaction, all heterosexual activity is conducted from the safety of the clique;
- stage 3 – formation of the heterosexual clique, some members engage in dating and retain membership of the same-sex clique;
- stage 4 – same-sex cliques slowly re-organise into heterosexual cliques;
- stage 5 – disintegration of crowd, loosely associated groups of couples who are dating or engaged.

From Dunphy's theory, it seems clear that structural change of groups can and does occur. The first change is the merging of young individual adolescents into same-sex cliques. This is followed by sporadic heterosexual contact, which is later followed by the formation of a heterosexual clique, and so on.

Perceptions of the Peer Group

Social psychology has generated a wealth of knowledge and theory relating to groups. Some developmental psychologists have applied such theory in an attempt to ascertain how adolescents view their peer group.

Gavin and Furman (1989) set out to examine whether there are any age and sex differences in adolescents' perceptions of the characteristics

of their peer group. They found that younger teenagers were more concerned about being in a 'popular' group than were older ones. The
researchers concluded that young adolescents view popularity as being
important, since it bolsters their own self-esteem and identity, both of
which are crucial as the teenager slowly begins to disengage from the
family (see also Emler and Reicher, 1995).

The results of the study also showed that younger adolescents
reported higher levels of conformity to group norms than older teenagers. Younger adolescents were also more likely to view their group
as lacking in permeability, and as being relatively stable, with a clear
hierarchical structure (leaders and followers). The impermeable nature
of peer groups is deemed important by group members who, no doubt,
see this as providing a sense of exclusivity (Gavin and Furman, 1989).

Status hierarchies, besides keeping others out, enhance the self-
esteem of the in-group. Middle adolescents, that is, those of about 14
to 16, are more likely to report negative or antagonistic interactions
between members than are younger or older adolescents. Such negative interaction may serve several important functions. According to
Gavin and Furman (1989, 832) these are:

- antagonisms toward others boosts the adolescent's own self-worth,
  which may also form the basis of negative behaviour toward outsiders;
- greater within-group dominance hierarchies result in confirmed
  leaders and followers, ultimately reducing aggression;
- antagonisms ultimately enforce similarity among members, non-
  conformers being punished.

Several changes in peer group perception that mirror Dunphy's
(1963) theory of group development occur in late adolescence. It would
appear that, as adolescents get older, group membership per se is
viewed as less important by members. This might explain the reduction
in antagonism among older adolescents that was previously noted.
Increasingly, groups are viewed as more permeable, while the pressures
to conform are reduced. Moreover, whereas very young adolescents
perceive peer influence as primarily concerned with friendships, older
adolescents are able to think more abstractly about the group, realising
that it symbolises certain attitudes and values (O'Brien and Bierman,
1988). Younger adolescents are more likely to define groups in terms of
activities and social behaviour, while older adolescents tend to view
group influences as far-reaching, i.e., not only dress style and illicit acts
but also attitudes and values. Whereas young adolescents view the group

as a source of friendship, older adolescents are more likely to describe it in terms of their own self-esteem (O'Brien and Bierman, 1988).

To summarise: perceptions of the peer group mirror adolescents' cognitive development. In the early years, perception includes belonging and friendship. In later years, the peer group is viewed more abstractly – it remains a source of friendship, but also comes to symbolise values and personal esteem.

Perceptions of peer pressure

It is generally accepted that adolescents tend to conform to peer norms and values (Costanzo and Shaw, 1966; Emler and Reicher, 1995; Gavin and Furman, 1989; Hopkins, 1994). When asked to nominate the peer pressures they experienced, adolescents in one study indicated that peer pressure tends to cluster in four broad categories, as listed in Table 4.3 (Brown et al., 1986). These categories include social activities (such as going to parties), misconduct (such as drug use or sexual activity), conformity (such as dress style), school-related activities (such as attitudes to academic matters) and family issues (relationships with parents, curfews, and so on).

TABLE 4.3   *Peer pressures encountered by adolescents*

Peer social activities
- Spending time with friends
- Going to parties
- Concerts and school events
- Pursuing opposite-sex relationships

Misconduct
- Drug and alcohol use
- Sexual intercourse
- Petty theft
- Vandalism
- Minor delinquent activities

Conformity to peer norms
- Dress and grooming
- Musical preferences
- Involvement in school
- Academic matters
- Extra-curricular activities

Involvement with family
- Relationship with parents

Source: Brown et al., 1986

Susceptibility to negative peer pressure

Why are some teenagers more likely to succumb to peer pressure of a negative kind? One body of research has investigated the consequences of adolescents who are left to care for themselves after school while their parents are still at work.

The importance of family and school experiences in childhood in helping us understand the susceptibility to negative peer pressure during adolescence should not be understated. A *social interaction* model has been proposed to explain these linkages (Dishion et al., 1991). It consists of the following three stages:

- stage 1 – begins with maladaptive parent–child interactions that are likely to result in anti-social behaviour, this has flow-on effects for school performance, this is also likely to lead to rejection by peers,
- stage 2 – failure in school, individual also does not succeed with the peer group,
- stage 3 – the failing, disliked and anti-social child selects those social settings that maximise social reinforcement, this appears to be exacerbated in those schools that stream adolescents on the basis of academic performance.

This model makes quite explicit the fundamental role that parent–child relationships play in determining adolescent behaviour and emotional adjustment. They include parenting style, communication between parent and teenager, parental maladjustment and family disruption.

Emler and Reicher (1995) have put the notion of 'peer pressure' into a new perspective. According to social identity theory, what drives young people to engage in certain behaviours is the degree to which they *identify* with particular groups of adolescents. Thus, for example, a teenager who shares the attitudes, values and beliefs of a delinquent group, is more likely to engage in deviant behaviours than a teenager who identifies with an academic group.

Peer Rejection

Why do peers reject some teenagers? Are there particular behavioural and emotional characteristics that lead some to be rejected? Firstly, it is

RESEARCH HIGHLIGHT 4.2
The specific functions of delinquent groups
Emler and Reicher, 1995

Why do some young people hang around delinquent groups? What is it about these groups that makes them so attractive to their members? According to Emler and Reicher a delinquent group fulfils some very important and specific functions for its members. These are:

anonymity – members engage in delinquent acts as anonymous group members; the behaviour is performed by 'the group' rather than by any specific individuals;

companionship – members share activities and do things together thus providing companionship for the individual;

reputation management – by engaging in delinquent behaviours a member's reputation among fellow group members is maintained;

security – the group provides a sense of security for the individual. It can act as a substitute for the family; individuals feel safe;

behavioural norms – delinquent behaviours reflect the attitudes and values of all group members.

important to distinguish between those who are neglected and those who are rejected by their peers (Asher and Dodge, 1986):

- neglected adolescents, although not disliked by their peers, do not have friends;
- rejected teenagers are disliked by their peers.

It is possible to gain a broad picture of the rejected adolescent by considering the characteristics of the popular teenager. In one study, young adolescents were administered a range of questionnaires, such as positive and negative sociometric nominations, measures of loneliness and social dissatisfaction and a measure of interpersonal concerns. Adolescents who were described as having low aggressive and disruptive behaviour were generally considered to be kind, trustworthy and cooperative (Parkhurst and Asher, 1992). The best-liked students were viewed as cooperative and compassionate. Rejected adolescents were thought of as aggressive, disruptive and lacking in qualities.

Some teenagers were thought of as 'controversial' by their peers and were rated high on negative interactional qualities.

Some important behavioural differences have been noted between rejected and non-rejected teenagers (Asher and Dodge, 1986):

- On the one hand, rejected teenagers appear to be disliked wherever they are. They are also likely to manifest aggressive and disruptive behaviour.
- Neglected adolescents, on the other hand, very often make a new start when they move to a new school or neighbourhood.
- Rejected children are likely to report higher levels of loneliness and social dissatisfaction than neglected teenagers.

These results have received some support by Scholte and colleagues (1997) who studied over 2000 Dutch 14-year-olds. Students who were accepted by their peers were described as agreeable, sociable, and low on openness to experience. They were also viewed as self-confident and low on aggression-inattentiveness (that is, they were not quarrelsome, irritable, or unfriendly). By contrast, the factor that best and most consistently predicted rejected peers was high aggression-inattentiveness (that is, being seen as quarrelsome, irritable, and unfriendly).

It is also possible to distinguish aggressive-rejected and submissive-rejected youth. Thus, some are viewed as aggressive and disruptive, while others are socially unassertive with low social interaction. Such a pattern of behaviour is referred to as *social withdrawal* with these teenagers tending to be easily victimised and bullied.

Aggressive-rejected and submissive-rejected adolescents dislike being teased by their peers. Evidence shows that the former group tends to overreact to teasing; they see it as a form of provocation. Submissive-rejected teenagers experience teasing as a form of criticism by their peers, which no doubt increases their feelings of loneliness, and their tendency to be withdrawn.

French and colleagues (French, Conrad and Turner, 1995) have also found evidence of two types of rejected youth: anti-social rejected (AR) and nonanti-social rejected (NAR) youth. It is possible to distinguish these groups as follows:

- AR youth are more involved with deviant peers than NAR youth,
- AR youth are more likely to use tobacco and alcohol,
- AR females in the 8th grade (13–14 years) scored higher on depression measures than NAR females,

- AR youth in the 10th (15–16 years) grade had lower achievement scores than NAR youth,
- AR youth in the 8th (13–14 years) grade were absent from school more often than NAR youth.

PARENTS vs. PEERS

A popular belief is that parents and peers have quite *opposite* demands and influences on the adolescent, and that there is an underlying tension between the two. This is not a surprising thesis given that the peer group is seen as providing a context for sociable behaviour and is seen as providing an emotional anchor for the teenager.

The view that adolescents 'choose' to conform to peer pressure, while abandoning the ways of their family, has been challenged. Such an 'either–or' process is not necessarily true, and parental and peer influences are not always contradictory (Coleman and Hendry, 1990) and may be complementary. Indeed, there is a surprising amount of overlap between parental and peer values and standards. It has been suggested that so-called negative peer pressure is not as influential as previously thought and may, in many instances, exert a positive influence on the adolescent (see Foster-Clark and Blyth, 1991).

This view is shared by Noller and Patton (1990). They suggest that most adolescents are not likely to reject their family, but would prefer to maintain warm and close emotional relationships with their parents. As they suggest (62): 'Adolescents will not be told what to do, but they are generally willing to talk things over with and listen to parents who are prepared to try and understand their position. They want to have more independence and autonomy, but within the context of a supportive family.'

Although adolescents slowly become emotionally autonomous from their parents and spend increasing amounts of time away from the family, some evidence suggests that the *quality* of time spent alone with mother or father does not change substantially. At the same time, adolescents may also begin to spend more time *alone* at home. This may take the form of studying, reading, watching television or listening to music. Although the ability to spend some time alone is an indication of psychological well-being (Larson and Richards, 1991), too much time alone may be an indication of depression.

That adolescents abandon the advice of parents and embrace totally the values and norms of the peer group is not entirely accurate.

We now know that teenagers seek advice from both peers and parents depending on the dilemma that they are faced with: adolescents tend to value the judgements of their parents with respect to weighty matters such as possible careers, decisions regarding further study, and so forth, while peers are important sources of information about dating, money, drinking, life style and such matters (Noller and Patton, 1990). O'Koon (1997) found that a strong attachment to parents helped adolescents deal with failure and assisted them in facing the future. Strong peer attachment, on the other hand, was useful for dealing with body image issues, social relationships, and matters related to sexuality.

Peers have the ability to help determine positive (Wentzel, 1998) as well as negative behaviours (Zhang, Welte and Wieczorek, 1997). Zhang and colleagues found that the nature of the influence that parents and peers have on teenagers is quite different. For instance, with respect to alcohol use by young people, it was found that the best predictors of this behaviour was parental attitudes in favour of use and peer alcohol behaviours. Considered together, the peer influence was more powerful than that of the parents.

BULLYING AT SCHOOL

Bullying has been identified as a significant problem in schools in the United Kingdom, the USA and Australia (Craig, 1998; Olweus, 1997; Pellegrini, Bartini and Brooks, 1999; Rigby and Slee, 1991). Olweus (1989, cited in Slee and Rigby, 1993, 371) defines bullying as follows:

- 'An imbalance of strength – physical and/or psychological,
- a deliberate intention to hurt the other where the aggressive act is largely unprovoked and
- repeated negative actions against the individual'.

Boys are generally more likely to experience physical bullying than girls especially in the lower grades. Female bullies also resort to physical aggression, but this is more typical of the higher grades (Craig, 1998). In some samples, bullies comprise up to 14 per cent, while victims of aggression may comprise about 5 per cent of the sample. Victims of other forms of bullying may comprise up to 18 per cent of a sample (Pellegrini et al., 1999).

Bullying can take different forms. One study among school students in Australia (Rigby and Slee, 1991) revealed four types of bullying:

- being called names,
- being picked on by other kids,
- being hit and pushed around by other kids,
- being made fun of.

This study found that boys were more likely than girls to experience physical bullying, while most teenagers were more likely to be called names. Boys were more likely to be the victims of different types of bullying, especially with respect to physical bullying.

Most youngsters are opposed to bullying at school. Certainly, there is great opposition to bullying with much support for the victim, particularly in primary school. However, opposition as well as support for the victims of bullying gradually decreases as teenagers move through high or secondary school (Rigby and Slee, 1991). The authors explain such diminishing support for victims thus (626): 'schools tend to inculcate stereotypically male values, which run counter to the development of empathic responses to others. Arguably increased exposure to such values may result in a lessening in sympathy for the victims of bullying'.

Just why does bullying occur at school? Can one predict with some certainty who is likely to bully or be bullied? Or does bullying occur in a rather haphazard fashion?

The Victim

Victims tend to have a history of yielding to the bully's demands and usually do not offer resistance (Perry, Kusel and Perry, 1988). Sometimes victims may resemble those that the bully has observed being bullied, or it is possible that the victim may, in some way, be provocative. Some victims reward bullies by actually acquiescing to their demands. Research has shown that victims tend to have low self-esteem, are socially isolated, are physically weak or are afraid to be assertive (Perry et al., 1988), while other evidence points to victims being more anxious and depressed than other students (Craig, 1998). It is not clear whether bullying precedes heightened anxiety or not. As Craig (1998, 129) explains, '(anxious) victims may exhibit an anxious vulnerability that may make them vulnerable to attack. Thus, anxious children are at risk for victimization and repeated victimization may heighten already high levels of social anxiety'.

One must distinguish between provocative (aggressive) and passive (non-aggressive) victims (Perry et al., 1988). Aggressive victims (those who deliberately start a fight) are most at risk for rejection by peers. These youngsters tend to be the most disliked members of a group, and are likely to suffer later maladjustment.

The Aggressor

Besides personality factors that characterise the bully and the bully/victim (see Research Highlight 4.3), other studies have identified hormonal and social influences on the aggressive behaviour of children and teenagers (see also Chapter 1). In an important review of the literature (Parke and Slaby, 1983), a link was noted between plasma testosterone levels and self-reports of physical and verbal aggression in 16-year-old Swedish boys. The higher the testosterone level, the more impatient

RESEARCH HIGHLIGHT 4.3
The personality profile of bullies and victims
(Mynard and Joseph, 1997; Slee and Rigby, 1993)

Do school bullies differ in their personality profiles from other students? Is it possible to predict who is likely to be a bully or a victim? Both studies cited here have used the Eysenck Personality Questionnaire to examine bullies and victims. Slee and Rigby found that bullies scored significantly higher on the extraversion dimension than victims and that bullies (perhaps not surprisingly) also scored high on the toughminded dimension (as measured by the P scale). Victims had low general self-esteem.

Mynard and Joseph categorised their students into one of four groups: bullies, victims, bully/victims, or not involved. Bullies were significantly more extraverted than victims, bully/victims and the not involved group. Bully/victims were significantly more neurotic than bullies and the not involved group. Finally, bully/victims as well as bullies were significantly more toughminded (P scale) than the not involved. Using other measures it was also found that bullies as well as bully/victims tended to have lower scores than other children on scholastic competence, global self-worth, behaviour conduct and physical appearance.

and irritable the boys were. Although some links between testosterone levels and aggression have also been noted in females, the effect is much weaker.

Evidence also indicates that aggression in youngsters may have social antecedents. Parke and Slaby (1983) note as influences the family, the peer group and the effects of television viewing. Thus, it has been demonstrated that the family sets the context in which children and teenagers learn to be aggressive. Excessive use of physical force on the child, or violence between parents may induce the child to act in an aggressive manner. These ideas have been supported by a recent study which found that bullying was associated with experience of a physical parental discipline style, negative peer influences, and residing in a neighbourhood where concern for safety is high (Espelage, Bosworth and Simon, 2000).

It is also possible that children and teenagers learn aggression from their peers. Peers may *elicit* aggression, or may serve as role models to other children who have a predisposition to act aggressively (see Chapter 1, social learning theory). Moreover, peers may reinforce aggressive behaviour. Research has also suggested that the viewing of violent television programmes may be linked to aggressive behaviour. Although countries differ in their regulation of the portrayal of violence on television, it remains a powerful socialising agent. When violence (however subtle) is portrayed, it is usually committed by a male figure. More often than not, victims tend to be females or males in much weaker positions, such as members of minorities (Parke and Slaby, 1983).

In conclusion, it is doubtful whether bullying will ever be completely eradicated in school. There are strong influences on children and adolescents acquiring aggressive behaviour, such as biological changes and social learning effects. Perhaps school authorities can attempt to counter those influences by rewarding children's acceptable behaviour more positively.

THEORETICAL CONSIDERATIONS

Two theoretical approaches appear to have important implications for this discussion. In the first place, close friendships as well as the larger peer group fulfil an important role in assisting the adolescent with the process of identity formation. Friends serve as a sounding board in a way that is quite different from parents. They reflect contemporary attitudes and values as well as dress and hairstyles. Friends and peers therefore act as a barometer against which the teenager is continually measured. Very often, parents and peers differ in their ideas about a whole range of issues. This serves a useful function for the adolescent, who must consider alternative arguments and propositions. This is a crucial aspect of identity formation.

Secondly, maladaptive parent–child relations may lead to rejection by peers. It was noted earlier that biological changes may be a strong influence on changed parent–child relations. Thus, biological changes are linked to peer rejection and, perhaps, bullying. What is required are longitudinal studies over several years to plot biological change in youngsters and associated parent-child relations and aggressive behaviour at school.

Thirdly, social learning theory is implicated in bullying in that children and teenagers are likely to learn such behaviours from others (parents or television shows) while still relatively young. For them, violence becomes an acceptable response, a way of dealing with a threatening situation or uncertainty. Finally, we noted that the peer group plays a crucial role in the adolescent's journey to adulthood. In this sense, it fulfils an important psychosocial function: assisting teenagers break the close emotional attachments to their parents.

SUMMARY

This chapter has highlighted the important role that friendships and peer groups play in the psychological development of the adolescent. As individuals move into adolescence, the peer group becomes increasingly important as a vehicle of social comparison. At the same time, the peer group is crucial in assisting the teenager become emotionally autonomous of the family to be able to assert his or her own independence. For those who do not have a warm relationship with their family, the peer group very often serves as an emotional anchor.

This chapter also discussed the importance of close friendships. A close friend acts as a confidant, someone to whom the adolescent can turn in the event of a problem or crisis. In short, close friends can be 'trusted'. Important sex differences were also noted in the nature and formation of close friendships.

Many of the studies reported here, as elsewhere in this volume, are based on English-speaking (mainly American) samples. There is a dearth of data using non-English-speaking, non-Western people. It would be interesting, for example, to replicate some of the studies reported here among Chinese teenagers. The family traditionally has a very important place in Chinese life. What is the role of the peer group in such situations? Are its functions similar to that reported for Western teenagers? Moreover, are there differences in the functions of the peer group between Hong Kong and mainland Chinese? Questions such as these need to be addressed in future research.

ADDITIONAL READING

Dunphy, D. (1963) 'The Social Structure of Urban Adolescent Peer Groups', *Sociometry*, 26: 230–76.
Hays, R. (1988) 'Friendship', in S. Duck (ed.), *Handbook of Personal Relationships: Theory, Research and Interventions*. Chichester: John Wiley and Sons.

EXERCISE

1   To what extent do adolescents use their parents and friends as a 'sounding board' for various issues? Interview five 16-year-olds and question them about this. Cover topics such as dress style, musical preference, dating, future career options, religious beliefs and political attitudes. Include other topics too, if you wish.

   Are there differences in the sorts of issues that adolescents believe parents and friends are qualified to deal with?

5

School Life

INTRODUCTION

Schools have a major influence on adolescent development. Not only are many friendships formed there but, as society becomes more complex, with increasing emphasis placed on the acquisition of specialist skills and training for jobs, so the importance of the school as a social institution is gaining in importance. Indeed, it has been suggested that this is happening at the expense of the influence of other social institutions such as the family and the church (Conger and Petersen, 1984).

More and more adolescents are choosing to complete their schooling. For instance, by the mid-1980s school retention rates were about 80 per cent in the USA, 84 per cent in Canada and about 90 per cent in Japan (Blakers, 1990). In Australia, retention rates have risen dramatically over the last twenty years. In 1981 it was a low 35 per cent, but by 1992 had risen to 77 per cent. By 1999 it had stabilised at about 72 per cent, with the retention rate much higher for girls (close to 80 per cent) than boys (just below 70 per cent) (Australian Bureau of Statistics, 1999). Such encouraging retention rates may be symptomatic of relatively high youth unemployment rates (see Chapter 10). On the other hand, they may simply reflect the view that higher levels of education are associated with higher social status and better-paid jobs (Blakers, 1990).

As the workforce becomes more sophisticated, more parents and teenagers see distinct advantages in completing school. Parents may view staying on at school as a means whereby their children can improve their prospects both socially and economically. Although many teenagers hold negative attitudes towards school and the curriculum (Poole, 1990), they nonetheless see a link between completing their studies, better qualifications and the increased likelihood of finding a job (Blakers, 1990). This view is borne out by the results of attitude surveys in different cultures (Britain and Australia) that show a recognition by adolescents that, by completing school, they enhance their job prospects (Furnham and Gunter, 1989; Poole, 1983).

In this chapter, various important psychological issues relating to school life and academic attainment will be discussed. It will begin by examining the transition to high or secondary school, before exploring some of the psychosocial correlates of academic performance and motivation. Attention will also be paid to school dropouts and the effects of gender and type of school on academic performance.

THE TRANSITION TO HIGH OR SECONDARY SCHOOL

The transfer from primary to high or secondary school is an exciting time for most young people. It is also a major life event for them. For some, it is a potentially stressful time and has the potential to negatively affect emotional adjustment (Dowling, 1980). The move to high or secondary school is often accompanied by a move away from close friends and familiar surroundings, and is associated with new expectations and teaching methods. Not only is the new school student surrounded by teenagers who appear to be a lot older and more confident, but there are also new curricula to select from, taught by unfamiliar teachers. Perhaps the biggest difference between primary and high or secondary school can be attributed to a difference in 'culture' (Yates, 1999). For many, this change can lead to strain and loss of self-esteem (Wall, 1977).

Wall has suggested that the first few weeks of high or secondary school are crucial in many respects. For many new students, this period may set the basis for future attitudes and behaviour. For instance, moving into a large and impersonal school separated from old friends and what is familiar may serve to lower the adolescent's self-esteem and confidence. This may then influence his or her approach to interpersonal relationships and academic performance, at least for the immediate future. Low self-esteem may give rise to negative attitudes to school which could increase truancy or other unacceptable behaviours (Rice, 1999).

Wall (1977) has noted several other crucial factors that impinge on the adolescent's adaptation to high or secondary school. He notes, for example, that the family plays a crucial role in helping adjustment to a new school (see pp. 104–7). It is also clear that young teenagers are at different stages of cognitive development with some, but not all, capable of abstract and formal reasoning. It is at this time, too, that teenagers are characterised by rapid physical and emotional changes, thus presenting them with a variety of challenges and developmental tasks. A range of different and complex challenges therefore confronts the new high or secondary school student: interpersonal, academic, cognitive and biological.

RESEARCH HIGHLIGHT 5.1
The transition to high/secondary school
Yates, 1999

Do the expectations that young students have of life in high or secondary school match their later experiences? Yates has gone some way toward addressing this question:

Some expectations of high/secondary school just before the transition:

- you can look after yourself, teachers won't look after you;
- more interesting subjects to do;
- different teachers every day.

The reality one year later:

- if you don't work no one follows up;
- miss teachers from the old school;
- teachers in high/secondary school don't seem to care.

One study (Dowling 1980) examined the relationships between adjustment one year after entering the new school and various assessments of children made towards the end of primary school. Before entering high or secondary school, students were administered measures of verbal reasoning, sentence reading comprehension, personality and teacher's ratings of adjustment such as: 'I think that this child will make a satisfactory social and emotional adjustment in secondary school'. A year after entering high or secondary school, Dowling assessed the adolescents, their attitudes toward school, their behaviour and general adjustment. He found that personality factors such as extraversion and introversion were weakest in predicting adjustment. The best predictors were teachers' ratings of adjustment to the new school. It should be pointed out, however, that the various predictive factors only explained 17 per cent of the variance in teachers' adjustment ratings. This suggests that other factors not considered in the research may have contributed to adjustment. Some of these may include attitudes towards school and the nature of parental support.

Although adjustment to high or secondary school has not generated much psychological research, this is not the case as far as the psychosocial correlates of academic attainment are concerned. It is to these and other issues that we now turn our attention.

ATTITUDES TO SCHOOL

Evidence shows that there are differences in the ways boys and girls perceive school. Overall, girls seem to have a much more positive attitude than boys, and this also seems to be the case for different cultural groups.

In one study conducted in the United Kingdom, over 2000 teenagers aged between 10 and 17 years were asked to share their views about school (Furnham and Gunter, 1989). Some questions were specifically directed at what adolescents expected from school. Table 5.1 shows the responses of all the respondents to a selection of questions. Generally, boys were found to be less optimistic and to have slightly more negative expectations about school than girls. Boys were more likely than girls to lower their expectations about school in order to avoid disappointment and were also more likely to expect that teachers would dislike them.

Similar findings were obtained in an Israeli study of over 2600 students (Darom and Rich, 1988). As predicted, girls tended to have more positive attitudes to school than boys. Moreover, teachers perceived the attitudes of girls to be more positive than those of boys, although teachers tended to overestimate these sex differences. To what

TABLE 5.1   *Sex differences in attitudes to school*

Attitudes		Respondents	
		Male	*Female*
1 You should not expect too much from school, for you would only be disappointed	Agree	49	41
	Neither	25	25
	Disagree	25	35
2 Students should not expect teachers to like them	Agree	49	33
	Neither	28	33
	Disagree	23	34
3 Most of the subjects I take are interesting	Agree	50	59
	Neither	25	18
	Disagree	25	23
4 It really doesn't matter how well you do at school	Agree	26	18
	Neither	17	12
	Disagree	57	70
5 I get bored and fed up with school and do not really enjoy anything connected with it	Agree	41	37
	Neither	28	25
	Disagree	31	38

Note: Results presented as percentages
Source: Furnham and Gunter, 1989

extent boys' relatively negative attitudes are determined by teachers' negative perceptions, or vice versa, has yet to be established.

Teenagers also have well-developed views about the structure and organisation of schools. Australian studies have shown that many are dissatisfied with the ways schools are run. They are not viewed as particularly inviting or supportive, and are seen to be organised along authoritarian lines, with an emphasis on discipline. Many adolescents find schools alienating and impersonal. Whereas primary schools are usually characterised as more supportive, high or secondary schools, with their system of rotating teachers, are not (Poole, 1990).

Adolescents' attitudes to school possess a certain structure (Furnham and Rawles, 1996). The following domains (with sample items) were uncovered based on a study of over 200 British school students:

- Anti-school – 'Some people require education for their jobs but for most of us it is a waste of time'.
- School necessity – 'Failure in examinations ruins a person's chances in life'.
- Usefulness of schooling – 'Technical and academic subjects should be offered in the same school'.
- Interest – 'Teachers are generally good at getting their ideas across'.

Attitudes to school are logically related to other belief systems. Thus, youth with less positive attitudes to school are less likely to believe in self-effort strategies for getting a job and appear to be more doubtful about career advice. Importantly, these young people also appear to be more externally and fatalistically oriented (Furnham and Rawles, 1996).

PSYCHOSOCIAL CORRELATES OF ACADEMIC PERFORMANCE

Academic performance at school is not only dependent upon the child's academic ability. There are many other psychological and social factors that help determine achievement, some of which will be discussed below:

The Importance of Family Life

Like so many other aspects of adolescent development, the family plays an important role in offering emotional support to adolescents and socialising them to do the best they can academically. Connel and his colleagues (1982) concur with this viewpoint by suggesting that (185–6):

RESEARCH HIGHLIGHT 5.2
Perceived quality of school life predicts Year 12 academic
performance
Mok and Flynn, 1997

Students' perceptions of school life are related to academic outcome during the final year of school. These authors studied the
attitudes and academic performance of over 4000 students attending Catholic schools in Australia. Better school performance was
found to be related to satisfaction with school, lower levels of
alienation from school, better relationships with school teachers,
higher self-esteem as well as a belief that school had some rele-
vance to life. These factors remained important after controlling
for personal, home and school background. Students in single-sex
schools tended to outperform those in co-educational schools,
while students from higher socio-economic status schools did
better than those from lower SES schools.

> Families are thought to shape the educational careers of their young mem-
> bers in a wide range of ways: the extent to which parents care about school-
> ing, the manner in which family members relate to each other . . . (methods of
> discipline), their material provision (for example, of a quiet place to study),
> and their internal structure (especially the state of the parents' marriage).

The extent to which the family can play a supportive role in the adolescent's school career depends very much on a range of factors. These
include parenting styles and the nature of the communication process
between parents and adolescents, the personality of the adolescent, and
other factors such as the family's social status and financial situation.
In the USA for example, black adolescents living in single-mother
households very often have to cope with factors such as large family
size, father's absence, crowding and mother's relatively low educational
level (Scheinfeld, 1983). In Australia, Poole (1983) has confirmed the
importance of social class. She found that higher social status families
are likely to have children who remain at school for a longer period of
time and obtain higher status jobs. She refers to this process as 'cultural
and social reproduction' (111).

In her longitudinal study of 1600 adolescents, Poole (1983) found
support for the importance of social-class factors in academic aspiration. She found that fathers in professional occupations were much

more likely than fathers in white-collar or blue-collar jobs to strive for university education for their children. There were also striking differences between the aspirations of the adolescents *themselves*. For instance, those with professional fathers were more likely to strive for university education than were adolescents with white-collar or blue-collar fathers (63.9, 43.4 and 32.1 per cent respectively). The reverse was true regarding adolescent aspirations for completing school: more adolescents from blue-collar than white-collar or professional families aspired to a school education only (19.1, 14.7 and 12.0 per cent respectively).

Similar findings have been noted in an African study (Cherian, 1991). This study assessed the links between the academic achievement of 1021 Xhosa-speaking students aged 13 to 17 years and their parents' aspirations. The parents were subdivided in terms of their level of education, occupation, income and socio-economic status. The findings supported the hypotheses: higher parental occupation, education, income and socio-economic status were associated with higher parental aspirations which, in turn, were associated with higher academic performance by the students.

Adolescents who are making academic progress perceive their families quite differently from those who are not making academic progress. Whereas those who are achieving academically tend to see their families as exhibiting cohesion and expressiveness, those who are underachieving are likely to describe their family as conflict-ridden and 'pressuring' (Masselam, Marcus and Stunkard, 1990; Steinberg, Elmen and Mounts, 1989).

Family cohesion and adaptability are important facets of family functioning (Masselam et al., 1990). Cohesion refers to the emotional bonding that the family displays, while adaptability refers to the extent to which family members are able to adapt to changing roles. Masselam and colleagues conducted a comparative study of two groups of matched adolescents. One comprised students who were not making academic progress at school, while the other comprised successful students. Significant differences were found in the perceptions of family functioning between the two groups of teenagers and their parents.

With respect to cohesion, adolescents making academic progress, as well as their parents, characterised their family as being significantly more cohesive than did adolescents who were not making progress. The two groups did not differ significantly with respect to adaptability. Respondents were also asked to give their *ideal* family rating on cohesiveness and adaptability. Significant differences emerged between the successful and unsuccessful students with respect to their *actual* and *ideal* scores. For the successful group, there was greater congruence between actual and ideal family functioning.

Parenting styles are also related to the academic achievement of teenagers. Research indicates that authoritative parenting is best associated with academic achievement, while authoritarian and permissive styles are not (Cohen and Rice 1997; Dornbusch et al., 1987; Glasgow et al., 1997; Taris and Bok, 1996). You will recall from Chapter 3 that an authoritative parenting style was found to be predictive of higher social and academic competence. Cohen and Rice (1997) found that, among teenagers with good academic outcomes, both teenagers and parents perceived parental behaviours as authoritative, but not permissive or authoritarian. In fact, authoritative aspects of parenting *facilitate* rather than simply accompany academic performance (Steinberg et al., 1989).

It has been suggested that an authoritative parenting style, in which much parental warmth and support are present, generates psychosocial maturity in adolescents (Steinberg et al., 1989). Psychosocial maturity is characterised by several features, one of which is a positive attitude to school work. Steinberg and colleagues found that psychosocial maturity increased the chances of academic performance in those homes classified as authoritative.

Influence of Family Disruption

The impact of family separation and divorce on the adjustment of children is well documented (see Chapter 3). Numerous studies have been conducted examining the effects of family disruption on various adjustment domains such as psychological and social adjustment, general conduct and self-esteem. In this section, the effect of family disruption upon academic performance will be considered.

Most research evidence in this area indicates that adolescents whose parents have separated or divorced do not perform academically as well as those from intact families. For instance, Bisnaire and associates (1990) noted the negative impact of father's absence on boys' academic performance. They also reported that children from one-parent families tend to be characterised by poorer socio-emotional development and lower academic achievement. An independent analysis (Wood, Chapin and Hannah, 1988) also highlighted the important role that the home environment plays in adolescents' academic success.

RESEARCH HIGHLIGHT 5.3
The role of significant others in adolescent
academic performance
Trent et al., 1996

Do parents' appraisals have a significant impact on the academic performance of their adolescent offspring? Trent and colleagues examined this question among 264 Australian 12-year-olds from six different schools. Teachers of these students were also assessed as to their views and, in 146 cases, so were both mother and father. There were no significant gender differences in how students rated their academic competence. However, the best predictors of boys' scholastic performance were students' perceptions of mother's intelligence, friends' support, father's perception of the student's ability, and teachers' perceptions of the student's ability. Among girls, however, only the student's perception of mother's intelligence was a significant predictor. Thus it would seem that boys use different sources to judge their scholastic competence, while girls rely heavily on one source only, namely, their mother. Parents therefore have different influences on their male and female children.

These findings were borne out by a separate longitudinal study (Zimiles and Lee 1991) which examined the academic attainment of school students from intact, single-parent and remarried families. Students from intact families significantly outperformed those from other families, although the differences between the groups were not large (see also Amato and Keith 1991). These results remained unaltered even after controlling for the effects of socio-economic status.

As noted in Chapter 3, not all adolescents who have experienced family disruption do poorly at school or are emotionally and socially maladjusted. Many factors have the potential to intercede and act as buffers against stress and disruption. Indeed, some researchers have commented on the interrelatedness of various systems in determining adjustment to divorce. For instance, at the micro level are found individual and family characteristics such as personal motivation and parental support. These interact with factors at the next level, the ecosystem, including social support networks and school factors. At the macro level are important factors such as ethnicity and socio-economic status (Mednick et al., 1990). In other words, the processes of adjustment to divorce and resultant academic achievement are quite complex with many factors interacting in quite unique ways for each individual. To suggest that family disruption will always tend to lower adolescents' academic performance is far too simplistic.

The divorce *experience* has an important impact on parents as well as on children. A single mother, for instance, who is experiencing financial, occupational, mental and physical stress and who is still in conflict with her ex-partner, may find it extremely difficult to cope. Furthermore, it is unlikely that she would be able to conceal this fact from her child. Such visible stress is likely to have a negative effect on adolescent academic performance (McCombs and Forehand, 1989; Mednick et al., 1990).

Other researchers have examined the role of factors such as mother's level of contentment and adolescent-peer relations. One team conducted an 18-year longitudinal study of the academic achievement of Danish adolescents who had experienced family disruption and divorce (Mednick et al., 1990). The authors examined reading and mathematics proficiency in the last two years of school and related these to various social and family matters. After partialling out the effects of socio-economic status and mother's educational level, several factors were found to predict academic performance. Table 5.2 shows that lower reading proficiency is related to mother's discontentment and adolescent's poor peer relations. Lower mathematics proficiency was associated with mother's discontentment, mothers' disorderliness, maternal employment instability and number of school changes.

This evidence indicates that mathematics proficiency may be more sensitive to family disruption and mother's level of adjustment than is reading proficiency. The authors argued that the ability of the single mother to cope with her situation is an important factor in determining

TABLE 5.2   *Social and family factors associated with low achievement in reading and mathematics*

Reading	Mathematics
Mother's discontentment	Mother's discontentment
Poor peer relations	Mother's disorderliness
	Maternal employment instability
	School changes

Note: Socio-economic status and mother's level of education have been partialled out
Source: Mednick et al., 1990

the academic performance of her children (see also Barber and Eccles, 1992). Mednick and colleagues (1990, 82–3) concluded that 'a decrease in the mother's ability to deal with her situation has a rather pervasive influence on her children's academic performance'.

The Role of Personality Factors

To what extent do personality factors predict academic attainment and achievement motivation? This is an area of enquiry that has generated substantial research endeavour.

A large body of literature has evolved which has examined the link between achievement motivation and academic performance on the one hand, and their personality correlates on the other. Many research studies have been conducted using either H. Eysenck's Big Three taxonomy (H. Eysenck and M. Eysenck, 1985) or, more recently, the Big Five taxonomy (Costa and McCrae, 1985). An early study yielded some interesting, albeit seemingly contradictory, results for primary school students and late adolescents. For example, extraversion was shown to be an important factor in academic attainment among primary school students, whilst introversion was important for older students (Entwistle, 1972). There are a variety of possible explanations for this. Perhaps able students become more introverted as they get older, while students who are less able become more extraverted. It is also possible that some extraverted students, perhaps because of excessive socialising, could fall behind as more complex academic skills develop (H. Eysenck and M. Eysenck, 1985).

Entwistle (1972) also showed that the relationship between personality traits such as extraversion and academic attainment is complicated by the effects of students' intellectual level, type of institution and the subject being studied (see also Seddon, 1977). Given our knowledge of the nature of extraversion, it is perhaps not surprising that they prefer (and excel at) academic activities based on verbal presentations rather than essay writing (Furnham and Medhurst, 1995). On the other hand, anxious students appear to be much less favoured toward verbal-based assessments.

Using the Big Five taxonomy, De Raad and Schouwenburg (1996) argued that agreeableness is a good predictor of the motivation to learn. They found that aggressive and withdrawn youngsters tend to have lower grades than non-aggressive and more extraverted students. Another important Big Five factor is conscientiousness that encompasses drive, carefulness, perseverance, endurance, being organised, and so forth. As one would expect, conscientiousness has been found to be negatively related to the number of re-examination or supplementary examinations that students apply for (De Fruyt and Mervielde, 1996).

Another factor related to academic outcome is 'locus of control'. Those who are said to be internally controlled believe that what happens to them does so as a result of their own efforts. In other words, they feel in control of the events of their lives. Externals, on the other hand, believe that fate and chance factors play a large role in their lives. It has been found that those who are internally controlled score higher academically than do 'externals' (for example, Fry and Coe, 1980; Heaven, 1990). In addition, research in the USA has shown that this relationship is more complex among black than white students. 'Internal' blacks seem to perform best when competing against a white, or when collaborating with other black students (Fry and Coe, 1980).

Another personality factor shown to be important in explaining academic performance among adolescents is social competence. Prosocial and responsible forms of behaviour are associated with academic attainment, whereas those who are rejected by their peers tend to be underachievers. On the basis of her research among 423 twelve- and thirteen-year-olds, Wentzel (1991) highlighted the importance of three aspects of social competence to academic attainment. These are:

- socially responsible behaviour (such as adhering to social rules and expectations),
- sociometric status (having friends),
- self-regulatory processes (such as planning and setting goals).

As predicted, it was found that all aspects of social competence were related to academic attainment. Importantly, socially responsible behaviour mediated the relationship between academic performance and factors such as peer status, goals, interpersonal trust and interpersonal problem-solving. There are three possible explanations for these findings (Wentzel, 1991).

- First, it is possible that socially responsible behaviour is itself an end goal of the educational process, and therefore associated with academic performance.
- Secondly, teaching strategies may influence socially responsible behaviour in adolescents.
- Thirdly, it is possible that academic performance is a direct result of socially responsible behaviour. Further longitudinal research would be required to determine such cause–effect relationships.

Such a study was recently conducted by Caprara and colleagues (2000). They tracked over 200 primary school children into early adolescence measuring their personalities and later academic performance. They found that prosocial children, that is, those who were higher on cooperating, sharing and consoling, were more likely to show better academic performance as young teenagers than those who were low on prosocial behaviours.

Causal Attributions for Success and Failure

The study of attributions or 'lay explanations' enjoys a central position in social psychology. Lay theories exist for most social events that we encounter in our daily lives. Thus, we each have particular beliefs about the possible causes of alcoholism, poverty, success, failure and so on. The study of attributions is important to psychologists, since attributions link the stimuli we encounter to individual behaviour (Ross and Fletcher, 1985). Attributions, therefore, have implications for behaviour.

It was earlier proposed that three dimensions underlie our attributions for success and failure (Weiner, 1979). These are controllability, locus and stability. Locus refers to internal dimensions (such as motivation) on the one hand and external dimensions (such as ability or luck) on the other. Stability refers to how persistent the cause is (for instance, 'Am I always lucky?'). For example, intelligence is an important factor in explaining academic success and is an internal and stable attribute. Table 5.3 shows that these dimensions can be further classified in terms of controllability or uncontrollability.

Research evidence shows that success in a task is usually attributed to internal stable causes, while failure is attributed to external causes. One study found that students who passed a course exam explained their

TABLE 5.3   *Causal dimensions for success and failure*

	Internal		External	
	Stable	*Unstable*	*Stable*	*Unstable*
Controllable	General effort	Attention Immediate effort	Teacher bias	Help from others
Uncontrollable	Ability	Mood	Task difficulty	Health ('flu')
	Health ('I'm sickly')	Maturity	Family	Luck

Source: Derived from Weiner, 1979

success in terms of their ability, while students who failed were more likely to explain their failure by resorting to external factors such as bad luck or task difficulty (Simon and Feather, 1973). Some exceptions to these general principles have been noted. Low-achieving individuals tend to attribute success to *external* causes (Chapman and Lawes, 1984). Research has also indicated that there are sex differences in attributional processes. Females, for instance, are more likely than males to make external attributions for success and failure and are more likely to view their fate as being determined by external rather than personal reasons.

Expectations of success and failure are also important. Irrespective of whether one expects to succeed or fail, research has shown that expected outcomes are usually attributed to stable causes, and unexpected outcomes to unstable ones. So students who expect to pass, but do not, are more likely to attribute failure to bad luck than to lack of effort (Simon and Feather, 1973).

Attributions for success and failure have been shown to be gender-biased. A common finding reported in the attributional literature is the tendency to attribute male success on typically male tasks to ability and failure to bad luck on his part. Females tend to be derogated when performing male tasks irrespective of outcome. There are no sex differences for male and female success when actors engage in stereotypically female tasks, however (Deaux and Emswiller, 1974). Much more recent research questions these early findings by not replicating the typical female-derogating and male-favouring attributions. This suggests either that social attitudes and expectations have changed over the years, or that prejudice toward females has become much more subtle (Hill and Augoustinos, 1997).

SCHOOL DROPOUTS

School retention rates in many developed nations are higher than 70 per cent. As noted earlier, it is not clear whether this is due to limited employment prospects for teenagers, or to a perception that high school education will ultimately enhance one's future job prospects. In an expanding economy, higher educational qualifications are normally associated with better occupational prospects (Power, 1984). However, this is not necessarily the case during a severe economic contraction or recession. Maintaining high retention rates, particularly during a time of limited employment, is a social and political imperative. As Power

(1984, 116) noted: 'Early school leavers face a greater risk of being unemployed than those successfully completing secondary school. Low retention rates have contributed to increases in the youth labour supply and hence to higher levels of youth unemployment'.

What are the factors associated with the decision to stay on at school? Several researchers (for example, Ainley, Foreman and Sheret, 1991; Pittman, 1991; Poole, 1983; Power, 1984; Zimiles and Lee, 1991) have reviewed this question. Power (1984) showed that school retentivity was determined by factors such as the type of school attended, parental encouragement and academic self-esteem. Perhaps unexpectedly, he found no evidence that parental socio-economic status and satisfaction of students with school were directly related to adolescents' decision to remain there. Instead, parental socio-economic status was directly linked to type of school and to parental encouragement. Both these factors were significantly related to the decision to remain at school.

Ainley and his colleagues (1991) have proposed a related model. They propose that several background or antecedent variables and intervening variables are related to school retention:

- The antecedent variables are factors such as socio-economic status of the family, parental expectations about whether a teenager should complete school, non-English-speaking background and type of school. Their evidence suggests that teenagers from higher socio-economic backgrounds are more likely to complete school than students from lower ones. Moreover, some teenagers from non-English-speaking backgrounds (for example, Hispanics in the USA) are more likely to complete school than native English speakers. Thus, these antecedent factors may have direct effects on educational plans.
- The intervening variables include achievement level and satisfaction with school and curriculum that may mediate the decision to remain in school. Unlike Power (1984), Ainley et al., (1991) found that satisfaction with school is an important factor in determining retentivity.

The role of socio-economic status in the decision to remain at school affects that decision in a unique way. It is the 'social' aspect rather than the 'economic' that determines the decision to remain at school (Ainley et al., 1991). That is, parents of high socio-economic status have certain attitudes, expectations and beliefs about the need to complete school and socialise their teenagers accordingly. They seem to encourage them in a way that parents from lower socio-economic groups do not. The role of this factor is particularly evident in Power's (1984) research, which found that parental encouragement has a direct influence on the decision to stay at school.

Compared to teenagers who leave school, those who decide to stay differ in their perceptions of what their parents expect of them. In one survey of Australian adolescents, for example, it was found that those who stayed at school were more likely to believe that their parents wanted them to enter lower or upper professional occupations. Adolescents who decided to leave school were more likely to believe that their parents were in favour of them following skilled manual or white-collar vocations (Poole, 1983).

Other writers have focused on the effects of family structure on school dropout rates. One major longitudinal study examined over 10 000 adolescents (Zimiles and Lee, 1991). The researchers divided their sample into either intact, single-parent or step-parent families. They found that students from intact families were up to three times less likely to drop out of school than those from other families. Moreover, significant interactions were observed between the gender of the adolescent and custodial parent. It was found that males tended to drop out of school less frequently when living with single fathers, while females tended to drop out less frequently when residing in a single-mother family. Importantly, the achievement scores of dropouts from single-parent and stepfamilies were found to be quite similar to those of dropouts from intact families. This seems to suggest that students drop out of school for reasons beyond academic ones.

With respect to family structure and dropout rates, one must note in conclusion that the findings reported here suggest a complex web of relationships that are partly determined by the gender of the teenager and custodial parent. Of added significance is whether the adolescent is in an intact family or not, as well as the custodial parent's decision to remarry. This could have possible negative implications for the emotional bond between parent and teenager. In that event, it may act as a catalyst in the decision to quit school (Zimiles and Lee, 1991).

GENDER, TYPE OF SCHOOL AND ACADEMIC OUTCOME

The relationship between gender, type of school and educational outcome has not only generated much scholarly research, but has also given rise to sometimes emotional debate. Perhaps this is inevitable where issues of gender and social class are involved (Jones, 1990). As others (for example, Connel et al., 1982) have noted, the debate concerns 'working class' and 'ruling class' schools.

A review of the literature soon reveals that the issues are indeed complex. Researchers have employed different methodologies and samples, and thus it is not surprising that research findings have tended to be equivocal. As Jones (1990, 153) noted, 'The intersection of class and gender in these variables makes the task of research very difficult and it is not surprising that there are now many studies which produce conflicting results'.

Single-sex versus Co-educational Schools

The question of whether adolescents should be educated in single-sex or co-educational schools has important policy implications (Marsh, 1989; Marsh and Rowe, 1996). Although co-education was first espoused as the ideal environment in which equal opportunity between the sexes could be made manifest, there is now some doubt among feminists and other writers as to whether girls perform optimally in such schools (for example, Byrne and Byrne, 1990; Jones, 1990; Marsh, 1989; Rowe, 1988). Jones, for example, has argued that class ideology is transmitted from the social structure of society into co-educational schools. As a consequence, class and gender interact to lower the academic and career aspirations of girls in such schools. By contrast, girls in single-sex (usually wealthy private) schools have access to better facilities, smaller classes and generally seem to perform better (although this may partly be determined by parents' social status in the case of wealthy, private schools).

Much research has focused on school type and gender differences in academic performance in subjects such as mathematics and science. Results have shown that boys in co-educational schools tend to outperform girls, while girls in government co-educational schools are less likely to enrol in higher level mathematics and science subjects (Jones, 1990). Some evidence has shown that girls from single-sex schools are more likely to prefer science subjects and they rate their performance in mathematics and science higher than do girls from co-educational schools. Girls from mixed schools, however, are more likely to prefer subjects like English. Boys from co-educational schools tend to prefer science subjects compared with boys from single-sex schools. On the other hand, boys in single-sex schools prefer subjects like English, although they are more likely to have higher self-esteem than males in co-educational schools (Foon, 1988). Thus, Foon concluded as follows (52):

> The type of school attended does seem to have differential consequences for students in terms of their stated preferences and rated achievement in subjects: those attending single sex schools seem to be less rigidly attached to traditional views... By contrast, attendance at co-educational schools appears to be associated with traditional subject preferences and related assessments of achievement in those subject areas.

Various explanations for girls' relatively lower performance in science-related subjects in co-educational schools have been advanced (Byrne and Byrne, 1990; Jones, 1990). Factors include school ethos, community attitudes, low aspiration, and negative teacher attitudes. As most school principals and department heads in co-educational schools are male, girls lack adequate role models (Byrne and Byrne, 1990; Jones, 1990). It has been argued that mixed classrooms have a negative impact on girls' self-esteem so that they tend not to take subjects such as mathematics and science offered at advanced levels. It is not clear whether lowered self-esteem is the result of being in a mixed class or not. Nonetheless, there is evidence to suggest that boys in such schools are much more confident in their ability to learn mathematics (Rowe, 1988). Future research should determine the source of this confidence, so as to initiate intervention strategies for girls.

There also appear to be particular classroom dynamics in operation whereby boys demand and receive more teacher attention (Jones, 1990; Rowe, 1988). This has led some researchers to conduct studies in which girls *within* co-educational schools have been placed in single-sex classes. One study (cited in Jones, 1990) conducted in Britain found that girls in such single-sex classes achieved better results in mathematics and science than did girls in traditional mixed classes. There is some support for this view from an Australian study which found significant gains in confidence over time for students in single-sex rather than mixed classes in a co-educational school (Rowe, 1988), although this has been disputed by Marsh and Rowe (1996).

Given methodological problems associated with the Rowe (1988) study, Marsh and Rowe (1996) re-analysed Rowe's results. Based on this re-analysis, they question the alleged benefits of single-sex classes and concluded as follows (159):

- 'the only significant effect of class type ... was in favour of mixed-sex classes (for attitudes in favour of equality of the sexes) ...

RESEARCH HIGHLIGHT 5.4
How good am I at mathematics and English?
Bornholt, Goodnow and Cooney, 1994

Do boys and girls differ in their perceptions of how well they do at school? More particularly, do these perceptions differ for maths and English? The authors asked 663 school students in the first four years of high/secondary school to complete standardised measures of reading comprehension and maths and to also provide general perceptions of their achievement in these two subject areas. They were asked about their current performance, future performance, their perceived ability, the effort they put in for each subject, and how difficult they find each subject.

Results showed no significant gender differences in actual test scores, but males significantly overestimated their maths and English performance. With respect to general perceptions of performance in the two subject areas, males overestimated their perceived current *and* future performance in maths, although there were no significant differences with respect to English. Males perceived themselves as having higher natural talent than females in maths leading to lower task difficulty requiring less effort. For English, girls perceived themselves as having more talent than boys leading to lower task difficulty for girls requiring less effort.

- girls in mixed-sex classes actually experienced larger gains for most outcomes...
- initially brighter students were more benefited by being in mixed-sex classes...
- differences that were found seemed to favour mixed-sex classes rather than single-sex classes'.

State- vs. Privately-funded Schools

The issue of state- vs. privately-funded schools and students' educational outcomes should not be divorced from our discussion so far. In a sense, they are closely intertwined, since many private schools are, in fact, single-sex schools. However, whereas the previous section focused primarily on issues relating to gender, this section will concentrate on

TABLE 5.4   *Academic attainment at different school types*

	Type of school		
	State	*Catholic*	*Independent*
Basic schooling			
Percentage completed	20	30	58
Mean years completed	9.6	10	11
Higher education			
Percentage participation	36	43	58
Mean years completed	2.9	3.2	3.8

Source: Graetz, 1990

the academic performance of students in state and private schools irrespective of adolescents' gender.

It now appears to be a well-established fact that students who attend private schools are more likely than their state counterparts to complete more schooling and to attend university (Jones, 1990; Byrne and Byrne, 1990). Support for the view that private school students perform better than their state school counterparts comes from a large-scale survey of Australian students (Graetz, 1990). This study found that private school students, on average, tend to spend more years at school (11 years) than state school students (9.6 years). It noted too that 58 per cent of independent school students were likely to proceed to university compared with 36 per cent of state school students. The main results are summarised in Table 5.4.

It is important to remember that it is not clear to what extent observed differences in outcome are due to *pre-existing* differences between students at co-educational and single-sex schools (Marsh, 1989). Some single-sex schools, it has been argued, are academically selective, attracting students with above-average ability. It is also likely that parental attitudes, values and social class may be implicated in student scholastic outcome. It is therefore difficult to attribute any differences in outcome solely to school type.

Of interest are the changes that have occurred in academic outcome between different types of schools over the last few decades. There has been considerable educational expansion. New schools and universities are associated with population growth and a question that arises is whether this expansion has benefited all segments of the population. In Australia those who attend private schools have benefited most from educational expansion (Graetz, 1990). Graetz divided his sample into

TABLE 5.5   *Academic attainment and school type over time*

		School type		
		State	*Catholic*	*Independent*
Basic schooling				
Percentage completed	pre-1950	6	10	28
	1950–69	12	19	55
	post-1970	35	52	77
Higher education				
Percentage participated	pre-1950	18	19	30
	1950–69	33	38	58
	post-1970	50	65	72
Highest attainments				
Degree	pre-1950	5	5	19
	1950–69	9	11	29
	post-1970	19	34	50

Source: Graetz, 1990

three cohorts, namely, pre-war (before 1950) post-war (between 1950 and 1969) and more recent (after 1970). The results of his analysis are shown in Table 5.5. It is clear that completion rates for basic education have increased by 29 per cent in the state sector for the whole period, but by almost 50 per cent in the private sector. There have been similar changes with respect to participation in higher education and the completion of first degrees.

In conclusion, Graetz (1990) makes an important observation about the long-term benefits of private schooling. He comments that up to the final year of school a private education bestows definite benefits and that, generally, adolescents attending such schools are distinctly advantaged. For academic performance beyond that, say at university level, school type makes little difference to academic outcome. Instead, according to Graetz, ability and social background are more important predictors of academic success.

THE TRANSITION TO UNIVERSITY

The relatively high rate of youth unemployment coupled with an increasing demand for a sophisticated and well-educated workforce has increased the demand for university education. Of course, not all school students make it to university, and even then some students will drop out. Who is likely to proceed to higher education? Are other factors besides academic ability important in predicting entry?

It is likely that many factors play a role in the decision to attend university. Some of these are economic, such as financial expectations and labour market opportunities. Others are sociological, such as peer-group influence and teacher encouragement. Hayden and Carpenter (1990) also identified the following factors:

- attracted by certain features of higher education system,
- did well at school (especially in science),
- received encouragement from parents and teachers,
- attended non-government schools,
- had better-off and better-educated parents.

Similar observations have been made in a longitudinal study of several hundred school-leavers over several years (H. Winefield et al., 1988). The adolescents were surveyed towards the end of their school careers and then four years later when they were in one of four comparison groups, namely, at university, unemployed, in satisfactory employment or in unsatisfactory employment. Of the adolescents rated 'definitely capable' of university study by their teachers, 43.4 per cent of the males and 32.9 per cent of the females proceeded to university. More males with high-status fathers than males with low-status fathers proceeded to university (46.3 per cent vs. 22.0 per cent), while for females the trend was 42.7 per cent vs. 28.1 per cent respectively.

This study also examined the effects of certain psychological factors. While at school, males in the four comparison groups were found not to differ significantly on measures of self-esteem or locus of control. However, females who proceeded to university had higher self-esteem and internal locus of control than other groups of females. Differences between the groups were also observed with regard to reported parental rearing patterns. Although there were no significant differences between the groups of males, females who entered university were much more likely than other groups of females to have had a father who encouraged university education and the achievement of success. The decision of females to attend university is therefore more closely related to certain personality attributes than it is among males. Thus H. Winefield et al. (1988, p. 189) noted that 'the pattern of sex differences found here suggests that the process of taking on a "student" identity is, for young women, dependent on considerable psychological resilience.'

THEORETICAL CONSIDERATIONS

Schools act as an important socialising agent in the lives of most adolescents. As such, they play an important role in the acquisition of social competence and adequate interpersonal skills, as well as friendships. Parallel with this influence is the role of the family. Supportive, yet authoritative parenting is likely to increase adolescents' psychosocial maturity, competence and self-esteem. This, in turn, is likely to enhance academic performance. Both the family and school, therefore, play an important role in academic performance and identity formation. The development of a vocational identity as well as the development of positive attitudes to work will, no doubt, be facilitated in those schools which are supportive and which encourage independence among students. These processes, moreover, are facilitated by families characterised by open channels of communication.

SUMMARY

More and more adolescents in developed countries are staying on to complete school. This is no doubt due to the increasing technological sophistication of society, with its greater demands for a well-educated workforce. Other factors such as limited job opportunities for youth also increase school retention rates.

The transition to high or secondary school can be a difficult period for some adolescents. This chapter reviewed some of the key factors crucial to academic performance in school. It was made clear, for instance, that supportive parenting styles assist teenagers in the transition to high or secondary school, thus enabling them to adjust to new demands with relative ease. The chapter also noted some of the most important socio-demographic characteristics of academic attainment, as well as the negative effects of family disruption. Research also shows that the expectations that young people have of high or secondary school are often not met.

Personality and attitudinal factors, it was noted, are also important in differentiating those who achieve academically and those who do not. There is a large body of literature that has reviewed the role of certain personality factors in academic achievement. Thus, for example, it was noted that extraversion may be an important factor for younger adolescents, while internal locus of control is not equally important for all racial groups in the USA. In addition, there are individual attributions, expectancies and values that also need to be considered when explaining academic performance among adolescents. Longitudinal research has shown that personality traits in childhood (for example, being prosocial) are important predictors of good academic outcome in early adolescence.

Attention was also paid to the critical issue of gender and school type. This is a delicate matter, since it touches on matters of ideology, social policy and social class and it is doubtful whether the last word has been written on this topic.

ADDITIONAL READING

Connel, R., Ashenden, D., Kessler, S. and Dowsett, G. (1982) *Making the Difference: Schools, Families and Social Divisions*. Sydney: Allen and Unwin.

Marsh, H. and Rowe, K. (1996) 'The Effects of Single-sex and Mixed-sex Mathematics Classes within a Coeducational School: A Reanalysis and Comment', *Australian Journal of Education*, 40: 147–62.

Poole, M. (1983) *Youth: Expectations and Transitions*. Melbourne: Routledge and Kegan Paul.

EXERCISES

1   Organise a class debate on the benefits/disadvantages of single sex vs. co-educational schools and state- vs. privately-funded schools.

2   After reading Poole (1983), interview a number of adults in full-time employment in your community. Select people from a wide range of occupations: professionals, white-collar workers, blue-collar workers. Talk to them about their schooling and other background factors. For instance, did they attend private or state schools? What schools did their parents attend? Did they or their parents attend university? Determine whether there is a link between certain types of schooling and current occupation. Were respondents more likely to attend university if their parents did? How important are these background factors in determining current occupation or are other factors (for instance, personality) important? Test for any other hypotheses you might have formulated. How do your results differ from Poole? What might explain such differences?

6

Mental Health

INTRODUCTION

This chapter deals primarily with depression and suicide among young people. Although the adolescent years can be fun-filled and challenging, for a few they are also traumatic. Some adolescents experience family and school-related problems, while others have relationship problems. To some, these problems seem insurmountable and daunting, such that the only escape is suicide. Suicide is one of the leading causes of death among teenagers, after accidents (Dusek, 1991). Worldwide, data show that suicide is the fourth major cause of death for this age group (Petti and Larson, 1987). It would also appear that the rate is steadily increasing.

There is much empirical evidence that links suicide to feelings of hopelessness and depression (for example, Suominen et al., 1997). As some writers have explained, suicide is normally not something contemplated on the spur of the moment (Conger and Petersen, 1984), but is usually the result of a long period of attempting to find solutions to trying problems, be they at school or of an interpersonal kind. To the teenager contemplating suicide, such an action appears the only viable solution to an increasingly hopeless and depressing situation. Very often, another bad event is enough to drive the teenager to suicide: a broken relationship, another bad grade at school, the death of a loved one, the separation of parents, may make an already unbearable situation worse, triggering a suicide attempt.

It is not surprising, then, that considerable research has been devoted to understanding the links between hopelessness, depression and suicide. In the present chapter, we shall note some of the important psychological correlates and antecedents of hopelessness and depression, and conclude by examining suicide. We begin with the nature of hopelessness.

HOPELESSNESS

Some authors regard hopelessness as central to understanding depression and, ultimately, suicide. Hopelessness can be defined (Kazdin et al., 1983, 504) as 'negative expectancies toward oneself and toward the future.' Minkoff and his colleagues (Minkoff et al., 1973, 455) define hopelessness thus: 'The person...expects or believes that nothing will turn out right for him, nothing he does will succeed, his important goals are unattainable, and his worst problems will never be solved'.

According to these definitions there appears to be a very strong cognitive element to hopelessness. It is quite likely that those who suffer from such feelings have a cognitive 'set' or a pre-existing expectation that things may not work out, that the future is likely to be disappointing and that failure is unavoidable. Close scrutiny of measures of hopelessness reveals that, in addition to the cognitive component, one's affect and motivation are also important in determining hopelessness (Beck et al., 1975). As will be discussed later, depression is also characterised by a negative cognitive set, an expectation that failure is imminent. In this respect, therefore, hopelessness is closely related to depression.

Kazdin and his colleagues (1983) developed a hopelessness scale for children modelled after a psychometrically sound scale used initially for adults (Beck et al., 1974). Sample items are 'I don't think I will get what I really want', and 'I want to grow up because I think things will get better'.

Evidence suggests that there is a close link between hopelessness, depression and suicide. Among adults, for example, research has shown hopelessness, depression and suicide to be closely interrelated (see Kovacs, Beck and Weissman, 1975; Minkoff et al., 1973; Wetzel, 1976). It has also been found that, when the effects of hopelessness are controlled for, the relationship between depression and suicide very often disappears. What this means is that hopelessness is a much stronger predictor than is depression of those who want to live (Kovacs et al., 1975; Wetzel et al., 1980), although this view has been disputed by others (for example, Asarnow, Carlson and Guthrie, 1987). These results are shown in Table 6.1.

Similar results are obtained with very young adolescents and those in pubescence. One research team conducted a study among a sample that had been admitted to an in-patient facility for disturbed children (Kazdin et al., 1983). As predicted, the authors found that feelings of hopelessness were related to depression and low self-esteem. They also found that scores on the measure of hopelessness were best able to differentiate between those children who repeatedly thought about or

TABLE 6.1 *Relationships between hopelessness, depression and suicidal intent*

Study	Suicidal intent with			
	Hopelessness	*Depression*	*Controlling for depression*	*Controlling for hopelessness*
Wetzel et al., 1980	0.76*	0.36*	0.72*	−0.10
Beck et al., 1975	0.38*	0.30*	0.24*	0.06
Kazdin et al., 1983	0.35*	0.20*	0.31*	0.02

Note: $p < 0.05$

had attempted suicide and those who had not. These findings are noteworthy since they suggest some similarities between younger respondents and those in adulthood.

It has been argued that individuals who display a negative attributional style (attribute negative life events to stable, global and internal causes) are at risk for suicide and that hopelessness mediates this effect. Researching this idea, Abramson and colleagues tracked college students for two and a half years (Abramson et al., 1998). Using hopelessness theory to underpin their research, it was found that students who displayed 'cognitive vulnerability' scored significantly higher on suicidability measures than did those who were low on cognitive vulnerability. As expected, hopelessness was found to mediate the effect of cognitive vulnerability on suicide.

Teenagers with little hope about themselves or their future can also be differentiated from hopeful adolescents in a number of other ways. Hopeless adolescents tend to be more anxious, and to have more school problems than hopeful ones (Kashani, Rosenberg and Reid, 1989). Hopeless teenagers also tend to be dysfunctional in areas related to friends and family. Indeed, on the basis of his longitudinal research among Chinese adolescents, Shek (1998) found that parent–adolescent conflict predicted later hopelessness, low life satisfaction and general psychiatric morbidity.

In summary, available evidence suggests that a strong case can be made for the view that hopelessness is an important element of the syndrome of depression and suicide. Of course, this does not suggest a *causal* link with depression or suicide. Hopelessness is a negative cognitive set which influences our expectations for happiness, success and well-being. When a situation is regarded as 'desperate' or 'impossible', the risk of suicide increases. If we are to reduce risk for suicide, therapists should attempt to change these distorted cognitive expectations (Minkoff et al., 1973).

DEPRESSION

First referred to as an affective disorder (Kovacs, 1989; Rowe, 1980), depression is now classified as either a mood disorder or as part of the adjustment disorders (APA, 1994). Depression involves changes in affect, ranging from positive (being elated) to negative. In its most serious form, extreme negative mood swings can become dysfunctional to the point where the individual is incapable of normal day-to-day activity.

Different authors use the term 'depression' in different ways (see, for example, Angold, 1988; Cantwell and Baker, 1991). Sometimes it is used to describe someone who is simply 'down in the dumps'. Sometimes, depression is used to refer to a pathological disorder. When thinking of depression in young people, Petersen and colleagues have suggested that we use the following classificatory system (Petersen et al., 1993):

- Depressed mood – teenagers will report being sad or 'down in the dumps'. Usually, there is an external reason for their feelings such as a bad grade at school or a relationship problem. Typically, these feelings can last from several days and may be associated with fear, anger, guilt and social withdrawal.
- Depression syndromes – depression can be viewed as part of a much larger problem which, according to Petersen and colleagues (1993) forms part of a behavioural syndrome. In other words, one can experience depression together with other problems such as high levels of anxiety, loneliness, a fear of being unloved, a fear of doing bad things, feelings of worthlessness, being nervous, and a sense of guilt.
- Clinical depression – According to Petersen et al. (1993) clinical depression is similar to major depression in adults. For teenagers to be diagnosed with clinical depression they must have experienced five or more of the following symptoms over a two-week period (156):

  * depressed mood or irritable mood most of the day,
  * decreased interest in pleasurable activities,
  * changes in weight or failure to make necessary weight gains in adolescence,
  * sleep problems,
  * psychomotor agitation or retardation,
  * fatigue or loss of energy,
  * feelings of worthlessness or abnormal amount of guilt,
  * reduced concentration and decision-making ability,
  * repeated suicidal ideation attempts, or plans of suicide.

Incidence of Adolescent Depression

When considering the prevalence rate of depression among adolescents, one should note at the outset that the vast majority of studies reported in the literature are based upon samples drawn from highly industrialised societies. It is not entirely clear to what extent adolescent depression occurs in other cultures (for example, China) and what the corresponding incidence rates are.

Just how widespread is depression among the teenage population? Reports of the incidence of depression vary quite widely, but studies which have used the Beck Depression Inventory suggest that about 5 per cent of youth will report feeling 'sad', while about 10 per cent report crying. However, with respect to much more serious forms of depression it has been estimated that about 4.7 per cent of teenagers have been so affected (Kashani et al., 1987). Among primary school children the prevalence rate of depression has been estimated to be about 5.2 per cent (Lefkowitz and Tesiny, 1985). Major depressive disorder was noted in 3.3 per cent of one adolescent sample (Garrison et al., 1997). It is estimated that about 8 per cent of adolescents suffer from some type of depression. Yet other writers report that about 22 per cent of adolescents report depressive symptoms, although these appear to be of a sufficiently mild and temporary nature not to be dysfunctional (Kashani et al., 1987).

Angold (1988) reported the incidence of some mild symptoms of depression in two samples and found that the incidence of a low appetite ranged between 5.3 and 8.3 per cent, feelings of irritability between 8.9 and 14.3 per cent, dislike of self 5.9 and 7.5 per cent, feelings of hopelessness/pessimism 2.6 and 6.1 per cent, feeling sad/miserable 2.9 and 5.4 per cent, and feelings of failure 4.9 and 11.1 per cent. Finally, some authors have reported a threefold increase in depression from preadolescence to adolescence (Fleming, Offord and Boyle, 1989), although this may simply reflect the fact that adolescents are better able to verbalise their feelings. It is also possible that the *manner of expression* changes as children get older, or that there are age differences in the susceptibility to stress (Rutter, 1986).

The incidence of depression among young people may be affected by cultural context. In Northern Ireland, for example, it has been reported that, based on the Child Depression Inventory, about 12 per cent of 11 to 25-year-olds have elevated levels of depression (Donnelly, 1995). Given the political violence so common, until the late 1990s, in some parts Northern Ireland, this is hardly surprising.

Depression Among Youth: Developmental Trends

Although very young children may feel 'sad' at the loss of a loved one, they are seldom able to accurately verbalise their sadness, grief or depression. However, by the time the child reaches adolescence, changes in cognitive development enable teenagers to verbalise and report their feelings more accurately.

The following developmental progression in depressive feelings has been noted (Rutter, 1986):

- middle of the first year of life – feelings of separation anxiety, or feelings of despair following admission to a hospital or institution;
- age 4–5 years – above feelings become less intense although they still experience 'sadness';
- puberty – characterised by an increase in depressive feelings and a change in sex ratio (see pp. 131–2); adolescent years marked by sharp increase in suicide rates.

RESEARCH HIGHLIGHT 6.1
Depressed adolescents: the transition to adulthood
Rao, Hammen and Daley, 1999

The authors tracked 149 12th grade female students for five years monitoring their risk for later depression. Students were selected from three state high schools in Los Angeles. Almost half (47 per cent) reported one or more episodes of major depressive disorder, with 30 per cent experiencing this within the first two years of leaving school. Of those reporting depression, the risk for a recurring episode was greatest during the first year. By the end of the follow-up period those who had experienced depression, compared to non-depressives, rated more poorly in their romantic relationships and academic work. In addition, partners of depressives rated their relationship as unsatisfactory. Thus, teenage depressives run the risk of maladjustment in adulthood. As the authors concluded: 'An implication is that women caught in depression-dysfunction cycles may be at considerable risk for recurrent depression and family-marital difficulties' (914).

In one study, the frequency of depressive symptoms in four populations of referred patients was compared (Carlson and Kashani, 1988): pre-school children, pre-pubescent children, adolescents and adults. It was found that symptoms of psychotic depression (such as delusions) tended to increase with age, with adults more likely to experience them than adolescents. Some symptoms, such as a lowering of self-esteem and a depressed appearance, were more likely to decrease with increasing age. Other symptoms appear not to be age-specific. These include poor concentration, insomnia, suicide ideation and suicide attempts.

Further research evidence supports the view that depression follows certain developmental trends in children and adolescents. One research team was interested in describing the depressive symptoms in three different age groups (8-, 12-, and 17-year-olds). Only the data for the 12- and 17-year-olds are reported in Table 6.2 (Kashani, Rosenberg and Reid, 1989). This table shows that several measures were used in the study and that each revealed certain age trends. According to the data, depression in older adolescents tends to be associated with such factors as being irritable, tired, agitated and not caring whether or not they get hurt. Among older adolescents depression is also associated with isolation from the peer group, not having energy, and not sticking up for oneself. Depression among younger adolescents tends to be

TABLE 6.2   *Frequency of depression-related items in two groups of adolescents*

Depression-related items	12-year-olds (%)	Rate of increase in 17-year-olds (%)
Child assessment schedule		
More tired than before	15.7	+126
Doesn't care whether hurts self	15.7	+146
Agitation or hyperactivity when sad	21.4	+61
Irritable a lot	21.4	+100
Birleson scale		
Not looking forward to things as much as used to	47.1	−34
Not liking to go out and play	24.3	+100
Having stomach aches	55.7	−25
Not having lots of energy	41.4	+63
Not sticking up for self	20.0	+25
Having horrible dreams	27.1	−11
Feeling very bored	92.9	−9

Source: Kashani et al., 1989

associated with not looking forward to things, having stomach pains, having horrible dreams, and feeling bored.

There are several factors that may explain the developmental changes in depressive affect among youth. They are (Rutter, 1986):

- hormonal influences – for example, irritability during the premenstrual cycle;
- genetic factors – refers to genotypical influences, but also the possibility that depression in adolescence differs genetically from depression in preadolescence;
- alterations in the frequency of stressors;
- vulnerability vs. protective factors – older adolescents who leave home are more at risk for depression;
- cognitive factors – girls more likely than boys to attribute failure to their own lack of ability.

Sex Differences in Adolescent Depression

Several studies (for example, Holsen, Kraft and Vitterso, 2000; Petersen, Sarigiani and Kennedy, 1991) have noted sex differences in adolescent depression with more girls than boys reporting depressive episodes (but see Garrison et al., 1997). This appears to be particularly the case during middle and late adolescence, with the biggest difference noted between early and late adolescents, particularly for girls (Holsen et al., 2000). In addition, the gender differences are larger for referred than non-referred teenagers, while among more representative samples of youth the gender differences are small. The biggest differences occur on ratings of depressed mood and anxiety/depression than on other symptoms such as sleep deprivation or loss of appetite (Compas et al., 1997).

In a large-scale Canadian study, the incidence of depression was noted to be higher for females for the less severe forms of depression, while no sex differences were noted in the incidence of more severe forms (Fleming et al., 1989). As the authors noted (652): 'This... suggests that perhaps female adolescents are more likely than males to report depressive symptoms, but no more likely than males to have a clinical syndrome of depression'.

The reported sex difference in depression persists into adulthood (Petersen et al., 1993). However, an alternate thesis has been suggested by Reinherz and colleagues who maintain that after 15 years of age males are more likely to experience *later* onset of depression (Reinherz et al., 1993).

What are the possible reasons for the observed sex difference in depression? The following have been given prominence by some writers (Avison and McAlpine, 1992; Compas, Orosan and Grant, 1993; Petersen et al., 1991, 1993; Rutter, 1986):

- In the first place, it is likely that early-maturing girls may develop a negative body image which, in turn, may be related to depression. Such a predisposition may be exacerbated if early maturing girls experience stressful events at home or school.
- Secondly, it has also been suggested that negative family events may serve as an antecedent for depression among girls, but not necessarily boys. Although this suggestion has not been adequately explained, it is held that some boys may develop particular coping mechanisms, while girls may not. Clearly, such a suggestion needs to be examined much more intensively.
- Another suggestion is that girls, much more than boys, ponder or ruminate over their depressed state which only serves to heighten their depression. It has been suggested that females are more alert than are boys to their moods and emotions and tend to focus more on their depressive symptoms. Thus, they experience their symptoms more acutely.
- Such an increased focus on symptoms is likely to enhance feelings of helplessness and negative self-evaluations. By contrast, males are more likely to engage in other activities and tasks with resultant lower levels of depression.
- Some authors have also commented on the relationships of self-esteem, mastery and social support with depression. Thus, it has been argued that, compared with boys, teenage girls' higher depression scores may be related to their generally lower self-esteem.
- Some of the factors associated with general developmental change may also explain sex differences in adolescent depression. Two important influences in this regard are hormonal factors and negative cognitive set. Hormonal changes are more likely to trigger depression in girls rather than boys, while it has been noted that girls are more likely to attribute negative events to an internal stable disposition.

Psychosocial Correlates of Depression

Which psychosocial factors are related to depression among teenagers? Research on this issue suggests that a wide range of factors is related to depression in youth, not least of which is the age of the adolescent. Among preadolescent girls, depression appears to be associated with anxiety and feelings of being persecuted. For girls aged 12–16 years, on the other hand, the important predictors of depression are withdrawal, being sensitive, feelings of shyness and timidity, and liking to be alone (Cantwell and Baker, 1991).

In most of its various forms depression has been found to have negative consequences for social and cognitive aspects of development. There is now evidence that depression is linked to a slowing of some aspects of cognitive development, while depression has also been found to have negative effects on the acquisition of age-appropriate verbal skills. Perhaps not surprisingly, depression in adolescence has also been found to be related to academic underachievement (Chan, 1997; Kaltiala, Rimpelae and Rantanen, 1998; Kovacs, 1989). Kaltiala and colleagues (1998) conducted an impressive large scale study of over 15 000 Finnish teenagers and confirmed the link between depression and poor school performance, after controlling for socio-demographic factors.

Depressed teenagers manifest particular social skills deficits. Available evidence indicates that those peers who rate teenagers as depressed tend to judge them as being more isolated and less effective in social interactions. Studies also show that depressed teenagers tend not to be preferred as work or playmates. They tend to regard themselves poorly and have low expectations of success (see Kovacs, 1989).

Some studies have compared adult depressives with adolescent depressives (see the review by Cantwell and Baker, 1991). These findings suggest that adolescents may experience less anorexia and weight loss, more psychomotor agitation and retardations, and more guilt and lower self-esteem. Very often, depressed adolescents are also characterised by anxiety and conduct disorders.

A review of the literature has suggested the following additional psychosocial risk factors for adolescent depression (Angold, 1988):

- Social class – some suggest that adolescents from lower social classes may exhibit higher depression, although the findings tend to be equivocal; more research is needed.
- Race – some reports suggest a 'depressive syndrome' among black adolescents, although findings are equivocal; more research is needed.
- Family psychiatric history – there appears to be a strong link between parental depression and adolescent disturbance.

Important buffers *against* adolescent depression are peer and parental support, as well as good individual coping responses. Some specific factors that have been identified are closeness with one or both parents, or with a good friend. Close links have been noted between teenagers' perceptions of parents as caring, and low depression scores among the adolescents themselves. This has led some writers to conclude that warm, communicative and caring parents instil confidence, mastery and high self-esteem in their children leading to low depression. A perception of parents as over-protective, however, appears to be linked to low levels of mastery and higher levels of depression (Avison and McAlpine, 1992). It has also been found that parental and peer support moderate the negative effects of such factors as early adolescent changes. Thus, parents and friends acts as a source of comfort and security in the changing world of the adolescent (Petersen et al., 1991).

It follows from the above that parenting style is implicated in adolescent levels of depression. From Chapter 3 you will recall that parental styles are differentiated into a number of different styles including authoritative, authoritarian, indulgent and neglectful. It has recently been demonstrated that, across different ethnic groups, the authoritative parenting style best predicts low levels of depression, while an unengaged style is predictive of depression (Radziszewska et al., 1996). Likewise, among both Chinese and American teenagers heightened depression is linked to low parental warmth and high levels of conflict with parents (Greenberger et al., 2000).

Negative self-perceptions

As noted earlier in the chapter, a negative cognitive set may be important in explaining a predisposition for depression. This line of reasoning is based on research findings that have shown a close link between low self-esteem and other factors such as hopelessness and coping skills. Such findings, noted by Asarnow and colleagues (1987, 361), have lent credence to 'the notion of a cognitive triad in depression that is characterized by negative views of the self, the world, and the future.'

Such negative cognitive biases in depression are generally regarded as quite important and have been examined in several studies of adults and adolescents. Specifically, studies have focused on factors such as locus of control, and the way in which causal attributions are made (Gladstone et al., 1997; McCauley et al., 1988). Evidence indicates that teenagers who perceive that they have little control over their life events (so-called 'externals') are more likely to be depressed than so-called 'internals', who perceive themselves as in control of their life events.

It has also been noted that depressed adolescents attribute the outcomes of negative events to internal, stable and global factors, and are therefore more likely to blame themselves for negative events. Depressed teenagers tend to attribute positive events to *external*, stable and global dimensions, that is, to causes beyond their control. They seem to be characterised by a negative cognitive set which, in addition to being related to depression, also has links to low self-esteem, loneliness and poor health outcomes (Abramson, Seligman and Teasdale, 1978).

These trends are clearly illustrated in Figure 6.1 in which the attributional scores of a group of depressed and never depressed adolescents are compared. The table shows that, compared to non-depressives, depressed adolescents made significantly more maladaptive attributions for negative events.

Stress, the family, and peers

There is a widely-held view among researchers that stressful events are an important determining factor in adolescent depression. Some of these stress factors are biological changes (being smaller/taller for one's age), cognitive development, social changes (moving from one town to

FIGURE 6.1 *Types of attributions made by depressives and non-depressives for negative events*

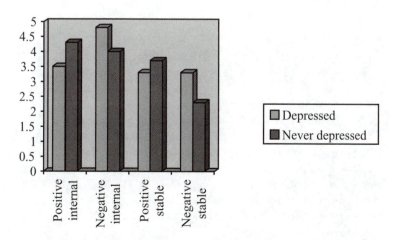

Source: Gladstone, Kaslow, Seeley and Lewinsohn, 1997

another), school transitions (changing schools), changes to the parent–child relationship (having parents who separate), changes in peer relationships (being left out of a group) and gender-role expectations (Gore, Aseltine and Colton, 1992). Younger teenagers appear to be more susceptible to the negative effects of stress than older youth (Siegel and Brown, 1988).

Family socialisation processes are also important in determining the likelihood of depression in children and teenagers (Cole and Rehm, 1986). Following the social learning model of Bandura (see Chapter 1), it is argued that adolescents adopt the reward and punishment models of parents. The authors note that depressed parents find it difficult to show affection for their children. Thus, parent–child communication is poor, with parents tending to reward their children less frequently. According to the model, depressed youngsters set high personal standards, are overly self-critical, and tend not to reward themselves. Such teenagers therefore find themselves in a vicious cycle attempting to achieve unrealistic goals with failure often the outcome. Such failure, combined with a negative cognitive set, only serves to increase the likelihood of depressive feelings among adolescents.

Research has examined the extent to which family structure and the socio-economic condition of the household act as buffers against life stress and consequent depression during adolescence. In a study of over 1000 teenagers in the USA, support was found for the view that the family can buffer the adolescent against the negative effects of stress (Gore et al., 1992). The researchers found that teenagers with a low

RESEARCH HIGHLIGHT 6.2
Family climate and teenage depression
Garrison et al., 1997

Garrison and colleagues found that family process rather than family structure is related to depression in teenagers. This is in line with much of the evidence discussed in Chapter 3. The authors sampled 359 school students and concluded that family support and cohesion acted as a buffer against teenage depression. Indeed, they found little evidence to suggest that depression is related to major life events, which is in contrast to the work of several other researchers.

standard of living were more likely to react negatively to stress events. They also found that teenagers whose parents had low levels of formal education were less likely to cope adequately with personal stress.

Other studies support these findings. For instance, among adolescent in-patients, high family and parental support tends to be related to low depression among teenagers, as is peer support. When family support was high, peer support was somewhat related to adolescent depression, but when parental support was low, peer support was *negatively* related to depression (Barrera and Garrison-Jones, 1992; see also Garrison et al., 1997). Thus, in the absence of parental support, the peer network acts as a buffer against depression by providing necessary emotional support.

Interesting applied research has also been conducted into the effects of stress on teenagers following major political crises such as the Gulf Crisis (Llabre and Hadi, 1997) and the war in the Balkans (Ajdukovic, 1998). In both these studies, teenagers had experienced severe stress in which their lives were at risk, culminating in post-traumatic stress disorder. In each case, high stress levels were associated with elevated levels of depression.

SUICIDE

Suicide is one of the leading causes of death among teenagers. Viewpoints differ and some regard suicide as simply a manifestation of destructive tendencies, while others suggest that suicide and suicide ideation may be a desperate plea for help. Although a single event such as the death of a loved one has the potential to lead to suicide, suicide may also result from years of psychological anguish and feelings of hopelessness. Thus, suicide ideation or attempted suicide is an undoubted signal to parents and teachers that the teenager is in need of immediate assistance.

Incidence of Adolescent Suicide

Many countries have recorded a steady increase in youth suicide rates over recent years. Table 6.3 shows the incidence of suicide for several countries with the rate for young Russian males the highest in the world, followed by New Zealand, Switzerland, Austria, Canada, and Australia. The suicide rate for young Russians has risen sharply in recent times. In 1981 the rates for males and females per 100 000

TABLE 6.3   *Suicide rates for males and females aged 15–24 years*

Country	Males	Females	Year
Russia	48.8	9.0	1994
New Zealand	39.4	5.9	1993
Switzerland	30.3	5.2	1994
Austria	25.4	6.6	1994
Canada	23.8	4.7	1993
Australia	23.7	3.7	1993
Scotland	21.5	5.6	1994
Northern Ireland	21.5	0.8	1994
Norway	21.9	6.0	1993
USA	21.9	3.7	1992
France	18.2	5.2	1993
Croatia	18.3	7.8	1994
Germany	13.9	3.7	1994
Bulgaria	13.3	5.0	1994
Sweden	12.0	6.6	1993
Japan	12.0	5.1	1994
Singapore	11.7	10.2	1994
England and Wales	10.0	1.9	1994
Israel	11.3	1.5	1993
Chile	7.6	2.4	1992
Hong Kong	9.5	8.7	1994
Netherlands	9.1	4.1	1994
Italy	6.8	1.8	1992
Mexico	5.9	1.3	1993
Portugal	4.8	1.9	1994

Note: Deaths are per 100 000 population
Source: World Health Organization, 1996

respectively were 37.1 and 6.5. In 1987 they were 22.6 and 4.9. By 1994 they had risen to 48.8 and 9.0 (World Health Organization, 1996). The suicide rate for males in Northern Ireland is considerably higher than that in England and Wales.

The Australian suicide rate for those aged 15–24 years is much higher for males than it is for females. Figure 6.2 illustrates this difference and also indicates the extent to which the suicide rate has increased over recent years. In 1981, the male suicide rate was just below 20 deaths per 100 000 population. By 1990 it stood at 27 deaths per 100 000 population (Australian Bureau of Statistics, 1991). In 1993 it was 23.7 per 100 000 population (Cantor and Baume, 1998). The suicide rate for females aged 15–24 years has tended to move up and down over

FIGURE 6.2   *Changes in suicide rates for Australians aged 15–24 years*

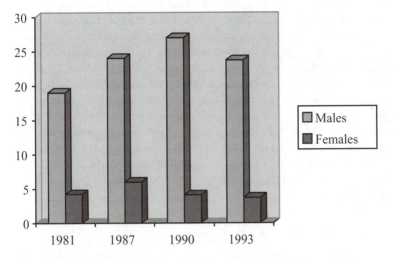

Source: Australian Bureau of Statistics, 1991; Cantor and Baume, 1998

the years. It reached a peak of about six deaths per 100 000 in 1987, but the average appears to be close to four.

There are important racial and ethnic differences in the incidence of suicide. For instance, the youth suicide rate is very low in Hong Kong (Ho et al., 1995), while data from the USA shows that the incidence rate for young whites is substantially higher than that for African–American youth. Rice (1999, p. 405) reports that white females aged 15–19 have a suicide rate about twice as high as their black counterparts (4.2 versus 2.1). The rate for white males is 18.5, while that of black males is 14.4. There are also differences in suicide rates across native-American groups. Thus, whereas the rate for Navajo Indians is 12 per 100 000, for some Apache groups it is 43 per 100 000 (Rice, 1992).

Theories of Suicide

Why do individuals commit suicide? Several psychological perspectives have been proposed which attempt to explain suicidal behaviour. Each of these will be briefly described below.

The psychoanalytical approach

This approach assumes an unconscious intention as the main motivation for suicide (Leenaars, 1990). It is argued that the suicidal person may experience a great sense of loss and rejection of a highly loved person or object. In such instances, suicide is seen as a way of coping with this loss. By killing themselves, they destroy the significant 'other' whose image is closely absorbed into the individual's psyche (Bootzin and Acocella, 1988). Very often too, the suicidal person may experience guilt or self-criticism or harsh attitudes toward the self. For such individuals, suicide is one way of dealing with this low self-esteem. Finally, this approach also suggests that suicidal individuals are unable to organise and synthesise their experiences. This may be so acute that sometimes the suicidal person becomes dysfunctional.

Cognitive-behavioural approach

According to this view, there is an important link between feelings of hopelessness, depression and suicide (Leenaars, 1990). Hopelessness appears to be associated with a negative cognitive set, with the future seen as unrealistically bleak and unpromising. In such individuals, thought patterns are characterised by possible errors such as overgeneralisation, selective abstraction, inexact labelling and so forth. Not surprisingly, the negative cognitive set may lead to suicide. According to this approach, suicide is viewed as positively reinforcing in that it elicits attention and pity (Bootzin and Acocella, 1988).

Social learning approach

The social learning approach suggests that suicide is learned in very much the same way one learns other behaviours. It is argued, for example, that suicide can be shaped by childhood experiences of punishment. Thus, aggression is expressed inwards toward the self, rather than outwards (Leenaars, 1990).

According to the social learning perspective, it is also possible that the suicidal person has not been adequately socialised into traditional culture. In other words, such individuals have not learned normal cultural values regarding life and death. Moreover, suicidal behaviour can be influenced (or reinforced) by subcultural norms as depicted on television, or as manifest by others known to the individual (so-called 'copy cat suicides') (Leenaars, 1990).

The biological approach

This perspective holds that mood disorders have a biological basis. Given the close relationship that is often observed between depression and suicide, some argue that suicide may be biologically based. It is argued that suicide, impulsiveness, and aggressive behaviour are associated with a decreased flow of serotonin from the brainstem to the frontal lobes of the cortex (Leenaars, 1990).

Attempted Suicide

Attempted suicide far outnumbers successful suicide. Although it is much more difficult to estimate the number of attempted suicides, some writers have estimated that the rate of suicide attempts is between 50 to 200 times greater than that of completed suicides (Dusek, 1991; Garland and Zigler, 1993; Mason, 1990). Females are more likely to attempt suicide than males, although males are much more likely to be successful.

Some hospital statistics support the observation that young females are much more likely to attempt suicide than young males. In Western Australia during 1985, for example, 14-year-olds (boys and girls) were admitted at the rate of 270 per 100 000 at-risk population. For boys, the figure was 70 per 100 000 at-risk population (Mason, 1990).

Are there any fundamental differences between suicide attempters and those who complete it? Are suicide attempters just seeking attention? In her review of this literature, Mason concluded that most commentators would now agree that there are few differences between the two groups. Indeed, about 40–50 per cent of completed suicides among teenagers had a history of earlier attempts.

Research shows that different socio-environmental and psychological-behavioural measures predict suicide ideation for males and females. One study of over 400 school students revealed that emotional and unemployment problems had direct effects upon suicide ideation for males. The absence of parental support had an indirect effect through emotional problems (Simons and Murphy, 1985). For the females in the sample, emotional problems and delinquent behaviour had direct effects upon suicide ideation. Absence of parental support as well as employment problems were found to have indirect effects through emotional problems, low self-esteem, hopelessness and delinquent behaviour. In conclusion, parental support and employment problems are important antecedents of suicide ideation. These findings have important implications for family communication and interaction as well as government policy. Simons and Murphy (1985, 431) state that 'programs and policies concerned with adolescent suicide should concentrate on strengthening the nurturing, supportive function of the family...[and] the employment problems faced by many teenagers'.

Method of Suicide

Males are much more likely than females to commit suicide by violent means, like using a firearm. Females are much more likely to kill themselves through poisoning (Cantor and Baume, 1998; Mason, 1990). The most successful method of suicide for both genders is through the use of firearms, followed by hanging and gassing (Garland and Zigler, 1993). In a review of all adolescent suicides in Finland for a one-year period, it was found that males were more likely to use firearms (45 per cent), hanging (27 per cent), and drugs (5 per cent). Females were more likely to commit suicide by drug use (33 per cent) and hanging (33 per cent), followed by firearms (11 per cent) (Marttunen, Aro and Lonnqvist, 1992). In Hong Kong, on the other hand, the most favoured methods are jumping from tall buildings, hanging, and self-poisoning (Ho et al., 1995).

Cantor and Baume (1998) have recorded the changes in suicide method for males and females in Australia. Table 6.4 shows these changes over a 20-year period from 1974 to 1994. For instance, hanging has become an increasingly preferred method for both sexes, while the use of firearms has remained relatively steady over time, peaking in the

TABLE 6.4   *Changes in method of suicide for Australians aged 15–24 years (1974–94)*

Method	1974		1994	
	Males	*Females*	*Males*	*Females*
Solids/liquids	3.1	2.6	1.9	1.0
Hanging	1.5	0.5	9.7	1.6
Drowning	0.2	0.2	0.3	0.0
Firearms	7.5	0.3	6.9	0.4
Jumping	0.7	0.3	1.3	0.4

Note: Rates are per 100 000 population
Source: Cantor and Baume, 1998

mid-1980s. The most preferred methods for Australian females currently are poisoning and hanging.

There have also been changes in the method of suicide for teenagers in England and Wales. Between 1970 and 1984 poisoning by 'other gases and vapours' (for example, domestic gas) increased from 2.4 to 5.7 per million population for males. Hanging, strangulation and suffocation increased from 7.9 to 13.4 for males (McClure, 1986). In Britain, the rise in suicides among teenage males to 1990 was largely due to a further rise in the rates of strangulation, suffocation as well as poisoning by car exhaust fumes (McClure, 1994).

Psychosocial Correlates of Suicidal Behaviour

Those who study suicide have noted several causes of adolescent suicide including biological, psychological and sociological factors (Diekstra and Moritz, 1987). Biological factors refer to bodily illness or certain disorders and physical handicaps, while psychological and sociological factors include a wide range of factors such as family discord,

---

RESEARCH HIGHLIGHT 6.3
Suicide among young people in Britain
McClure, 1994

McClure (1994) studied the suicide rates of young people in England and Wales for the period 1960–90. For males, suicide rates have shown a dramatic increase. For instance, in 1960 it was 30 per million population among 15 to 19-year-olds, but only 15 per million population among females. By 1990 this had increased to 57 per million for males. Among females it was 14 per million. Suicide rates among 10 to 14-year-olds in England and Wales have remained relatively low and constant over this period. For males and females respectively, the rates were 1.8 and 1.0 per million for the years 1960–70, 1.5 and 1.2 for 1971–80, and 1.5 and 1.0 for the years 1981–90. Just under half of the deaths among 15 to 19-year-old males in 1990 was by car exhaust fumes with a substantial rise also in hanging, strangulation and suffocation. Most of the deaths due to 'unspecified means' are the result of jumping off high places or lying in front of moving vehicles.

TABLE 6.5   *Psychosocial factors associated with suicide among youth*

Primary risk factors

1 Affective disorders. These include major and bipolar depressive disorder. These disorders appear to be over-represented in those youth who have attempted or completed suicide.
2 Previous attempt. Prior attempts at suicide are a good predictor of future attempts.
3 Hopelessness.

Secondary risk factors

1 Substance abuse, especially alcohol abuse, amphetamine and cocaine withdrawal as well as use of sedatives, hypnotics and anxiolytics.
2 Personality disorders. These are especially important in the presence of substance abuse.

Situational risk factors

1 Family functioning and history. These include broken homes, family history of psychiatric problems, family history of suicidal behaviour, and childhood abuse.
2 Social relationships. This refers to the quality of social support and peer relationships.
3 Exposure to suicide or the 'ripple' effect
4 Life stressors.
5 Homosexuality

Source: Stoelb and Chiriboga, 1998

sexual and emotional abuse, depression and hopelessness, school problems, unemployment, poverty, and substance abuse (Mason, 1990).

More recently, Stoelb and Chiriboga (1998) suggested that the factors associated with youth suicide be classified as primary risk factors, secondary risk factors, and situational risk factors. These factors, many of which overlap with those mentioned by Mason (1990) above, are described more fully in Table 6.5.

Many research studies have tended to focus on the importance of these factors in isolation. Thus, for example, Ben-Ari and Gil (1998) studied the perceptions of life and death of gay adolescents, while Garnefski and Arends (1998) demonstrated that adolescents who experienced sexual abuse are more likely than other teenagers to have elevated levels of suicidal thoughts. In New Zealand, it was shown that the risk for serious suicide attempts increases as levels of unemployment rise, although the relationship was found not to be a causal one (Beautrais, Joyce and Mulder, 1998). These same authors also found that the most significant predictors of suicide among the young are relationship breakdowns, other kinds of interpersonal problems and financial concerns (Beautrais, Joyce and Mulder, 1997). In Australia, Sibthorpe and colleagues found that 45 per cent of a sample of homeless and potentially homeless youth had attempted suicide by drug overdose (Sibthorpe et al., 1995). In a retrospective study De Wilde and colleagues found that life stressors were important predictors of suicide, although different stressors are important at different stages of the lifespan (De Wilde et al., 1992).

Graham (1996) found sexual abuse to be a significant factor in the etiology of adolescent suicide and concluded that this factor is more important than living in a dysfunctional family. Another study found feelings of hopelessness to be a better predictor of youth suicide than a dysfunctional family (Levy, Jurkovic and Spirito, 1995), although family problems were found to be significant among female suicides in Hong Kong (Ho et al., 1995). School problems were the most important predictor of high suicide ideation scores among one US sample (Sieman, Warrington and Mangano, 1994).

The Rural Adolescent

It is believed that rural adolescents face greater stressors than do urban ones (for example, Forrest, 1988). Those who live in small provincial towns or communities are largely dependent on single economies such as farming, fishing or mining, and face unique problems. Many such communities are isolated and these teenagers face higher levels of unemployment and distance from resources and facilities that teenagers in the cities take for granted. For instance, entertainment is very often limited, with many teenagers describing life as 'dull'. Moreover, there is added stress on farming families, due to current low commodity prices and emigration to more populated areas (Cullen and Connolly, 1997).

The suicide rate among rural adolescents has shown a significant increase in recent years (Bush, 1990; Forrest, 1988). It was noted earlier that the suicide rate among Australian males has risen sharply. Bush (1990) has suggested that this increase is due largely to the accelerating suicide rate in rural areas. In the Sydney metropolitan region, for example, the adolescent male suicide rate rose from 3.4 per 100 000 in 1966 to 3.8 per 100 000 in 1986. In the rural shires of New South Wales, however, the rate rose from below 3.5 in 1966 to 21.6 per 100 000 in 1986.

This dramatic rise in the male suicide rate in rural areas can perhaps best be understood in terms of social context. Bush (1990) suggests that men in rural areas face declining opportunities for employment. In addition, rural social networks tend to be close-knit and supportive, yet also conservative and prescriptive. Bush makes the point that what these young men need are new role models and a belief that there are alternatives to a life on the land which would generate more diverse social networks. Indeed, Cullen and Connolly (1997) have remarked that many rural suicides lack social and interpersonal ties.

THEORETICAL CONSIDERATIONS

There are at least three theoretical perspectives worth considering when thinking about depression and suicide in adolescence. One is the biological. Evidence indicates that hormonal influences are critical in triggering depression and that the effect may be stronger for girls than boys. It is not entirely clear why this is the case. The fact remains that, beginning with puberty, depression rates for girls show a marked rise. As Rutter (1986) reminds us, during the premenstrual phase, many women suffer irritability and depression, while the latter has been found to be associated with the use of oral contraceptives. Parents and counsellors should therefore be cautious when recommending the use of such contraceptive methods.

Secondly, it is abundantly clear that the family network acts as an important buffer against depression and suicide. All adolescents will face challenges of one sort or another, some of which may seem insurmountable at the time. It is the role of the family to provide much-needed emotional support and adequate role models for their teenagers. Understanding and caring parents can greatly assist those who face difficulties, thus acting as a barrier against hopelessness, depression and suicide. There now appears to be some evidence that peer influences are also implicated in depression. How parental and peer influences interact to moderate stress in relation to suicide ideation remains unclear.

Finally, one must also bear in mind the possibility, as psychologists have indicated, that suicide may result from an unconscious desire or motivation to compensate for a great loss. It is, of course, extremely difficult to test such a link, although there does seem to be a link between depression and feelings of loss. It is therefore highly likely that a link will also exist between suicide and feelings of loss and rejection.

SUMMARY

This chapter has reviewed the link between hopelessness, depression and suicide. Hopelessness, it was observed, is characterised by a negative cognitive set: namely, a belief that the future is bleak and unpromising, and that life is devoid of much value. Importantly, such an attitude is also characteristic of some mood disorders, whilst some depressives suffer from suicide ideation. There is thus an important thread that strongly links the three concepts.

The chapter also noted the alarming increase in youth suicides in many countries. It is not clear why these countries should show such dramatic increases. There appears to be no overall pattern that could be suggestive of particular causes of youth suicide cross-culturally. Future research should therefore attempt to uncover the different factors that account for the youth suicide rate across different cultures.

ADDITIONAL READING

Cullen, A. and Connolly, J. F. (1997). 'Aspects of Suicide in Rural Ireland 1978–1994', *Archives of Suicide Research* 3: 43–52.

Fleming, J., Offord, D. and Boyle, M. 'Prevalence of Childhood and Adolescent Depression in the Community: Ontario Child Health Study', *British Journal of Psychiatry, 155* (1989) 647–54.

Lester, D. (1990) *Current Concepts of Suicide*. Philadelphia: The Charles Press.

Rutter, M., Izard, C. and Read, P. (1986) *Depression in Young People: Developmental and Clinical Perspectives*. New York: The Guilford Press.

EXERCISE

1 Are there marked city/rural and sex differences in suicide in your region? Try and obtain official statistics for your state or county and note the following:

- city/rural suicide rates,
- sex differences in suicide rates,
- sex differences in method of suicide,
- age differences in suicide rate,
- note the trends in these for a 5- and 10-year period.

What do these data suggest to you about adolescent suicide?

7

Sexuality

INTRODUCTION

We live in an age in which we are overwhelmed by material and information of a sexual nature. The AIDS epidemic has raised the consciousness of many adults and adolescents about sexually transmitted diseases, and 'safe sex'. Sexually explicit material, not available a generation or two ago, is now freely obtainable. Glossy magazines depict idealised body shapes, fashions and trends. Understandably, some adolescents may feel pressurised to make themselves as sexually appealing as possible. In addition, societal norms about sexuality are rapidly changing with increasing numbers of teenagers becoming sexually active. The gap which has traditionally existed between boys and girls with respect to their sexual activity is also rapidly decreasing (Moore and Rosenthal, 1993).

The onset of sexual awareness coincides with puberty. Whereas boys begin to show an interest in girls in a *sexual* way, girls are more interested in boys in a *romantic* way (Harris and Liebert, 1987). It is during puberty that the body undergoes rapid change in terms of size, height, weight and distribution of body hair. The various hormones being released into the bloodstream at this time prepare the child physically for adult sexuality (Gallois and Callan, 1990). The first menstruation and first ejaculation are major psychological events that herald the end of childhood and signal to the young adolescent the imminence of adulthood. In this move towards adulthood, the adolescent is not only engaged in identity formation, but must also come to terms with his or her own sexuality. This needs to be meaningfully integrated into the self-identity with as little conflict and turmoil as possible (Conger and Petersen, 1984).

Puberty and its associated rapid changes also have implications for adolescents' self-perceptions of attractiveness and sexual desirability. Furnham and Stacey explain as follows (1991, 106):

the mass media constantly present fashionable types of beautiful people for adolescents (as well as adults) to compare themselves with. Adolescents often worry about their looks and physical attractiveness, and their capacity to appeal sexually. If there is a failure to meet current standards of acceptable looks, then this may well become an important personal problem.

Why is it that some adolescents engage in sexual intercourse at an earlier age than others? Are there specific identifiable causes of such behaviour? Are such teenagers more affected than others by hormonal, family or other social influences? Or is it simply a matter of chance as to who is likely to engage in sexual intercourse? These and other issues will be discussed in this chapter.

ATTITUDES TO SEX

Adolescents have quite clearly formed beliefs about sex-related matters. This has been demonstrated in a number of surveys. In a large-scale study of over 2000 British adolescents aged 10 to over 17 years, respondents were asked about the desirability of a range of sexual matters such as premarital sex and heterosexual relationships. Almost half of all respondents felt that society should tolerate all types of sexual relationships, not just heterosexual ones. Almost three-quarters approved of premarital sex. Just over 20 per cent of adolescents agreed that the main reason for having sexual relations should be to have children (Furnham and Gunter, 1989). The large-scale British study by Johnson and colleagues (Johnson et al., 1994) found that about 80 per cent of 16 to 24 year-olds disapproved of a married person having sex with someone other than his or her partner. In contrast to Furnham and Gunter (1989) almost 70 per cent of young males disapproved of male homosexuality, while the disapproval rate among females was substantially lower.

Because not much is known about the sexual attitudes of those living in China, a recent report based on the attitudes of Chinese youth is of considerable interest (Kaufman, Poston, Hirschl and Stycos, 1996). They surveyed over 5000 students in grades seven to twelve in Sichuan province and reported the following:

- Over 65 per cent of males and almost 80 per cent of females agreed or strongly agreed with sex before marriage.
- Almost 25 per cent of males and 17 per cent of females agreed that anyone has the right to use birth control measures to avoid pregnancy.

- Close to 45 per cent of males and females suggested that they would use birth control measures whenever they needed to.

Are there gender differences in attitudes to specific sexual behaviours? In one study (Wilson and Medora, 1990), over 600 university students in the USA were surveyed to determine their attitudes towards premarital sex, masturbation, homosexuality, extramarital sex, oral-genital sex, anal sex and sexual fantasising. Overall, both males and females approved somewhat of premarital sex when the couple is in love or engaged. They were also approving of oral-genital sex and sexual fantasising, although males and females disapproved somewhat of homosexuality and extramarital sex. There were, however, significant differences in attitude between the sexes. Males and females differed significantly on premarital sex for casual couples, extramarital sex, oral-genital sex and anal sex. On all of these, males reported more favourable attitudes. The findings are summarised in Table 7.1.

BEING IN LOVE

Most adolescents report their first experience of being in love around age 12 years, although there is a tendency for this to increase among students in the higher grades (Montgomery and Sorell, 1998). How do young people describe being in love? Perhaps not surprisingly, the

TABLE 7.1   *Attitudes of undergraduates towards sexual behaviour*

Sexual behaviours	Mean scores	
	Males	Females
Premarital sex – couple casually acquainted	2.90	3.76*
Premarital sex – couple in love	2.36	2.56
Premarital sex – couple engaged	1.89	1.99
Masturbation	2.96	3.16
Homosexuality	4.11	4.13
Extramarital sex	3.86	4.11*
Oral-genital sex	1.76	2.28*
Anal sex	2.80	3.36*
Sexual fantasising	1.66	1.79

Note: $n = 641$
*males and females differ significantly. Low scores indicate favourable attitude
Source: Wilson and Medora, 1990

themes that are touched upon vary quite considerably as shown by the following (Montgomery and Sorell, 1998, 683–4):

- Lack of experience and maturity. Some adolescents acknowledge that 'real' love only happens much later and that many adolescents are not mature enough for a relationship.
- What is love? Adolescents appear to have specific ideas on love vs. infatuation, love vs. sexual attraction, love vs. self-promotion, and love vs. loving (see Table 7.2).
- Love is friendship. Some see love as a stronger form of friendship.
- Love is mysterious; it is difficult to understand. For some, love is 'confusing', 'complicated', and 'difficult to determine'.
- Love hurts. For a small number, love is a painful experience leading to no desire for further close commitments, at least for the foreseeable future.
- Reciprocity. It seems a small number of boys are incapable of 'reading' messages about the relationship from their partner.
- Love endures. A small number commented on the enduring nature of the experience.

THE SEXUAL TIMETABLE

Introduction to sexual intercourse appears to be a gradual process. Normally, adolescents first experiment with kissing and hugging before they proceed to 'light' and then 'heavy' petting (Harris and Liebert,

TABLE 7.2 *Adolescents' perceptions of the true nature of love*

Love vs. infatuation
Most high school kids just say they are in love; they don't know what 'true love' is

Love vs. sexual attraction
'Being in love has nothing to do with sex'

Love vs. self-promotion
Teenagers in relationships are having them 'for self esteem . . . or they do it for the challenge'

Love vs. loving
'When you love someone you know about their faults and you realize that they may not be exactly as you want them to be, but you love them in spite of it'

Source: Derived from Montgomery and Sorrell, 1998, pp. 683–4

1987). There also appear to be racial and cultural differences in this regard. There is a developmental sequence from necking, to feeling parts of the body directly, to sexual intercourse for white 12 to 15-year-olds in the USA. Among blacks, however, fewer seem to engage in the various petting activities that precede intercourse (Miller and Moore, 1990). Rosenthal and Smith (1997) found age differences in the acceptance of sexual practices among Australian youth. Whereas only about 2–3 per cent of 12- to 14-year-olds thought that sexual intercourse was appropriate for them, among 15- to 17-year-olds the approval rate was much higher (approaching 65 per cent).

Adolescents are becoming sexually active at an increasingly younger age. This view is supported by a number of studies from different countries. For instance, a representative sample of Danish teenagers aged 16–20 showed that about one-third had experienced sexual intercourse by age 16 (Wielandt and Boldsen, 1989). Surveys of teenagers in the USA suggest that by age 15 years about half of black men had experienced sexual intercourse. For Hispanic-American men it was 16.5 years, while for whites it was 17 years. For black, Hispanic and white women respectively, the ages were 17, 18 and 18. For each racial group 90 per cent had experienced sexual intercourse by about 22 years of age (Michael et al., 1994). White American youth of both sexes report significantly more sexual partners over their lifetime than do Asian-American youth (McLaughlin et al., 1997).

Johnson and her colleagues (1994) surveyed the sexual attitudes and lifestyles of almost 20 000 Britains. Just over 4000 were aged between 16 and 24 years of age. The median age of first intercourse for women aged 55–59 years was 21, while for women aged 16–19 it was 17. Among older men the median age at first intercourse was 20, while it was 17 for younger men. Thus, there has been a consistent shift towards decreasing age for first sexual intercourse. British youth (16–24 yrs) also appear more promiscuous than those who are older (25–34 yrs). Among the younger group 11.2 per cent of males and 2.5 per cent of females had sex with 10 or more partners over the last five years. The figures for the older age group were 5.8 per cent and 0.8 per cent respectively. In Australia large-scale surveys of teenagers suggest that close to 50 per cent of Year 12 students have had sexual intercourse with lower rates for younger students (Lindsay, Smith and Rosenthal, 1997).

For many teenagers first intercourse can usually be described in one of the following ways (Mitchell and Wellings, 1998):

•   It is unexpected – this is usually so for younger teenagers.

- It is not anticipated, but it is not a shock – in hindsight, both sexes are able to recognise cues that sex was always likely to occur.
- It is anticipated, but not wanted – in these cases negotiations about sex, if present, are usually very limited. Typically, the female succumbs to the male script. Later, women seem to express some ambivalence about what has happened.
- It is planned – these adolescents are older and in a steady relationship. For them sex is the next logical step in the development of their relationship.

INFLUENCES ON SEXUAL BEHAVIOUR

How do teenagers first learn about sex? Is the motivation to engage in sexual intercourse due to hormonal influences, or do social factors such as the influence of family and friends play an important role in shaping adolescent sexual behaviour? Let us consider some of these issues.

The Role of Family and Friends

Numerous studies have examined the relative effects of family and friends on adolescent sexual behaviour. Although both factors are important socialisation influences (Miller and Moore, 1990), it has been argued that the family sets the social context within which the adolescent will learn about sexuality (Tucker 1989, p. 270). Factors such as mother's adolescent sexual experience, the educational level of parents, the sexual activity of older siblings, communication within the family and parents' attitudes and values towards adolescent sexual intercourse have all been linked to the sexual behaviour of adolescents. Thus, for example, it has been found that early sexual experience of an adolescent mother may increase the likelihood that her adolescent daughter will also engage in sexual intercourse at a relatively young age.

Not all research supports the importance of family factors on adolescent sexual behaviour. A study of white and Asian American youth (McLaughlin et al., 1997) found that family factors (for example, perceived parental warmth and acceptance) were far less important as predictors of early sexual behaviour than factors such as the adolescent's perceived level of physical attractiveness and success in forming romantic relationships. One exception was noted among white females. Family conflict in decision-making predicted sexual activity for this group.

Parents' *marital status changes* determine adolescents' transition to sexual behaviour. Teenage males and females incorporate family structure and family disruption in different ways as manifest in their transition to sexual activity. On the basis of a longitudinal study among several hundred white teenagers in the USA, it was found that girls who remained in intact families had a 15 per cent chance of beginning sexual activity. Girls who moved from intact families to single-mother families increased their risks of sexual activity to 31 per cent. Boys who remained in intact families had a 24 per cent chance of beginning sexual activity, while boys who moved to single-mother families were much more likely to initiate sexual activity (a 70 per cent chance) (Newcomer and Udry, 1987).

Boys *remaining* in single-mother families only had a 25 per cent chance of being sexually active by Time 2, which leads one to conclude that it is the *disruption* of family life rather than the *type* of family which is an important predictor for male adolescents. Among girls, moving into blended families appears especially risky for the initiation of sexual behaviour, while girls *remaining* in single-mother households had a 38 per cent chance of being sexually active by Time 2. This leads one to conclude that the break-up of the family unit, rather than its type, is the important key to understanding adolescents' transition to sexual behaviour. It is quite likely that during marital or family break-up, partners are too concerned with their own personal problems to adequately supervise their children. It is also likely that single mothers (most of whom have custody), are sexually active and dating men, thus providing a particular role model for their adolescents. Newcomer and Udry (1987) concluded as follows: 'For boys the loss of control is associated with the disruption inherent in the loss of the father from the household, while for girls the loss of control is associated with the state of not having a father in the household and not the disruption per se'.

Single fathers who have custody of their teenagers are also presumably sexually active. Because most children reside with single mothers, few research studies have examined the sorts of role models that single fathers provide for their adolescents.

Parent–adolescent Communication

Several studies have highlighted the importance of parent–adolescent communication on the sexual behaviour of teenagers (for example, Jaccard and Dittus, 1991; Rosenthal, Feldman and Edwards, 1998; Whitaker and Miller, 2000). Although family communication about sexual matters is important not least because of the implications for health status, research evidence suggests that parents' communications may be less effective. The problem, as Rosenthal and colleagues pointed out (Rosenthal et al., 1998), is that such communication is nearly always about biology, rather than decision-making.

It would seem that the mother is the primary source of information regarding the menstrual cycle and contraception, at least as far as the daughter is concerned. Parents also appear to differentiate between their sons and daughters with respect to the *content* of their sexual discussions. For example, there are some matters of a sexual nature that fathers simply don't discuss with their daughters. On the basis of several research studies, Mueller and Powers (1990) summarised these differences in content, which are shown in Table 7.3. It is clear that mothers tend to discuss a whole range of issues with their daughters. With her son, a mother discusses matters related to sexual morals, bodily changes and birth. Fathers discuss birth and abortion as well as homosexuality with their sons, although fathers' discussions with daughters tend to be much more superficial. Thus, there appear to be specific 'gaps' in communication; gaps which appear much larger among younger rather than older teenagers (Pistella and Bonati, 1998).

TABLE 7.3 *Parent–adolescent communication about sex*

Mother with daughter	Mother with son
• Menstruation	• Sexual morals
• Dating and boyfriends	• Bodily changes
• Sexual morality	• Birth
• Conception	
• Sexual intercourse	
• Birth control	
• Bodily changes	
• Homosexuality	
• Abortion	

Father with daughter	Father with son
• Least intense and least intimate discussions about sex	• Birth
	• Homosexuality
	• Abortion

Source: Mueller and Powers, 1990

TABLE 7.4   *Communicating about sex: mother–teenager patterns*

Characteristics	Communication style				
	Avoidant	Reactive	Opportunistic	Child-initiated	Mutually interactive
Initiation	Neither	Mother	Mother	Teenager	Mother and teenager
Predominant communicator	Neither	Mother	Mother	Mother and teenager	Mother and teenager
Comfort level of mother	Very low	Low	Moderate	High	High
Topics discussed:					
Psychological issues	No	No	Yes	Yes	Yes
Non-penetrative sexual practices	No	No	No	Yes	Yes

Source: Rosenthal, Feldman and Edwards, 1998

What communication styles do mothers use when they communicate with their teenagers about sex? One research team (Rosenthal et al., 1998) enquired about the role that parents play, the nature, style and frequency of sex communication, and so forth. Five communication styles were uncovered: avoidant, reactive, opportunistic, child-initiated, and mutually interactive. These are shown in Table 7.4 where the major characteristics of each are also displayed. It is clear that, compared to the avoidant style, a wider range of topics is discussed in the mutually interactive style. Moreover, neither mother nor teenager in the avoidant group is likely to initiate a conversation about sex.

To conclude this section, little research has been done on parent–adolescent sex communication in single-parent families. Do fathers with whom adolescent daughters reside, for instance, provide the sex information that is usually provided by the mother in intact families? More research is needed in this area.

Influence of Friends

Adolescents' perceptions of peer norms and expectations about sexual behaviour as well as the behaviour of friends are important in predicting adolescent sexual activity. Boys are more likely to learn about menstruation from their friends than from their parents, while girls are more likely to learn about menstruation from their mothers and friends

RESEARCH HIGHLIGHT 7.1
How communication by parents and peers influences adolescent sexual behaviour
Whitaker and Miller, 2000

These authors were interested in the communications that teenagers have with their parents and peers about sex. More particularly, they were interested in the joint effects of these different communications on sexual behaviour. Their participants were over 900 teenagers at risk for contracting HIV. It was found that those teenagers who talked with their parents about sex were more likely to initiate sexual activity later rather than earlier and were also more likely to have fewer partners. If peers were perceived to be engaging in sex early, this was likely to increase the chances of the participants engaging in sex. It was also found that peer norms to engage in sex were greatest on those teenagers who tended not to talk with their parents about sex. Teenagers who discussed condom use with their parents were more likely to use condoms, while this trend was strengthened in those teenagers who talked with their parents about condoms compared to those who did not.

than from their fathers (Amann-Gainotti, 1986; Mueller and Powers, 1990). Other sources of sex-related information include school nurse, doctor, television, radio, movies and magazines (Pistella and Bonati, 1998).

It would seem that, in many instances, peer group pressure rather than parental norms and values is an important factor in the adolescent's *decision* to engage in intercourse for the first time. Indeed, there is evidence of a close relationship between reported sexual behaviour of adolescents and their friends, although it has been suggested that the importance of how friends are perceived may be overstated (Smith, Udry and Morris, 1985). It could be that peer influence *interacts* with pubertal development in determining teenage sexual behaviour (see pp. 158–61).

Once adolescents are sexually active, it would seem that parental views are important as far as the continued use of contraception is concerned. Parents who are tolerant of adolescent sexual activity are more likely to have adolescents who use contraception. Adolescents with more tolerant parents are less likely to experience stress about engaging in sexual intercourse, and are therefore more likely to use contraception (Baker et al., 1988).

Hormonal vs. Non-hormonal Influences

According to one viewpoint, an increase in sexual activity during adolescence is not learned, but is rather the result of uncontrollable endocrinological influences (Paikoff and Brooks-Gunn, 1990; Udry et al., 1985). Endocrinological changes occurring during puberty are the result of two processes. These are *adrenarche*, by which androgens are produced, and *gonadarche*, by which the hypothalmic-pituitary-gonadotropin-gonadal system is reactivated (Paikoff and Brooks-Gunn, 1990). Not only do these changes in endocrinological levels have the capacity to lead to early sexual intercourse, but they have also been used to explain other changes in behaviour and mood (Buchanan, Eccles and Becker, 1992; Paikoff and Brooks-Gunn, 1990).

Changes in hormone level can affect adolescent behaviour in four possible ways (Buchanan et al., 1992).

- First, hormone levels simply rise in concentration and have a direct and overwhelming impact upon behaviour.
- Secondly, it is possible that, as hormone levels rise (notably sex steroids and gonadotropins), the adolescent adapts by adjusting behaviour.
- Thirdly, it is possible that there are 'irregular' effects. In other words, the rise in hormone levels could be inconsistent or spasmodic, resulting in mood swings and rapid changes of behaviour.
- Finally, each of these factors may interact to varying degrees with one another, as well as with numerous social factors (for instance, family, peer and school relations) in influencing behaviour.

The view that early sexual activity, notably intercourse, is determined primarily by hormonal influences is not endorsed by all social scientists. Psychologists with a more psychoanalytic bent have tended to explain behavioural change during adolescence by focusing on the individual's internal drives. A range of emotional conflicts, sexual instincts, and Oedipal complexes motivate the adolescent to engage in various 'deviant' behaviours, ranging from compulsive eating to sexual intercourse (Buchanan et al., 1992).

RESEARCH HIGHLIGHT 7.2
The psychological factors associated with sexual behaviour
Cooper, Shapiro and Powers, 1998

Cooper and colleagues recently demonstrated that the causes and correlates of sexual behaviour among young people are quite complex. There is no single reason as to why adolescents engage in sexual behaviour. Rather sexual behaviour serves a wide range of psychological functions including (1530):

- enhancing physical and emotional pleasure;
- coping with negative outcomes;
- achieving intimacy with a particular person;
- gaining the approval of others and avoiding censure.

The authors developed a measure of these major domains which, when factor analysed, yielded the following components: enhancement, intimacy, coping, self-affirmation, partner approval, and peer approval. What is noteworthy is that these components were later found to be linked in logical and predictable ways with certain personality traits. For example, neuroticism was significantly positively associated with high scores on the coping, self-affirmation, and partner/peer approval sub-scales. Thus, the emotionally unstable were in greater need of self- and partner-approval.

There are racial and cultural differences in the extent to which adolescents engage in sexual intercourse (Miller and Moore, 1990). This suggests that other non-hormonal factors are also important in understanding why adolescents engage in sexual intercourse. Some researchers (for example, Paikoff and Brooks-Gunn, 1990; Brooks-Gunn and Furstenberg, 1989) suggest that, even if hormonal effects on sexual behaviour are clearly demonstrated, one still needs to consider the effects of social and other contextual factors. They argue that hormonal and non-hormonal factors interact in a variety of complex ways to produce behaviour.

Acknowledging the importance of non-hormonal factors, it has been argued that a biosocial model is most useful for understanding adolescent sexual behaviour (Udry, 1988). Both biological and social factors are important in predicting whether adolescents will engage in early sexual intercourse. Hormonal factors act as social signals, heralding that the adolescent is now physically ready to engage in sexual activity. However, a variety of factors co-determine the propensity of a teenager to engage in intercourse. Included are motivation (hormones, libido, etc.), physical attractiveness and social control (restrictions, familial controls, opportunities, etc.) (Udry and Billy, 1987) and other psychological factors (see Research Highlight 7.2). Research has shown that early maturing girls (a biological influence) are much more likely than other girls their age to have older friends who, it is believed, will increase the risks of early initiation into sexual activity, smoking, and possible drug use (Brooks-Gunn and Furstenberg, 1989).

The biosocial model was tested among a large sample of teenagers in the USA (Udry and Billy, 1987). The respondents were asked a wide range of questions about their behaviour and attitudes, while parents and friends were asked to rate the teenagers on various behavioural and other dimensions. Important sex and race differences were observed. For example, social controls were not as important in predicting sexual intercourse for white males and black females, while the sexual behaviour of white males was found to be strongly related to hormonal effects (namely androgens). There was, however, a strong social effect for white females with their non-coital sexual behaviours being determined by androgenic hormones. It was also found that white females who participated in sports and had a father living at home were less at risk for early sexual intercourse than others. An important predictor for black females' transition to sexual intercourse was attractiveness. In addition, black girls were found to engage in sexual intercourse at an earlier age than their white counterparts, although the authors are at a loss to explain this.

Results such as these lend support to the biosocial approach to understanding sexual behaviour among adolescents. Not only are hormonal levels important, but they also interact with social factors in unique and important ways. Udry and Billy (1987, 852) concluded that:

> The effects of hormones on males' behavior are much stronger than on females because, as males mature, their androgen levels go up by a factor of 10 to 20, while, in females, androgen levels hardly double, with males and females starting from the same prepubertal levels. In males, the hormone levels may overwhelm the social controls.

Further support for the biosocial approach comes from a study by Smith, Udry and Morris (1985). They found that increased sexual motivation among a sample of teenagers was related to levels of pubertal development as well as the sexual activity of best friends. Thus, there was an important interaction effect between the social and biological factors, which influence sexual behaviour. Smith and colleagues concluded that research that ignores the contribution of biological factors may be overstating the effects of social factors.

CONDOM USE AND THE THREAT OF AIDS

Contraception has traditionally been important in the context of adolescent pregnancy. Although teenage pregnancy continues to be of major concern, the focus has shifted somewhat in recent times. With the advent of the AIDS crisis, one particular form of contraception, namely condom use, has become the focus of renewed research attention and is considered to be paramount in the prevention of HIV infection and other sexually transmitted diseases (STDs).

Female adolescents have among the highest rates of gonorrhea, cytomegalovirus, chlamydia cervicitis and pelvic inflammation (Brooks-Gunn and Furstenberg, 1989), while black teens in the USA have higher rates than Hispanics or whites (Buzi, Weinman and Smith, 1998;

RESEARCH HIGHLIGHT 7.3
Ethnic differences in STDs in the USA
Buzi, Weinman and Smith, 1998

205 female adolescents who attended health clinics in Houston, Texas, were screened for STDs. Of the sample, 72.7 per cent were black, 9.8 per cent were white, and 17.6 per cent were Hispanic. It was found that:

- white teenagers had more sexual partners than either blacks or Hispanics;
- blacks, but not whites or Hispanics, were more likely to present with syphilis;
- the most frequent infections for the whole group, on a percentage basis, were chlamydia (50.2), trichomoniasis (32.2), gonorrhea (10.2), condyloma (10.2), syphilis (6.3), herpes (4.9), and lice (2.4).

see Research Highlight 7.3).These diseases are likely to be exacerbated by early sexual activity and inconsistent condom use. Thus it has become imperative that adolescents be educated about the risks of 'unprotected' sex; indeed, failure to reduce risky sexual behaviour among adolescents may dramatically increase the number of adolescents diagnosed with STDs or as HIV-positive.

Survey results suggest that condom use by adolescents has been steadily rising. In Britain, teenagers are now much more likely to use condoms or the pill than other forms of contraception (Johnson et al., 1994). Although rates of condom use have risen sharply in recent times, they are still relatively low (Brooks-Gunn and Furstenberg, 1989), and vary between ethnic and racial groups (Strunin, 1991). Many adolescents seem to be apathetic and irresponsible about condom use and the risks associated with unsafe sex. Indeed, one Australian study found that 83 per cent of respondents agreed that condoms generally prevent the spread of AIDS and STDs (Barling and Moore, 1990). However, only 38 per cent of them also agreed that AIDS was something they had not thought a lot about, while 30 per cent felt that it was of no concern to them, since their best friends were unlikely to be HIV-positive.

There are two major theoretical approaches to understanding contraceptive behaviour among adolescents. These are cognitive or decision-making models and socialisation models (Balassone, 1991). Let us briefly review the role of cognition.

The Role of Cognitive Factors

The practice of contraception among sexually active adolescents has been quite firmly linked to cognitive development and various aspects of formal reasoning (Gordon, 1990). In the first instance, it would appear that some adolescents do not comprehend the different forms of contraception that are available. Secondly, some do not properly evaluate the consequences of their actions so that, quite often, the pregnancy is 'unexpected' and unanticipated. Furthermore, it is clear that some adolescents do not take their partner's needs into account with some males failing to appreciate the risks of pregnancy to their female partners (Gordon, 1990, 348–9), while 'adolescent females may romanticize their boyfriends' position by perceiving unprotected intercourse as an affirmation of love and commitment to a relationship'.

Evidence also indicates that some adolescents cannot adequately reason about chance and probability. In other words, these teenagers seem to think that a single act of unprotected intercourse is less risky than several such acts. Again, they appear quite surprised at the 'unexpected' pregnancy or infection. Such deficits in cognitive functioning have been referred to as *global developmental delay*. These teenagers also very often underachieve at school, which may be suggestive of an environment that is deficient in opportunities for abstract thinking (Gordon, 1990).

Teenagers make decisions about contraception in different *social contexts* and these need to be taken into account when predicting condom use. Thus, adolescents' perceptions about risk and responsibility for pregnancy as well as their subjective feelings about embarrassment are important factors in contraceptive decision-making.

In a survey of almost 2000 15 to 19-year-old males in the USA, it was found that normative beliefs predicted condom use, that is, males who believed it is the male's responsibility to prevent pregnancy were more likely to use them (Pleck, Sonenstein and Ku, 1991). Their *personal* concerns about pregnancy were found to be less important. In other words, concern about fathering a child *per se* was less important than normative beliefs about pregnancy prevention. Males who believed that their partner was not using the pill were also more likely to use a condom. In addition, frequency of worry about AIDS, rather than actual perceived risk of HIV infection, was more likely to lead to condom use. Males who perceived their partner as wanting them to use a condom, and as being appreciative of this, were more likely to use one. On the

TABLE 7.5   *Males' costs–benefits of condom use*

Preventing pregnancy: personal costs–benefits
- Concern about pregnancy increases condom use
- Belief that female uses pill reduces condom use

Preventing pregnancy: normative belief
- Belief that males have responsibility for reducing pregnancy increases condom use

Avoiding AIDS
- Concern about AIDS increases condom use

Partner expectations
- Request by females raises condom use
- Belief by females that they can get males to use condoms increases use

Embarrassment and reduction of pleasure
- Perception of not being embarrassed increases condom use
- Belief that sexual pleasure will not be negatively affected increases condom use

Source: Pleck, Sonenstein and Ku, 1991

other hand, males' embarrassment or belief that pleasure would be reduced was likely to reduce condom use (see Table 7.5).

Not all males will suggest using a condom during sexual intercourse; very often it may be up to the female to suggest some form of contraception. Others might not even discuss the question of contraception, and appear to blatantly disregard the risks of pregnancy and STDs. It is this attitude of denial and irresponsibility which led Moore and Rosenthal (1991a) to comment as follows (164): 'Adolescents are reputed to be highly susceptible to this kind of thinking, that is, the illusion that although others may suffer the consequences of dangerous and risky actions they are somehow immune.'

Risky Sexual Behaviours

There would seem to be a discrepancy between adolescents' knowledge of safe sex and their actual behaviour. A survey of undergraduate non-virgins (mean age = 18.5 years) found that almost 10 per cent were engaging in unprotected vaginal intercourse with casual partners, while 15 per cent were engaging in withdrawal. Among regular partners, the frequencies were 13 and 27 per cent respectively (Rosenthal, Hall and Moore, 1992). Thus, some teenagers are engaging in more risky behaviours with partners described as 'regular'. One study of adolescents attending community-based agencies in New York and Los Angeles found that females were more likely to engage in unprotected sexual behaviours, while males reported having had more partners (Murphy, Rotheram-Borus, and Reid, 1998). The situation seems more critical among those young people who present themselves to clinics for the detection and treatment of STDs. These youth, it would seem, are much more likely to engage in unprotected vaginal sex (57 per cent of cases) (Heffernan, Chiasson and Sackoff, 1996).

Although it appears that Hong Kong adolescents have relatively low levels of risky behaviours (Davis et al., 1998), there is very little discussion about HIV/AIDS and related issues: 85 per cent of respondents had not discussed HIV/AIDS with their family, while 60 per cent had rarely or never raised this problem with their friends. Instead, most information was derived from television and newspapers. Moreover, about 15 per cent of the sample believed that Westerners were more at risk of contracting HIV/AIDS than Asians and that the disease was really a problem for IV drug users, homosexuals, and prostitutes.

Attitudes to AIDS precautions are linked to the likelihood of engaging in risky sexual behaviour. Moore and Rosenthal (1991b) in

Australia found that females were more positively disposed to AIDS precautions than were adolescent males (see also Parsons et al., 2000). Females with negative attitudes to precautions were more likely to engage in risky sex. Males with a more fatalistic attitude towards AIDS and those with multiple partners were more likely to engage in risky sexual behaviour (Moore and Rosenthal, 1991b).

Finally, which factors best predict whether young gay men will practise safer anal sex? The following were found in a study of 100 young gays attending a community centre (Rotheram-Borus et al., 1995):

- a perception of being susceptible to the HIV virus,
- possessing positive attitudes to safer sex,
- having perceptions of greater self-efficacy,
- greater self-control in sexual situations.

Are there particular personality traits that discriminate those that engage in safer sex from those who do not? Evidence indicates that a link exists between personality disposition and the likelihood of engaging in risky sexual practice. Important factors are beliefs about personal control and self-efficacy (Joffe and Radius, 1993; Moore and Rosenthal, 1991a). Moore and Rosenthal found that only 6 per cent of the late adolescents in their study thought that they could *moderately* control their chances of getting AIDS, while 17 per cent thought they could *completely* control them. It was also found that belief in personal control was related to various types of sexual behaviour such that a perception of low personal control accompanied moderate- to high-risk sexual behaviour. In other words, adolescents who took a more fatalistic approach to diseases such as AIDS were less likely to employ safe sex strategies.

The importance of a sense of control has been alluded to in several other reports. Females are especially at risk for HIV infection as they are less likely to insist on condom use with regular partners than with casual ones. Thus, females tend to shift the burden of responsibility (or control) on to their partners. Male respondents tended not to distinguish between casual and regular partners, perhaps because they view HIV infection largely as a problem for homosexuals rather than heterosexuals (Crawford, Turtle, and Kippax, 1990).

How is one to understand these findings? One argument is that females are *traditionally* more dependent and less proactive in sexual matters than are many males (Heaven, Connors and Kellehear, 1992). For example, males may be relatively more comfortable with the practice of buying condoms (or asking for them from a clinic) as a preventive

RESEARCH HIGHLIGHT 7.4
Denial and the risks of HIV/AIDS
Ben-Zur et al., 2000

HIV/AIDS denial increases the chances of not engaging in safe sex and thereby contracting the disease. The following are likely to occur:

- Denial prevents the accumulation of appropriate knowledge.
- Denial helps strengthen negative attitudes and strengthens barriers to buying condoms.

measure in sex. This attitude is probably less common among females. Traditional sex roles that encourage males to be active and females to be passive and supportive in dating and sexual practices may predispose females with a lower sense of control to take less preventive measures against risk of infection. Indeed, as Seeman and Seeman (1983) found, lower sense of control may also be associated with less self-initiated preventive care.

Implicit Personality Theories and Risky Behaviour

A question that often arises is why adolescents engage in risky sexual behaviours even though they are knowledgeable about HIV transmission. An important qualitative study using focus group discussions found that college students use *implicit personality theories* when judging the riskiness of potential sexual partners. As summarised in Table 7.6, respondents use several strategies to judge the HIV status of partners. The risks that these students run is that these constructions of another's HIV status are likely to be incorrect, uninformative, and unreliable – and can prove fatal (Williams et al., 1992).

ADOLESCENT SEX OFFENDERS

It has been reported that about 20 per cent of all rapes and some 30–50 per cent of all child sexual abuse cases are committed by adolescents (Davis and Leitenberg, 1987). Alarming as these statistics are, the authors suggest that they may, in fact, under-represent the true picture.

TABLE 7.6   *Implicit personality theories used in judging HIV status of potential partners*

Judgements of riskiness of sexual partners
1   Known and liked partners are viewed as not risky: ('I knew my partner really well before we had sex, so I didn't have to worry about her sexual history').
2   Risky people dress provocatively, hang around bars, tend to be older, are from large cities, and are keen for sex; ('If they're dressed up like a slut . . . they're usually a slut').
3   Respondents tend only to use condoms with partners they don't know well: ('If you just met, then you use a condom . . . if it's long term you aren't going to worry').

Assessments of personal risk
1   Respondents often thought themselves generally not at risk: ('Personally, I'm not really worried about AIDS on this campus').
2   Respondents feel personally not at risk: ('I'm not gay').

Reasons for unsafe sex
1   Alcohol
2   Lust: ('In the heat of the moment you don't think about it [AIDS]').

Beliefs about condoms
1   Condoms interfere with sex;
2   they are unpleasant to use;
3   they are inconvenient;
4   they have undesirable implications – that is, you don't trust your partner.

Source: Williams et al., 1992

As they point out, not all offences lead to convictions and not all victims and their families report assaults. This may be because, very often, the offender is known to the victim and the family. Indeed, some parents may even regard the incident as 'insignificant', thinking of it as mere 'sexual exploration' and 'experimentation'.

Most adolescent sex offenders are male. Studies reveal that the most common offence is fondling ('indecent liberties') accounting for about 59 per cent of cases. This is followed by rape (about 23 per cent of cases), exhibitionism (11 per cent), and other non-contact offences (for instance, indecent phone calls, 7 per cent). Assaults against similar-age adolescents or those who are older usually involve rape (67 per cent of offences). Among younger children, however, rape only accounts for 24 per cent of offences (Davis and Leitenberg, 1987).

According to many reports, victims are often known to the offender. In one study of incarcerated adolescents, for example, it was found that in 55 per cent of cases the victim was known to the offender in some way. Moreover, child victims rather than older ones are more likely to be known to the offender. Indeed, very often victims may be family members (20 per cent in one report; Davis and Leitenberg, 1987).

Sex offenders also manifest other behavioural and adjustment deficits with many adolescent sex offenders having also been charged or convicted of other delinquent offences.

Adolescent sex offenders can usually be described in terms of a particular family history, social and psychological maladjustment, and a record of physical and sexual abuse. One study found adolescent sex offenders, compared with non-offenders, to be socially isolated, to engage in assaults more frequently and to be more resentful (Valliant and Bergeron, 1997). Steele and Ryan (1991) elaborated on some of the family and personal characteristics of juvenile sexual offenders. Their life histories share many common themes such as lack of empathic experience and lack of available coping models. Some families display low levels of affect, and greater family secrets and distorted attachments, while the offender's role in the family appears to be as a focus for others' guilt and shame (Ryan, 1991). Sex offenders may also show less emotional bonding to peers and be estranged in their relations with others. Quite often the mother-son relationship of these boys shows poor levels of communication with the families being described as 'dysfunctional' (Blaske et al., 1989).

As females do not commit many adolescent sex offences, there is a dearth of research in this area. One exception is a report by Fehrenbach and Monastersky (1988). According to their observations, sexual offences among females do not form part of a syndrome of delinquent behaviour, as so often seems to be the case with boys. Most offences are against a younger victim who, more often than not, is someone known to the offender. Whereas a large proportion of male offenders commits acts of exhibitionism, indecent phone calls, and so forth, this does not appear to be the case among female offenders. Finally, whereas male offenders quite often have a history of physical or sexual abuse, this tends not to be a causative factor for female offenders. As the authors note (Fehrenbach and Monastersky, 1988, 151): 'prior sexual abuse alone does not explain why a girl would become an offender. Many more girls than boys are sexually abused as children, yet most offenders are male.'

ADOLESCENTS IN PROSTITUTION

Juvenile prostitution has shown a steady increase over recent years. It is estimated that in the ten-year period, 1970–80, juvenile prostitution increased from 24 to 74 per cent in New York City (Schaffer and

DeBlassie, 1984). Large increases have no doubt also occurred in all other large cities across the world. Of concern are the enormous physical and emotional risks involved, such as rape, murder, STDs including HIV infection, and pornography. In some developing countries where control of prostitution is less effective, STD rates are almost 50 per cent in brothels with condom use being very low (Joesoef et al., 1997).

Social scientists have speculated on the reasons for adolescent prostitution. The following have been suggested (McMullen, 1987; Schaffer and DeBlassie, 1984):

- alienation from the family, rejection by the family;
- parental abuse (psychological, sexual, physical and spiritual);
- limited employment opportunities for lower class women, some teenagers might also be attracted to prostitution through economic need;
- a sense of hostility (for example, anger at being rejected by their family), a sense of adventure and drug abuse.

Because of their age, adolescent prostitutes are relegated to the streets, and tend not to work in hotels and parlours. Most are under supervision of a pimp who, in a limited number of cases, might provide a sense of security and some shelter (Schaffer and DeBlassie, 1984). Although young male and female prostitutes may be in prostitution for similar reasons, they also differ in some very important ways. Whereas female prostitutes engage in heterosexual intercourse, most male prostitutes participate in sex with other (usually older) males, even though they would normally regard themselves as heterosexual (Schaffer and DeBlassie, 1984).

SEXUAL ORIENTATION

Although this chapter has focused chiefly on heterosexual relationships, a relatively large proportion of teenagers will, at some stage, adopt a homosexual orientation. It has been estimated that up to one-third of male adolescents beyond 16 years of age have had at least one homosexual experience up to orgasm (Miller and Dyk, 1993).

There is some doubt as to whether a homosexual orientation can be established or identified in adolescence (for example, Remafedi, 1987; Savin-Williams, 1991). According to this view, homosexual experience is part of normal sexual experimentation and growing up. Any inclination to be attracted to someone of the same sex, it is argued, will in most cases be outgrown. Glasser (1977) asserts that it is only possible to be labelled gay or lesbian *after* adolescence. According to this view, there is very little relationship between homosexual experience during adolescence and self-description as a homosexual during adulthood.

Is it possible to identify a homosexual orientation in the teen years? Although many adolescents may not directly label themselves as gay or lesbian, it is possible that they experience a feeling of 'being different' and of being attracted to others of the same sex. This can be a time of great confusion for these teenagers whose desires are at odds with the heterosexual world in which they live. Very often they are not able to understand their inner feelings, which run counter to general social norms and expectations. Among these youth, the label homosexual, gay or lesbian is only used later (around 19 years of age). It is not until some years later (around 23–28) that many will disclose their homosexual orientation to significant others (Remafedi, 1987). It is perhaps only a very small proportion of young teenagers who actually label themselves as homosexual, but this can occur as young as 14 years of age (Remafedi, 1987).

It has been reported (Garnets and Kimmel, 1991) that males and females are first aware of being erotically attracted to members of the same sex at different ages. For males, this can occur between the ages of 12 and 13, while for females it can happen between 14 and 16. Garnets and Kimmel (1991) suggest the following developmental milestones for homosexual identity development:

- initial awareness of same-gender affectional-erotic feelings – around 12–16 for gays and lesbians,
- initial same-gender sexual experience – earlier for gays (about 14 years) than lesbians (about 20 years),
- self-identification as lesbian or gay – late adolescence/early adulthood for both gays and lesbians,
- initial same-gender sexual relationship – early adulthood for both gays and lesbians,
- positive gay or lesbian identity – mid to late 20s.

The awareness of being attracted to others of the same sex can, for some, be a traumatic experience. Very often there is no one in whom to confide – least of all friends and parents. These teenagers' sexual urges do not fit with social or personal expectations. They are often very confused and suffer emotional distress. This may have a negative impact on school performance, and emotional upheaval may also lead to other behavioural problems, such as loneliness, suicide ideation, victimization, violence, drug and alcohol use, and running away from home (see Faulkner and Cranston, 1998; Martin and Knox, 1997).

There seems to be a growing awareness of, and openness to, different sexual orientations. Discrimination against people on the basis of sexual preference has been outlawed in some countries, and gay support groups have been established in many centres. Compared with previous generations, society seems more accepting of gay people, and it is now much easier for gays and lesbians to come to terms with their own sexuality and 'come out'.

Should one attempt to modify the behaviour or attitudes of an adolescent who 'comes out' or is suspected of being gay? Most writers would say no. Although techniques for behaviour change were attempted in the 1950s and 1970s, their effectiveness was always disputed. As Remafedi (1991, 505) explains: 'conventional wisdom suggests that sexual orientation is resistant to change and that attempts to change should be resisted, so as not to compound identity confusion, shame, and intrapsychic injury.'

THEORETICAL CONSIDERATIONS

Although few researchers actively set out to test the major theories as described in Chapter 1, three relate to the work examined in this chapter. These are biological theory, Erikson's identity formation theory and cognitive development. There is clear evidence that biological changes occur during puberty. These take on various forms, including endocrinological and physical changes. They have an impact not only on the teenager's emotional state (for example, moodiness or depression), but also on parent–child relationships and sexual behaviour. Research evidence points to the influence of both hormonal and non-hormonal factors on sexual behaviour.

Synonymous with adolescent sexuality is identity formation. With biological change comes an awakening of sexual feelings and urges, an awareness of a sexual force within the adolescent. It is both exciting and intriguing and, at first, shrouded in mystery. An important developmental task is the exploration of this new dimension of the self and the discovery of just who one is sexually. Sexual identity cannot be divorced from one's self-identity, and in this regard, a loving and supportive family is important in facilitating self-discovery.

During the adolescent years, the teenager is undergoing cognitive development. As we noted, this has implications for sexual decision-making. Younger adolescents, it seems, are less able to reason about risk and probability and are therefore more likely to engage in sexual behaviour regarded as risky for HIV infection and pregnancy.

SUMMARY

In this chapter we considered some important issues relating to adolescent sexuality. From the evidence reviewed here, it is clear that adolescents are engaging in sexual intercourse at an increasingly young age. Sexuality is an important issue affecting all adolescents, and it was argued that they must come to terms with their own sexuality and incorporate it into their self-identity with as little disruption as possible.

This chapter reviewed findings that point to the importance of hormonal and non-hormonal factors (particularly the influences of family and peers) in explaining why some adolescents become sexually active. It seems clear that hormonal factors alone cannot explain sexual behaviour among adolescents and that a range of non-hormonal ones may need to be considered as well. Some reports have suggested that hormonal and non-hormonal factors interact in complex ways in determining adolescent sexual behaviour.

AIDS is a major crisis which all of us, including adolescents, must confront. Unfortunately, many adolescents seem unperturbed by the risks of unprotected sex. Indeed, many appear irresponsible. According to some reports, many adolescents do not practise safe sex and are putting themselves at risk for HIV infection and other STDs. Although adolescents appear knowledgeable about safe sex strategies, this is not matched by their behaviour.

Of further importance is the observation of links between risky behaviours and attitudes to AIDS precautions and certain personality traits. Those adolescents adopting a more fatalistic attitude are more likely to engage in risky behaviour and therefore increase their risk of HIV infection. Future research should concern itself with how all adolescents might be encouraged to change their behaviour and adopt safe sex practices.

ADDITIONAL READING

Brooks-Gunn, J. and Furstenberg, F. (1989) 'Adolescent Sexual Behavior', *American Psychologist*, 44: 249–57.

Cooper, M. L., Shapiro, C. M. and Powers, A. M. (1998) 'Motivations for Sex and Risky Sexual Behavior among Adolescents and Young Adults: A Functional Perspective', *Journal of Personality and Social Psychology*, 75: 1528–58.
Newcomer, S. and Udry, J. (1987) 'Parental Marital Status Effects on Adolescent Sexual Behavior', *Journal of Marriage and the Family*, 49: 235–40.

EXERCISES

1 The literature suggests that, although adolescents are aware of the risks of HIV infection, they tend not to practise safe sex. Can you think of some strategies to encourage sexually active teenagers to take precautions against HIV infection?
2 Replicate the Wilson and Medora (1990) study referred to in the chapter (see also Table 7.1). If you obtain similar findings, what can you conclude?

8

Adolescents as Parents

INTRODUCTION

Adolescents are becoming sexually active at an increasingly young age. Whereas in 1974, 9.9 per cent of all US females aged 15–19 years became pregnant, by 1985 this figure was 11 per cent (Miller and Moore, 1990). More than one million pregnancies in the USA in 1990 were recorded to women under the age of 20 years (Rice, 1999). This rise in pregnancy rates has all sorts of social and economic ramifications. For instance, many teenage parents need welfare assistance (Spitz et al., 1996), while women who had their first child in their young teens are more likely to suffer educational, employment and income deficits (Grindstaff, 1988; Rodriguez and Moore, 1995; Spitz et al., 1996; but see Furstenberg

---

RESEARCH HIGHLIGHT 8.1
The risks associated with early pregnancy
Hanson, 1990

The National Longitudinal Survey of Youth was conducted by the Ohio State University Center for Human Resource Research and compared various outcomes for pregnant and never pregnant teenagers. Some important comparisons between these two groups have been summarised by Hanson (1990):

The probability of . . .	Never pregnant	Pregnant
being a school dropout	.04	.455
being currently in school	.901	.446
receiving aid to families	.001	.050
currently living with both parents	.736	.369
being currently married	.014	.254

FIGURE 8.1 *Birth rates for Australian mothers aged under 20 years*

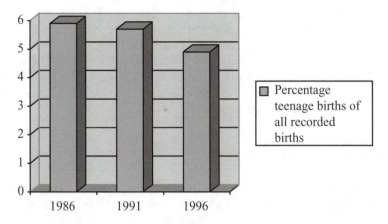

Source: Australian Bureau of Statistics, 1999

et al., 1987). In 1989 the USA spent $21.6 billion providing assistance to teenage mothers (see also Research Highlight 8.1).

Although the rates of pregnancy and sexual intercourse appear to be rising, paradoxically actual birth rates have fallen among teenagers in some Western nations. In Australia, for instance, birth rates for women under twenty have shown a steady decline over recent years (Australian Bureau of Statistics, 1999). This is not to suggest that Australian adolescents are now less sexually active than they were a few decades ago. These trends, reflected in Figure 8.1, may simply reflect the availability of legalised abortion in some Australian states.

There are different fertility rates for white and Aboriginal teenagers in Australia (Hart et al., 1985). Whereas the reproduction rate for all teenagers aged 15–19 years in South Australia in 1981–82 was some 25 births per 1000 women, the Aboriginal rate was 140.4. Ethnic differences in fertility have also been noted in the USA. Spitz and colleagues (1996) observed that, among 18–19 year olds, birth rates for black females were almost twice that of white females. Among 15–17 year olds, it was almost three times that of white teenagers. (See the exercise at the end of this chapter).

Although birth rates among teenagers have declined over recent years, many more teenagers than before are having babies outside marriage. Furstenberg and colleagues (1989) reported that by the early 1980s almost two-thirds of white teenage mothers in the USA were unmarried when they fell pregnant. This compares with less than one-third in the early 1950s. By the early 1980s, 97 per cent of black teenagers in the USA were single when they became pregnant. In Australia more women (of all age groups) are now having babies outside marriage. Whereas only 16.8 per cent of all births were outside marriage in 1986, this had risen to 27.4 per cent by 1996 (Australian Bureau of Statistics, 1999).

This chapter will examine the psychosocial characteristics associated with teenage pregnancy, as well as the resolution of pregnancy. It will also discuss birthing outcomes, the psychological adjustment of children and research into teenage fathers.

THE RISK OF EARLY PREGNANCY

Teenage mothers are having more babies compared with a generation ago. Moreover, the younger adolescents are when having their first child, the more likely they are to have another child while still a teenager (Meyerowitz and Malev, 1973). Slightly more than one-half of white girls in the USA who become pregnant by the age of 14 years will be pregnant again by age 18. Among black adolescents, slightly more than one-half will be pregnant again by 17.

Various psychosocial factors have been found to be associated with teenage pregnancy. Although some reports show that teenage mothers are more likely to have lower self-esteem, to be alienated from their own mothers and isolated from female friendships, others dispute this (Robinson and Frank, 1994). Some teenage mothers are quite likely to be underachievers at school, to have unmarried sisters with children, and to exhibit feelings of inadequacy and unworthiness. They are also likely to have a history of skipping school, delinquency and rebellion. They are also likely to be dissatisfied with family relationships and their body image, while others appear to be externally controlled (or fatalistic) and to lack purpose in life (Meyerowitz and Malev, 1973; Ralph et al., 1984; Walters et al., 1986).

A British study of over 2000 women found that, compared with those who had their first child between the ages of 20 and 24, teenage mothers (aged 15–19) were more likely to have parents with relatively low levels of formal education, and to come from blue-collar families (Kiernan, 1980). These parents were also less likely to be concerned about their teenagers' education. Once pregnant, adolescent mothers were less likely to undertake vocational training.

Farber (1991) cites evidence that teenage mothers are likely to come from lower socio-economic backgrounds and from single-mother families. They are also more likely to begin sexual activity at an earlier age. One study compared pregnant teenagers with never pregnant ones and found that pregnant girls scored significantly higher on 'powerful other' locus of control, and started intercourse earlier. This led the authors to conclude as follows (Morgan, Chapar and Fisher, 1995, 286):

> The powerful other locus of control finding might indicate that adolescents who are dependent on others for health decision-making are also more susceptible to peer pressure or even more dependent on authority figures than are others, which might place them at higher risk for unintended pregnancy than more self-reliant peers.

Holden and colleagues found the following differences between pregnant and non-pregnant girls (Holden et al., 1993): Pregnant girls:

- had lower scores on mathematics and English and had also failed more classes,
- had lower perceptions of their self-worth,
- were more likely to have a close friend who was also pregnant,
- tended not to use contraceptives on a regular basis and also engaged in intercourse more frequently.

Different racial, ethnic and socio-economic groups have different antecedents for pregnancy. Whereas *externality* has been shown to correlate with teenage pregnancy in most cases (for example, Meyerowitz and Malev, 1973), there is evidence of a link between *internal locus* of control and teenage pregnancy among some black adolescents in the USA (Ralph et al., 1984). It is suggested that black females, more than whites, may deliberately choose to become pregnant.

There is compelling evidence that pregnant teenagers tend to romanticise their relationship. Black teenagers in the USA have the highest romanticism scores, while Asians tend to have the lowest scores (Medora, Goldstein, and von der Hellen, 1994). Possible reasons for Asians' lower scores may be the fact that (in the USA) they have a low divorce rate, tend not to have births outside marriage, and tend to have more conservative sexual attitudes.

PREGNANCY RESOLUTION

Very few teenagers deliberately choose to become pregnant. As Furstenberg and his colleagues (1989) so aptly put it (314): 'Indeed, if teens

RESEARCH HIGHLIGHT 8.2
Who becomes pregnant?
Garrett and Tidwell, 1999

Many studies have been conducted over the years comparing teenagers who have been pregnant with never pregnant ones. Garrett and Tidwell recently summarised some of this literature. They found that adolescent females who have been pregnant can be characterised as follows (91):

- dysfunctional family (for example, strained relationships, abuse, parental substance abuse, early loss of father, lax parental control);
- problematic mother–daughter relationship (for example, maternal rejection, maternal inconsistency, over identification with mother who was also a teenage mother);
- peer relationships (for example, being a follower, poor interpersonal skills);
- low use of contraception (for example, romanticising the current relationship, significant partner influence on low contraceptive use, hoping to 'permanently bond' with partner);
- race (blacks in the USA more likely than whites to have had intercourse, blacks become sexually active at a younger age than whites).

had to take the pill to become pregnant, relatively few would elect to do so.'

Social scientists have long been interested in the decisions unmarried pregnant teenagers make regarding the resolution of their unintended pregnancies (Eisen and Zellman, 1984). It has been reported that about 40 per cent of pregnant teenagers decide to have an abortion, 13 per cent will miscarry, while almost half will give birth. Of these, fewer than 10 per cent will give their child up for adoption. Of those who give birth, most will raise their child as single mothers, at least in the short term (Farber, 1991).

The Decision to Keep the Baby

One researcher conducted in-depth interviews with black and white adolescents aged 15–20 who decided to keep their babies (Farber,

1991). For them, this decision was viewed as ethical and responsible – 'the right thing to do'. Other scholars in this area have identified six factors which adolescents rate as very important in their decision to keep their babies (Warren and Johnson, 1989). These are:

- the partner desired the baby,
- a fear of the abortion procedure,
- equating abortion with loss of a part of self,
- getting married,
- resistance to the family's wishes for abortion.

Adolescents' decisions about various aspects of pregnancy are very much in line with familial and personal values in such matters as abortion, adoption, sanctity of life and so on. It would also seem that, among more affluent adolescents, a struggle very often develops over the right decision. Among lower class teenagers it seems to be generally accepted that pregnancy results in motherhood, while possible alternatives such as abortion and adoption are not discussed with family members in too much detail (Farber, 1991).

One sixteen-year-old white lower class teenager described her decision to keep her baby in the following terms (Farber, 1991, 713):

> My dad was telling me, you know, 'It's your decision to make. If you want to keep it, fine. If you want to abort it, I'm going to tell you right now – we don't like the idea of your having an abortion. And we don't like adoption either...' So they finally decided that I would keep the baby. Then we went over to [her boyfriend's] house, and his mother comes out and she said, 'I know what it's like. I wasn't married to Thomas's father. I was young and pregnant. Tell me how I can help you out. If you need anything, you've got people to help you out.'
>   Then finally it hit me: 'Hey, there's nothing I can do about it.'

There appears to be no one single reason why adolescents decide to keep their babies. Very often, rather than calculating their own self-interest, they respond to psycho-emotional needs and the expectations and desires of their own family. They also consider moral and ethical issues. Values, beliefs and attitudes about pregnancy and its resolution appear to be bound up with class and race. Thus, more whites than blacks consider abortion (at least in the USA), while poorer teenagers are much more likely quickly to reject abortion as well as adoption (Farber, 1991). It has also been observed that blacks in the USA are generally opposed to abortion and adoption. This has recently been confirmed after in-depth interviews with young black adolescents (Pete and DeSantis, 1990): Both adolescents and their parents viewed abortion negatively and thought that it was the girl's responsibility to have the baby.

Custer (1993) examined the reasons behind white females' decision to keep their baby rather than place it for adoption. Social sanction against adoption was a powerful factor. Mothers were also fearful of the psychological discomfort that would follow adoption and that they would agonise over what had happened to their child. There was pressure not to give a 'blood relative' away while another contributing factor was accepting responsibility for one's actions and learning to live with the consequences of 'messing around'.

Adolescent girls, while making these important decisions about whether to keep their babies or not, or to terminate their pregnancies, very often desire greater cohesion or 'enmeshment' with their families. As has been remarked, this is quite unusual, since most adolescents seek more involvement with peers and greater independence from their parents (Geber and Resnick, 1988). This desire reflects, no doubt, the peculiar position in which pregnant adolescents find themselves and may be an important coping mechanism in a stressful situation. Of course, not all adolescent parents-to-be are likely to respond in this way. As the authors found, those who are alienated from their families are not surprisingly much less likely to seek support from them.

The Decision to Place for Adoption

Not many teenage mothers place their children out for adoption in the USA, Canada or Australia (Daly, 1994; Farber, 1991). It is estimated that less than 5 per cent of pregnant adolescents who carry to term will place their baby for adoption (Custer, 1993; Daly, 1994; Sobol and Daly, 1992). The adoption figures among black teenagers in the USA are much lower than those for whites, although it is not clear whether racial differences exist in other societies. Although white American teenagers have always preferred adoption compared with blacks, it would seem as though this option is losing its appeal. The reason for this is not clear. It could be that teenagers who in the past would have favoured adoption are now able to have legalised abortions.

Those adolescents who place their babies for adoption usually have the support of their families. Teenagers whose mothers favour adoption are very much more likely to choose adoption, while those who choose adoption are less likely to know other teenagers who are single parents (Herr, 1989; see also Research Highlight 8.3). This highlights the socialising influence of the peer group in transmitting values and attitudes regarding sexuality (Miller and Moore, 1990). It has also been noted that adolescents who place their babies for adoption tend to be older than those who keep their children. They also tend to come from financially better-off families and have higher academic motivation. They usually uphold traditional family values and live at home with both parents (Sobol and Daly, 1992).

A summary of the relevant research literature suggests that three factors influence a teenager's decision to place her baby for adoption (Sobol and Daly, 1992): these are individual social, and organisational factors (see Table 8.1). Individual factors include the desire to complete school, the young mother's emotional preparedness and lack of financial resources. Social factors include peer influences as well as the mother of the pregnant adolescent. Finally, there are several organisational factors influencing the decision not to place, such as the availability of abortion and social welfare benefits.

TABLE 8.1   *Factors influencing decision to place baby for adoption*

To place	Not to place
Individual Factors	
Unprepared for parenthood	Not emotionally prepared to place child
Wanting to finish high school	Not prepared to after carrying child to term
Not emotionally ready	
No financial resources	
Not able to provide home environment	
Social Factors	
Mother likely to encourage placement	Black family values (don't abandon baby)
Peers likely to be encouraging	
Mother more influential than teenager's partner	
Organisational Factors	
	Not familiar with administrative procedures
	Counsellors don't provide all the information
	Teenagers concerned about confidentiality
	Availability of abortion
	Society accepting of unwed parenthood
	Availability of welfare

Source: Sobol and Daly, 1992

According to Sandven and Resnick (1990), informal adoption following out-of-wedlock teenage pregnancy is quite common among black
families in the USA. They argue that this practice originated with slav-
ery; informal adoption being seen as a *mutual obligation system*, a way
of coping with poverty and a way of demonstrating a commitment to
the survival of the group.

Sandven and Resnick interviewed 54 urban black adolescents who
had recently made an adoption or parenting decision about their infants.
They found that 20 teenagers chose informal adoption, although parent
and child remained with the original family unit (the so-called 'shared'
group). Nine mothers chose informal adoption by which the child
received primary care from another person (the so-called 'gift' group).
Twenty-five mothers decided to raise their child outside the original
family unit (the 'exclusive' group).

It was found that most of these teenagers did not *want* to become
pregnant while there were some noted differences between the three
groups of mothers. For instance, the girls in the 'shared' group
expressed positive feelings towards their mothers. Thus the mothers
of these girls seemed to play an important role in helping them
decide to keep their babies and to remain in the original family unit.
These girls, therefore, had the added benefit of family support in
raising their children. Although some of the girls in the 'exclusive'
group appeared independent and motivated, others were disorgan-
ised and rebellious. The authors concluded that the girls probably
had had family interactions that were 'problematic' (Sandven and
Resnick, 1990). Finally, it was found that the girls in the 'gift' group
had a history of drug, alcohol and sexual abuse. They tended to be
younger than the other mothers and had experienced problems at
school.

Kalmuss (1992) challenges the view that the demand for formal
adoption among black adolescents in the USA is low. It is argued that
available data do not support such a perception and that research
should be conducted to determine answers to a variety of questions,
including:

- knowledge and attitudes among blacks about formal adoption,
- perceptions of support in the black community for adults who adopt
  unrelated infants,
- the assumptions that black teenagers have about demand in the
  formal adoption system,
- black teenagers' attitudes toward adoption.

Finally, Namerow and colleagues (1993) studied the factors that influence a young woman's decision to keep her baby or to place it for adoption. Multivariate analyses showed that the most important predictors were not factors such as race or whether the pregnant woman was on welfare or not. Rather, her decision was influenced by factors such as:

- Adoption socialisation influences. Those who themselves were adopted or had relatives who had been adopted were more likely to place their child for adoption.
- The role of significant others. Mothers are particularly influential – their values and beliefs have a large influence on the teenager's decision.
- The role of the boyfriend. His encouragement one way or the other is also influential.
- The role of expectancies and values. If women believed that by keeping their baby their goals would be attained, they were then more likely to do so.

The Decision to Terminate the Pregnancy

Spitz and colleagues (1996) studied the abortion rates among US teenagers during the 1980s and concluded as follows:

- rates for all aged 15–19 years remained relatively stable,
- abortion rates for the 18 to 19-year-olds is about twice that of the 15 to 17-year-olds,
- Sexually experienced teenagers showed a decline in abortion rates, the biggest decline was among 15 to 17-year-olds.

Several studies have revealed that those adolescents who decide to terminate their pregnancy tend not to have dropped out of school and usually have higher educational aspirations than girls who decide to keep their babies (eg. Eisen et al., 1983). In the USA, it is usually young white or older black adolescents who choose abortion. Those who opt for abortion are also more likely to have mothers with higher educational levels who tend to supervise their adolescent daughters more closely (Farber, 1991). In addition, girls who decide to have an abortion tend to be less religious and less likely to have friends who are teenage mothers. They are also more likely to receive support from their sexual partner, mother and close friends (Furstenberg et al., 1989; Miller and Moore, 1990).

Demb (1991) conducted in-depth interviews with a small number of inner-city black adolescents a week after they had had an abortion. Their ages ranged from 13 to 17. Although their circumstances were quite different, the following underlying characteristics were detected:

- First, the decision to abort was not taken lightly. All girls experienced a certain amount of distress, even though some might try to hide their emotions. Indeed, some can be so successful at this that adults very often think of them as 'unfeeling'.
- Secondly, some adolescents receive counselling about the options available to them, although it is not clear to what extent this differed for different racial and socio-economic groups.

It would appear that, for girls who decide to terminate their pregnancy, adoption is not considered to be a serious option. As Demb (1991, 101) observed: 'The girls tended to take the position that if they were to have a baby it would make no sense to give it away.'

Many adolescents experience negative emotional reactions prior to the actual abortion. Warren and Johnson (1989) reviewed several reports that suggest that many adolescents experience anxiety, hostility, depression, guilt and shame. Following abortion, however, these negative emotions tend to decrease; indeed, some teenagers even experience relief. Interestingly, it has been noted that black teenagers in the USA report lower pre-abortion anxiety than do their white counterparts, although blacks find the *decision* to have an abortion much harder to make than do whites. Other studies have also shown that those females who have the support of their partner find it much easier to decide to terminate their pregnancy.

Satisfaction with the Decision

How satisfied are teenagers with their pregnancy resolution decision? Not many researchers have examined the attitudes and adjustment of adolescent mothers following pregnancy resolution. In one study, 299 white and Mexican-American adolescents aged 13–19 years were interviewed six months after the birth of their children or the termination of their pregnancies (Eisen and Zellman, 1984). The authors were interested in the adolescents' reported satisfaction with their decision, and whether this was influenced by any demographic, economic or psychosocial factors.

RESEARCH HIGHLIGHT 8.3
The long-term consequences of placing or parenting
Namerow, Kalmuss and Cushman, 1997

Are there significant differences in the long-term outlook of those young women who decide to keep their baby compared to those who place their baby for adoption? These authors tracked over 400 young mothers interviewing them four years after the birth of their child. They found that those who placed their baby for adoption were advantaged in a number of ways:

- they completed more formal education;
- more were in paid employment;
- more were employed outside the home;
- they were less likely to receive public assistance;
- they reported more satisfactory relationships with their partners;
- they were less likely to have had another pregnancy;
- they were more likely to be legally married (by contrast parenters were more likely to be in *de facto* relationships, divorced or separated);
- parenters were more likely to be satisfied with their decision to keep the baby than were placers with their decision to place their baby for adoption.

A high proportion (82 per cent) of teenage mothers in the sample said that they would make the same decision again. There were no age or ethnic group differences. The authors found that satisfaction was consistently high across the various resolution groups. For example, 80 per cent ($n=148$) said that they would choose abortion again, 87 per cent ($n=57$) were prepared to choose single motherhood again, while 80 per cent ($n=36$) said that they would marry again. Those who were happy with the abortion decision were more likely to be older and to have a mother with a relatively high level of education. These adolescent mothers were also likely to have good school grades and to use contraceptives consistently *after* abortions.

Those adolescents who said that they would choose single motherhood again, were more likely not to have attended school during the six months after delivery. This finding underlines the difficulties faced by young single mothers who attempt to complete school. They have to cope with being mothers, students and teenagers, as well as very often coping with child-care facilities that are inadequate (Eisen and Zellman, 1984) as well as other contingencies. What is more, the mothers of these teenagers also usually endorse single motherhood.

One can conclude that, in terms of post-decision satisfaction, there is no best or worst decision. Pregnant teenagers need professional counselling in which all their options are made clear to them. The circumstances of each adolescent are different, and they should be encouraged to make a decision that best reflects their own values and beliefs, as well as their personal aspirations. Their decision should not reflect parental pressures. Only by so doing is the mother likely to be satisfied with the decision she has taken (Eisen and Zellman, 1984).

BIRTHING OUTCOMES

Pregnant teenagers are at greater risk for birthing complications than other women. The death rates for babies born to mothers younger than 15 years are higher than for babies born to mothers aged 15–19 years. Moreover, children born to mothers under the age of 20 are more likely to suffer from various birth defects and injuries (Sprinthall and Collins, 1988).

The young mother is also quite likely to have a difficult pregnancy and birth. Teenagers tend to suffer excessive or poor weight gain, premature rupture of membranes and intra-uterine growth retardation, to name just a few problems. They are also likely to manifest higher toxemia and related complications, and to have prolonged labour (Sprinthall and Collins, 1988). Risks among prostituting adolescents are even greater. One study detected various sexually transmitted diseases among the mothers, while 22 per cent of mothers' infants were premature. Several were diagnosed with respiratory distress syndrome, drug effects, sepsis, intra-uterine foetal demise and positive toxicology screens (Deisher, Litchfield and Hope, 1991).

Studies of pregnancy among teenagers have noted birthing complications such as lower birth weights (Lee and Walters, 1983) and increased risk of prematurity (Davis, 1988). In a noteworthy large-scale study of almost 50 000 births to women of various age groups in Australia, the association between a wide range of risk factors (such as birth weight) and outcome was examined (Correy, Kwok, Newman and Curran, 1984). It was found that, when adolescent births were compared with those for women over 18, significant differences in outcome emerged

TABLE 8.2   *Comparison of birth outcomes to adolescent mothers and mothers aged 18 years and older*

	<16 years (n = 188)	<17 years (n = 693)	<18 years (n = 1719)	≥18 years (n = 46591)
Mean birthweight (g)*	3143.42 (SD ± 556.14)	3202.15 (SD ± 528.80)	3212.00 (SD ± 597.27)	3345.19 (SD ± 575.47)
Birthweight < 2500 g*	21 (11.2%)	65 (9.4%)	151 (8.8%)	2609 (5.6%)
Gestation period < 38 weeks	26 (13.8%)	88 (12.7%)	221 (12.9%)	3330 (7.2%)
Apgar score (at 1 minute) below 7*	38 (20.2%)	132 (19.0%)	312 (18.2%)	5459 (11.8%)
Congenital abnormalities	7 (3.7%)	19 (2.7%)	48 (2.8%)	913 (2.0%)
Perinatal mortality*	5 (2.7%)	22 (3.2%)	48 (2.8%)	720 (1.6%)
Hypertension in pregnancy (transient hypertension in labour excluded)*	41 (21.8%)	131 (18.9%)	293 (17.0%)	6406 (13.8%))
Antepartum haemorrhage (placenta praevia excluded)	1 (0.5%)	16 (2.3%)	47 (2.7%)	1007 (2.2%)
Caesarean section*	13 (6.9%)	38 (5.5%)	92 (5.4%)	3684 (7.9%)
Forceps delivery*	58 (30.9%)	178 (25.7%)	432 (25.1%)	9667 (21.5%)

Note: *Groups differ significantly
Source: Correy et al., 1984

for nearly all risk factors (see Table 8.2). Women younger than 16 tended to have children with lower birth weight and lower apgar scores and were also more likely to have had a forceps delivery and to suffer hypertension during pregnancy. Interestingly, those younger than 16 and older than 18 years were more likely to deliver by Caesarean section.

From Table 8.2 one is led to believe that negative birthing outcome for teenage mothers might be the result of their relatively younger age. Further statistical analysis of the data, however, modifies this view. It was found that, when teenagers were *matched* with older women in terms of marital status and socio-economic level, most of the significant differences observed in Table 8.2 disappeared. To illustrate this point, Table 8.3 compares the birth outcomes of adolescents and adults aged 18–34 years in socio-economic Category 5 (that is, unemployed and unskilled workers). Only two significant differences now emerged between the teenagers and the older group. The table shows that adolescents were *less* likely to undergo Caesarean section and forceps delivery than older women. There were no other significant differences between the age groups (Correy et al., 1984).

TABLE 8.3   *Comparison of adolescent and adult (18–34 years) birth outcomes in social class 5*

	Adolescents			Adults
	<16 years (n = 156)	<17 years (n = 529)	<18 years (n = 1159)	18–34 years (n = 4720)
Mean birthweight (g)	3140.28 (SD ± 560.94)	3207.69 (SD ± 590.04)	3211.67 (SD ± 580.02)	3214.31 (SD ± 576.30)
Birthweight <2500 g	20 (13.1%)	51 (9.6%)	101 (8.7%)	404 (8.5%)
Gestation period <38 weeks	22 (14.4%)	66 (12.8%)	140 (12.1%)	494 (10.4%)
Agpar scores (at 1 minute) below 7	32 (20.9%)	105 (19.8%)	216 (18.6%)	782 (16.6%)
Congenital abnormalities	7 (4.6%)	14 (2.6%)	30 (2.6%)	135 (2.9%)
Perinatal mortality	4 (2.6%)	18 (3.4%)	30 (2.6%)	123 (2.6%)
Hypertension in pregnancy (transient hypertension in labour excluded)	29 (19.0%)	104 (19.7%)	214 (18.5%)	1057 (22.4%)
Antepartum haemorrhage (placenta praevia excluded)	0 (0.0%)	9 (1.7%)	29 (2.5%)	138 (2.9%)
Caesarean section*	9 (5.9%)	29 (5.5%)	66 (5.7%)	482 (10.2%)
Forceps deliveries*	44 (28.8%)	139 (26.3%)	303 (26.1%)	1721 (36.5%)

Note: *Groups differ significantly
Source: Correy et al., 1984

These results suggest that other factors besides age are important in determining birth outcome for teenagers. Not only is socio-economic and marital status important, but so too are antenatal care, alcohol and cigarette use and diet (Correy et al., 1984; Davis, 1988). For instance, evidence shows that some adolescents are less likely than other pregnant women to visit health care facilities on a regular basis. Rather, many of them seem to prefer symptom-specific care when antenatal care and monitoring is especially important during the crucial first trimester of pregnancy (Davis, 1988).

PARENTAL PRACTICES

Do teenagers exhibit certain parental qualities not evident in other groups of parents? Although there is a relative dearth of research, there is some evidence pertaining to teenage parents' knowledge of child development and their attitudes to parenting as well as teenagers' behaviour toward the child (Brooks-Gunn and Furstenberg, 1986; East, Matthews and Felice, 1994; Hanson, 1990).

Some evidence suggests deficits in the interaction patterns of adolescent mothers (Christ et al., 1990; Culp et al., 1991), who appear less verbal and responsive than older mothers. In one study, researchers were interested in the responses of adolescent and non-adolescent mothers, matched for their level of education, during feeding and play times (Culp et al., 1991). It was found that adolescent mothers showed less delight and were less facially and verbally responsive than were older mothers when feeding. During play times, adolescent mothers were found to be less patient, inventive and had a less positive attitude. It was concluded that intervention strategies might be appropriate for adolescent mothers, and that they be taught to be more verbally and emotionally responsive.

Importantly, teenage mothers do exhibit emotional *warmth* to their offspring, and do not differ in this regard from older mothers. At the same time, however, adolescent mothers have been observed to provide less *stimulation* to their children as measured by the HOME (Home Observation for Measurement of the Environment) inventory, although they tend to be no less responsive to their children's needs than older mothers.

Very young adolescent mothers report lower acceptance of their children (East, Matthews and Felice, 1994). In general, younger adolescent mothers tend to have unrealistic expectations regarding child development, underestimating their child's cognitive, language and social functioning abilities. Even when controlling for the effects of socio-economic background, it would seem that teenage mothers have inappropriate expectations about developmental milestones (Brooks-Gunn and Furstenberg, 1986). Hanson (1990), studying a rather small group of pregnant teenagers, found that, although they tended to be empathic with respect to children's needs, they were more likely to have unrealistic expectations about their developmental capabilities and to favour the use of corporal punishment. One-quarter of the respondents viewed their babies as helping to fulfil some of their own unmet needs.

Although it would appear that many young mothers exhibit parenting deficits, it would be inaccurate to assume that this applies to *all* mothers. Nonetheless, it should be recognised that young mothers are at greater risk for poor parenting which would be indicated by the presence of one or more of the following (Miller et al., 1996):

- poor cognitive readiness to parent,

- poor parenting attitudes and values,
- poor parenting knowledge.

PSYCHOLOGICAL ADJUSTMENT OF CHILDREN

Psychological research has been concerned with the emotional, cognitive, and behavioural well-being of children born to teenage parents. Writers have noted certain behavioural and emotional deficits in these children. Some have reported particular psychosocial and cognitive deficits such as acting-out behaviour and problems with self-esteem (Oppel and Royston, 1971), learning problems, hostility and impulsivity (Kinard and Reinherz, 1984). Children of teenage mothers have also been found to perform poorly at school (Dubow and Luster, 1990).

Evidence suggests that teenage mothering has negative effects on children's academic performances. Indeed, differences between the children of adolescent and older mothers are noticeable in the pre-school years (Brooks-Gunn and Furstenberg, 1986). Moreover, by the time these children reach high or secondary school, they are likely to have relatively lower academic aspirations than other adolescents, and to show signs of maladjustment. For instance, one study cited found that 49 per cent of adolescent mothers interviewed reported that their children had been suspended from school.

In a noteworthy three-year longitudinal study, researchers studied the effects of young mothers' cognitive readiness on the outcomes of their children (Miller et al., 1996). The prenatal attitudes, values and knowledge of pregnant women aged 14–19 years were assessed, as were the emotional and intellectual outcomes of their children three years later. The mothers tended to have below average IQ, to come from lower socio-economic groups, while most had completed Year 10 (aged 15–16 years) of school. It was found that mother's perceptions of her role as a parent and of her child predicted children's outcomes at three years. Specifically, mothers who reported high stress levels and their children as being difficult, also reported their children as depressed and anxious at three years.

Not all children born to teenage parents exhibit behavioural or emotional deficits, of course. There is an enormous amount of variability among children born to teenage mothers and many children show adequate emotional adjustment and school performance. Several risk factors predict negative adjustment in these children, while several protective factors act as buffers against negative adjustment. These are listed in Table 8.4.

TABLE 8.4   *Predictors of positive and negative adjustment in children of teenage mothers*

Risk factors	Protective factors
Many siblings	Quality of home environment (i.e. cognitively and emotionally supportive)
Father-absent homes	High intellectual ability of child
Poverty	Positive self-concept
Maternal maladjustment	
Maternal education less than twelve years	
Low maternal age at child's birth	
Urban residence	

Source: Dubow and Luster, 1990

Dubow and Luster (1990) studied 721 children aged 8–15 years who were born to teenage mothers. Included in the inventory were a range of risk and protective factors as well as several measures of behavioural and academic performance. Results showed that the children scored higher than the general population on the behavioural problem index, while also being weaker than average in terms of intellectual performance. As expected, however, several protective factors were found to buffer them against emotional maladjustment. The following were identified as being particularly important: an emotionally supportive home, the child's verbal intelligence and self-esteem. Of these, self-esteem seems particularly important as it is related to social competence, independence, inquisitiveness and assertiveness in children. Thus, programs that aim to enhance the self-esteem of children of teenage parents may be particularly beneficial. The authors concluded as follows (402): 'the children in this study who experienced multiple stressors were at greatest risk...the risk of developing problems increased linearly with the number of risk factors to which children were exposed.'

Finally, it is important to note that research in this area has been characterised by various methodological problems (Kinard and Reinherz, 1984). In many cases select groups of children attending various clinics and assessment centres have been studied (see Christ et al., 1990), while in other cases sample sizes are small (see Miller et al., 1996). In other cases the maternal age of the mother when giving birth has been defined inconsistently, depending on whether the first-born is the focus of study, or not. On other occasions, age groups have also been inconsistently defined: that is, researchers disagree on the meaning of 'young' and 'older' adolescents. Finally, researchers have used different measures of the behaviour under consideration, while not all have considered the importance of risk and protective factors (Dubow and Luster, 1990).

ADOLESCENT MOTHERS IN ADULTHOOD

There is a general belief that teenage mothers are at a decided disadvantage economically, educationally and occupationally. Not many studies have tested this claim longitudinally although a notable exception is one study that spanned seventeen years (Furstenberg and colleagues, 1987).

They concluded by saying that the view that teenage mothers are all caught up in a cycle of poverty and welfare dependency is an oversimplification. Although many such mothers, in fact, do perform less well on many indicators than those who postponed motherhood, there are those who manage to complete school, find a job and thus escape the poverty cycle. For example, the authors noted that most of the schooling that occurred after the birth of the first child took place late in the longitudinal time span. Whereas only 8.8 per cent of the sample had some post-school training early in the study, this had risen to 24.7 per cent later in the study.

Relationships with men tended to be less than satisfactory. It was found that 24 per cent of the sample were in their second or third marriages, and that only 16 per cent were still married to the father of the first child. Support was found for the general view that teenage mothers have several children, with half of the mothers having at least four. They tended to be born in the first few years of the study while most mothers were still relatively young. Only a small proportion of respondents (about one-fifth) used contraception on a regular basis.

Another commonly held view is that, after the birth of the first child, teenage mothers are reliant on welfare assistance. According to the longitudinal study reviewed here, about two-thirds of the mothers were no longer dependent on subsidies in the latter segment of the research. In view of these and other findings, Furstenberg et al. (1987, 9) noted that there is

> tremendous variation in outcomes of early parenthood ... many women have not all followed the predictable course of life-long disadvantage, even if they are not doing as well as their peers who postponed parenthood ... The failure to take account of pre-existing differences may have led to an overestimation of the impact of premature parenthood on the life course of women.

TEENAGE FATHERS

In reviews of teenage parenthood, fathers are very often ignored, with most attention being devoted to teenage mothers. One reason for this may simply be that increasing numbers of infants are now being raised in teenage single-mother households. Yet another reason might be that there is some dispute as to just how many babies born to teenage mothers have fathers who are teenagers. There is evidence to suggest that almost one-half of babies born to teenage mothers have fathers older than twenty years (Robinson, 1988a; 1988b). A further reason might be that adolescent fathers have tended to be neglected because of Western society's 'mother-centered bias' (Parke, Power and Fisher, 1980). As Parke and colleagues noted (88): 'This neglect of the father stems, in part, from our assumption concerning the primacy of the mother-infant relationship'.

Who are likely to become teenage fathers? Fagot and her colleagues found the following factors to be the best predictors (Fagot et al., 1998):

- low school graduation rates,
- daily tobacco use,
- marijuana and hard drug usage.

What other features distinguish teenage fathers? Like their peers, they tend to use contraception inconsistently, but differ from non-fathers in that they are more likely to accept teenage pregnancy as something that is not out of the ordinary. They are also more likely to favour abortion and themselves to be the children of teenage parents (Robinson, 1988b). With respect to marriage and child-rearing, evidence shows that teenage fathers, like teenage mothers, are quite likely to have inappropriate developmental expectations of their children (Harris, 1998; Parke et al., 1980), although fathers do not differ in this respect from non-fathers (Robinson, 1988a). Harris (1998) found that most of her teenage parents could not estimate the amount of sleep a young child requires, nor could the fathers give correct answers to questions regarding medical care.

Many teenage fathers have very little contact with their children (Fagot et al., 1998), although those who do decide to live with their partner and infant face strains no different from those on teenage mothers. It has been suggested that teenage fathers experience the same emotional cycle of elation and despair faced by teenage mothers (Robinson, 1988a). Teenage fathers have reported being sad, anxious, fearful, depressed, happy, overwhelmed and shocked. Although teenage fathers face higher unemployment rates and school difficulties (for example, Marsiglio, 1986), Harris (1998) found that most of the teenage fathers in her sample were already educationally 'off-track' by the time of the pregnancy.

Although signs of depression and stress among teenage fathers have been noted, they do not differ significantly on a number of personality traits from older fathers with teenage partners (Robinson, 1988b). In addition, teenage fathers suffer the stress of being separated from their peer group as well as the added strains of assuming new roles and responsibilities (in some cases, marriage), for which they might not be prepared. Teenage fathers are also likely to have a poor academic record prior to parenthood and to find a job before most other boys (Neville and Parke, 1991).

Teenage fathers (and mothers) find the changed roles and new responsibilities most difficult to deal with. Robinson (1988a) explains their predicament in the following terms (56):

> teenagers have an even more traumatic time because of the premature role transition. Prospective fathers, having to deal not only with the worries of pregnancy but also with the stresses of normal adolescent development as well as the unscheduled developmental tasks of adulthood, face a triple developmental crisis ... They either forego further education or attempt a 'triple-track' pattern of undertaking education, work, and parenthood simultaneously, and in some cases they take on marriage as a fourth accelerated task.

Some data suggest that many teenage fathers show an interest in their sexual partner and child (Harris, 1998; Robinson, 1988b; but see Fagot et al., 1998). Some fathers attend antenatal clinics with their partner, continue to date after the birth of their child, and some maintain regular contact. In one study (cited in Robinson, 1988b), two-thirds of the fathers contributed towards the support of both mother and child. This has been confirmed by another report showing that many adolescent fathers want to remain involved with their children and show financial concern (Elster and Hendricks, 1986).

Finally, not many of these teenage couples will marry. In fact, only about 10 per cent will, with many of these alliances ending in divorce. Many such marriages are characterised by conflict, resulting in a divorce rate for under-18s that is three times higher than that for couples who had their first child in their twenties (Robinson, 1988b).

THEORETICAL CONSIDERATIONS

Several developmental tasks during the teenage years were noted in the first chapter. Paramount among these is the development of a strong sense of self, as well as the development of a vocational identity. For some teenagers this is a slow, yet steady, process. It is suggested here that adolescent parenthood impedes these important developmental tasks. According to the literature cited, many teenage parents exhibit certain psychosocial problems. It is quite likely that pregnancy and parenthood lead to identity diffusion and unnecessarily delay the attainment of identity achievement.

SUMMARY

Although adolescent birth rates have declined in some Western nations, it is not clear to what extent this has happened in other countries, notably those in Eastern Europe. Future research should document these trends in non-Western nations as well as the attitudes and beliefs of these teenagers concerning aspects of parenting and child-rearing.

More and more adolescent mothers are keeping their babies. Together with abortion, this accounts for the vast majority of pregnancy resolution decisions. Adoption appears much less popular, notably among black teenagers in the USA. It is generally agreed that pregnant teenagers need professional counselling regarding pregnancy resolution, and that they should be encouraged to make a decision that best reflects their personal circumstances as well as their own values, beliefs and aspirations.

One must express concern at the risks that the children of teenage mothers face concerning their prospects for emotional adjustment and school outcome. The risk and protective factors are well documented. It is hoped that intervention programmes can be instituted so as to enhance protective factors such as positive self-esteem while offsetting some of the risk factors. Such intervention programmes could have important effects on child well-being.

We should not lose sight of the importance of intervention programmes for adolescent fathers (Elster and Hendricks, 1986). Although many young fathers want to be involved in decision-making regarding their child, they are often prevented from so doing by the mother's parents or by the mother herself. For those who maintain close contact with mother and child, intervention strategies may be needed to make the young father aware of vocational and educational opportunities, and to help him build a strong and supportive social network.

ADDITIONAL READING

Dubow, E. and Luster, T. (1990) 'Adjustment of Children Born to Teenage Mothers: The Contribution of Risk and Protective Factors', *Journal of Marriage and the Family*, 52: 393–404.
Fagot, B. I., Pears, K. C., Capaldi, D. M., Crosby, L. and Leve, C. S. (1998). 'Becoming an Adolescent Father: Precursors and Parenting', *Developmental Psychology*, 34: 1209–19.
Furstenberg, F., Brooks-Gunn, J. and Morgan, S. (1987) '*Adolescent Mothers in Later Life*.' Cambridge: Cambridge University Press.
Spitz, A. M., Velebil, P., Koonin, L. M., Strauss, L. T. et al. (1996). 'Pregnancy, Abortion, and Birth Rates among US adolescents – 1980, 1985, and 1990', *Journal of the American Medical Association*, 275 (13): 989–94.

EXERCISES

1   Birth rates were shown to vary across ethnic groups. Why should this be the case? Research the possible explanations for cultural differences in birth rates.
2   Consider some of the risks to psychological and emotional adjustment that may result from unwanted teenage parenthood. Contact your local community health centre and seek their cooperation in trying to locate young teenage mothers/fathers. If you can manage to interview these parents, examine the circumstances surrounding their parenthood. Was it planned, what support was received from both sets of parents, did they complete school, are they currently employed, what plans do they have for the future, and so forth? To what extent do your findings support those reported in the literature? What can you conclude about teenage parenthood?

9

Orientation to Authority and Delinquency

INTRODUCTION

The term 'juvenile delinquency' refers to illegal acts committed by young people (Eysenck and Gudjonsson, 1989). When using the term delinquency we include a wide range of varying behaviours that differ in their levels of seriousness. Thus delinquency includes such acts as gaining access to entertainment without paying, the fire-bombing of letter boxes, and interpersonal violence. Also included are break-and-enter and theft.

It is important to bear in mind that the age of legal responsibility for being delinquent varies from country to country. In England and Wales, for example, a juvenile is a person under the age of 17. At the same time, it is also held that children under the age of 10 years cannot be found guilty of an offence, and that rape cannot be committed by a boy who is under the age of 14. In the USA, on the other hand, 17 is regarded as the age of transition to adulthood in most states (Eysenck and Gudjonsson, 1989).

It would appear from media reports that juvenile crime is on the increase. Certainly, there have, of late, been some very well publicised incidents where we have been alarmed by the young age and the extent of the violence of some offenders. Who can forget the abduction and subsequent murder of a child by two young boys in Liverpool, UK and the school shootings in Colorado, USA? However, we are reminded by West (1967) that juvenile crime is commented upon by nearly every generation. To illustrate this point, he cites the following example, taken from a report published in England in 1818 (West, 1967, 33): 'The lamentable depravity which, for the last few years, has shown itself so conspicuously amongst the young of both sexes, in the Metropolis and its environs, occasioned the formation of a Society for investigating the causes of the increase of Juvenile Delinquency'.

This is not to suggest that the seriousness of delinquency has been overstated. On the contrary; delinquency causes serious hurt, emotional distress and enormous financial loss. It therefore warrants serious and careful analysis by psychologists and other professionals. Fortunately, however, it would seem that delinquent and criminal acts are committed by a minority of adolescents. Evidence (Rigby, Schofield and Slee, 1987) indicates that, by and large, many adolescents are reasonably accepting of institutional authority.

In this chapter we shall review some important theories of criminality and delinquency, as well as the social and personality factors related to these behaviours. We begin by first examining general orientation to authority among adolescents.

ORIENTATION TO AUTHORITY

From a very early age, young children have to learn to cope with individuals who are placed in positions of authority. Children are socialised in the context of the family and have to develop relationships with parents who represent institutional authority. It is from parents that children hear the word '*No!*' for the first time. It is with parents that children first experience the thwarting of their desires and behaviour. How they respond and adapt to such constraints may have important implications for later adolescent behaviour vis-à-vis institutional authorities. Indeed, it was noted earlier (see Chapter 3) that differences in parenting style are related to adolescent behaviour outcomes, including problem behaviour, misconduct and drug use.

During adolescence the parent–child relationship changes in nature. Adolescents are much more questioning of authority than younger children, although this is regarded as a normal part of adolescent development and identity formation. It is expected that teenagers will, within established boundaries, experiment with different roles, behaviours and ideas (see Chapter 2). Teenagers are caught between their own desires and impulses on the one hand and the demands of friends and peer groups and the constraints of parents on the other. Each set bounds or rules for acceptable behaviour, within which development must occur. For some individuals, however, the boundaries are too constraining. Some overstep the mark and go beyond what is normally regarded as acceptable behaviour.

It has also been demonstrated that there is a *generality* of attitude to authority. This suggests that adolescents who are accepting of the police are also likely to be accepting of other authority figures. Such individuals are also likely to hold relatively conservative social and political beliefs and to engage in pro-authority behaviours (Reicher and Emler, 1985; Rigby and Rump, 1979; Rigby et al., 1987).

Researchers (Reicher and Emler, 1985) have identified various subdimensions of attitudes to authority. These are:

- alienation from the institutional system,
- absolute priority of rules and authorities,
- bias vs. impartiality of authorities,
- relationship to school rules and authority.

Theories of Orientation to Authority

Several theories have been put forward to explain the development of orientation to institutional authority. However, the following perspectives were noted as important (Rigby, 1990): psychoanalytic theory, identity formation theory, cognitive developmental theory and social factors. As many of the relevant issues pertaining to these broad theories were discussed in the first chapter, these perspectives will only be briefly summarised here.

The psychoanalytic perspective

According to this view, adolescence is marked by a dramatic rise in sexual and instinctual feelings. This results in inner conflict, causing the teenager to seek closer ties with the peer group and to break emotional and constraining links with the family. Thus the teenager seeks to strive for, and to attain, independence. In so doing, many adolescents question authority figures and the nature of authority itself.

Identity formation theory

Marcia's identity statuses were reviewed in Chapter 2. Characteristic of the moratorium phase is the fact that adolescents are not committed to a set of beliefs, values, or ideology. Although the moratorium phase is regarded as essential for final identity achievement, some teenagers appear totally alienated from society. Relationships with peers and parents are viewed as meaningless (Rigby, 1990) with the result that some engage in delinquent and other forms of anti-social behaviour.

Cognitive developmental theory

Younger children are much more likely than adolescents to be accepting of parental and other authorities. Adolescents, capable of abstract reasoning, are more likely to question authority. Research evidence has shown that adolescents who disagree with their parents about various strategies for resolving problems are more likely than others to have reached relatively advanced levels of identity achievement (Peterson, 1990).

Social influences

There are some important social determinants of orientation to authority (Rigby, 1990). Included are the role of the peer group and the decline of patriarchal authority. The influences of the peer group are well known, and their links to delinquency will be discussed below. With respect to the decline of patriarchal authority, it is suggested that the socio-economic basis of the family has slowly shifted over the generations to the mother, while the role of the father has been trivialised. This has resulted in a breakdown of respect for authority figures. However, little empirical support for this position has been offered (Rigby, 1990).

Orientation to Authority: The Role of Individual Difference Factors

A considerable amount of research has examined the personality correlates of orientation to authority. Independent studies have all tended to agree that negative orientation to authority is associated with a particular constellation of personality and individual difference variables. Included are such traits as impulsiveness, religiosity, extraversion, achievement motivation, venturesomeness, Eysenckian psychoticism, risk-taking and external locus of control. Perhaps not surprisingly, several of these (for example, psychoticism and venturesomeness) have also been identified as important predictors of delinquency.

Acceptance of authority is related to high levels of religiosity. It was found among Australian teenagers that Catholic adolescents who were accepting of authority were more likely to (a) believe in God, and (b) attend church regularly (Rigby and Densley, 1985). In another study, it was noted that those who perceive themselves to be internally controlled were more supportive of institutional authorities. In explaining these findings, it was concluded that the possibility exists that internals (those who believe that what happens to them occurs through their own volition) feel sure enough of themselves *not* to feel threatened by institutional authorities (Heaven, 1988).

Another study examined the relationships between orientation to authority, beliefs in certain values and particular personality dimensions (Heaven and Furnham, 1991). Following an earlier lead (Feather, 1982), it was argued that values, although abstract in nature, are *normative*: that is, they act as frames of reference that guide behaviour and attitudes. Values are therefore a useful tool which aid our understanding of human behaviour. It was expected that an endorsement of values would be significantly related to all aspects of orientation to authority. Specifically, it was suggested that conservative values would be related to a positive orientation. In addition, the authors were interested in the relative influence of personality factors such as extraversion, neuroticism and psychoticism.

The contribution of personality (namely, psychoticism) to total variance explained was rather limited for both the attitudinal and behavioural aspects of authority. With respect to negative attitudes to authority, for instance, endorsement of values made a modest contribution of 8 per cent to variance explained, followed by pro-authority behaviour (16 per cent) and psychoticism (3 per cent). With respect to pro-authority behaviour, values explained 22 per cent of the variance, followed by attitudes to authority (14 per cent) and psychoticism (6 per cent).

These results show the close links that exist between attitudes to authority and behavioural dispositions. Secondly, the results show that, although the contribution of personality (in this case psychoticism) to explaining orientation to authority is significant, its overall contribution is rather small. It is therefore likely that other factors not measured here are important in explaining orientation to authority. Such factors are likely to include peer influences.

As negative attitudes to authority can be viewed as symbolic of general counter-conformity, it is reasonable to expect that adolescents who have them are likely to engage in a range of anti-authority behaviours, such as smoking. Support for this thesis was obtained from a study of 193 adolescents (Heaven, 1989). It was observed that smoking in females was related to general negative attitudes to authority as well as negative attitudes to law. Among males, smoking was related to negative attitudes to the army. These results suggest that, for females, 'law' is traditionally associated with male power, dominance and male authority. Feminist theory predicts that rebellious females will reject such manifestations of 'male power'. Likewise, if one assumes that 'army' is traditionally associated with things masculine, and with authority and discipline, one can expect that young males' rebelliousness will be directed toward this image (Heaven, 1989).

Orientation to Authority and Delinquency

According to some reports, adolescents who reject institutional authority are likely to commit acts of delinquency. There are significant associations between negative attitudes to authority and self-report
delinquency measures (Heaven, 1993; Reicher and Emler, 1985; Rigby,
Mak and Slee, 1989). Among males it has been observed that negative
attitudes to authority have significant and direct effects on self-reported
delinquency (Heaven, 1993).

Some writers (see Emler and Reicher, 1995; Reicher and Emler,
1985) have questioned the role of personality factors suggesting that
psychologists have tended to overlook the importance of some contextual factors. It is suggested that delinquent acts reflect a *negative quality*
in the relationship between the adolescent and wider society. Reicher
and Emler (1985, 16l) 'propose that juvenile delinquency may be
regarded as the reflection of a negative relationship between the young
person and the system of social regulation ... called "legal-rational
authority", or, more simply, between the young person and formal
authority'.

According to this view, therefore, the very nature of the relationship between adolescent and authority figures is damaged to such an
extent that the teenager is likely to engage in a variety of anti-social
behaviours.

JUVENILE DELINQUENCY

The actual extent of juvenile delinquency is unclear, although many
suspect that official figures under-represent the true situation. Official
figures are also very sensitive to changes in method of reporting, definitions of crime and age of legal responsibility. Nonetheless, nearly all
writers would agree that delinquency is a serious problem with huge
associated financial costs. School vandalism, for instance, costs many
millions of dollars every year. Large sums of money are required all
over the world for policing and the administration of juvenile justice
systems. In the USA during the 1980s it cost $1 billion per year to main-
tain the juvenile justice system (Patterson, DeBarsyshe and Ramsey,
1989).

Incidence of Delinquency

In the USA there was a 42 per cent increase from 1992 to 1994 in the number of people under 18 years arrested for crime. Those under 18 years made up 18.6 per cent of all arrests in the USA in 1994 (Rice, 1999). Although boys are four times more likely than girls to engage in delinquent behaviours, the number of females involved in behaviours such as gang activity and drug trafficking is steadily increasing. In the USA those offenders under 18 years were responsible for the following crimes (Rice, 1999):

* murder 16%
* rape   16%
* robbery 28%
* car theft 45%
* arson   49%

In Australia's most populous state, New South Wales, 12 540 males were charged with criminal offences in the Children's Courts in 1989–90, compared with only 2117 females. Table 9.1 gives a break-down of some of these offences for the two sexes. Thus, for instance, there are only small sex differences in the incidence of some behaviours such as robbery and extortion, while the sex differences are much larger for others such as motor vehicle theft and shoplifting.

TABLE 9.1 *Male-female breakdown of some criminal matters before the Children's Courts, New South Wales, 1989–90*

Type of offence	% Male	% Female
Against the person	12.8	15.1
Robbery and extortion	1.3	1.1
Break, enter and steal	15.9	7.6
Fraud	1.9	6.5
Motor vehicle theft	12.1	7.8
Shoplifting	3.7	12.6
Property damage	8.2	5.0
Firearms and weapons	1.1	0.2
Drug	4.1	3.5

Source: NSW Bureau of Crime Statistics and Research, 1991

Measuring Delinquency

Given the difficulties associated with studying juveniles in detention and in the justice system generally, it is not surprising that some researchers have resorted to studying delinquency among 'normal range' youth using self-report measures. Is this an appropriate methodology? Empirical evidence suggests that a close relationship exists between officially adjudicated and self-reported delinquency (Emler and Reicher, 1995; Shaw and Scott, 1991), while Emler and Reicher (1995) have commented on the satisfactory levels of reliability and validity that can be achieved with self-report measures.

Such measures also serve a very useful function in that they are able to detect many offences that go unrecorded. Indeed, Emler and Reicher (1995) assert that self-reports of offences exceed official records and documented crime by a substantial margin.

The Structure of Problem Behaviour

Delinquent behaviour is part of a syndrome of problem behaviour (Donovan and Jessor, 1985; Donovan, Jessor and Costa, 1988; Jessor,

---

RESEARCH HIGHLIGHT 9.1
Using self-report measures to gauge delinquency
Mak, 1993

Mak has proposed a self-report delinquency measure that has been shown to be internally consistent and also adequately discriminates adjudicated delinquent from non-delinquent adolescents. It comprises the following dimensions:

1　cheat (for example, vandalism)
2　status (for example, running away)
3　fight (for example, using a weapon)
4　vehicle (for example, stealing a bicycle)
5　drugs (for example, using LSD)
6　theft (for example, shoplifting)
7　harm (for example, beating someone)
8　driving (for example, drink driving)
9　disturb (for example, using graffiti).

Donovan and Costa, 1991). According to this view, delinquent behaviour is usually associated with other problem behaviours such as alcohol use, illicit drug use and sexual promiscuity. Jessor and his colleagues (Jessor et al., 1991) have proposed a theory of psychosocial risk and suggest that a range of different factors play an important role in determining the extent to which adolescents will engage in problem behaviours.

The factors comprise three domains. The first group comprises social background factors and includes major life events or educational status. Social psychological factors refer to such factors as the adolescent's values and beliefs and the adolescent's perceptions of family functioning. The final cluster is referred to as the behavioural system and includes conventional behaviours (such as attitudes to school).

It is now believed that a single common factor accounts for various problem behaviours in both male and female adolescent groups. This common factor or underlying theme, which explains the syndrome of problem behaviour, is *unconventionality* in personality and social attributes (Donovan and Jessor, 1985). It is also clear from the available evidence that one can rank-order behaviours from those most, to those least, determined by unconventionality as follows:

- number of times drunk in past six months,
- frequency of marijuana use in past six months,
- general deviant behaviour in past six months,
- sexual intercourse experience.

Some factors will act as buffers against problem behaviours. Following our discussion of the family in Chapter 3, one can predict that families that show open and warm communication and in which parents adopt authoritative parenting styles are less likely to have children who engage in problem behaviours. Mechanic (1991, 638) put it in the following terms: 'children who grow up in decent neighbourhoods and well-integrated families, who have parents and other close role models who communicate interest, caring, and support, but also convey high but realistic expectations and standards, are substantially protected against significant risks'.

Besides the possible influence of personality and social attributes on problem behaviour, there may be other explanations for such a syndrome of problem behaviour. In the first instance, engaging in these behaviours may be one way of achieving a particular set of goals. Secondly, such behaviours are quite often learned together, and continue to be performed together. Thirdly, they often occur in social contexts where other adolescents are present, resulting in peer pressure on the individual. Questions of *social ecology*, or the context within which behaviours are performed are therefore important (Donovan and Jessor, 1985).

Jessor's suggestion that problem behaviours are learned and performed in the presence of others is an important one and supported by Emler and Reicher (1995). We will take this up again later (see The Importance of Delinquent Groups).

The Stability of Delinquent Behaviour

Are anti-social and delinquent children likely to manifest delinquent behaviours as adolescents? According to some studies, this is highly likely. One review (Loeber, 1982) found evidence for this so-called *stability hypothesis*, especially for those young males who were initially rated as extremely anti-social. For example, it was noted that, of boys about 8–9 years of age who were judged to be above the 95th percentile in rated aggressiveness, 38.5 per cent were judged to be in the same percentile 10 years later. Likewise, girls with conduct disorder at age 13 years were found to engage in criminal behaviour and manifest other behavioural problems at age 18 years (Fergusson and Woodward, 2000).

Although anti-social and delinquent behaviour tends to be stable over time, there do appear to be changes in the sorts of behaviours engaged in (Loeber, 1982). Stealing in the home, truancy and the use of alcohol and drugs tend to increase between middle childhood and age sixteen. Fighting, disobedience, and lying, on the other hand, tend to decrease across the adolescent years.

In a study of over 500 Swedish males, it was found that delinquency and alcohol misuse tend to be associated in young males aged 10 years. Indeed, of those youngsters who did not engage in alcohol use, only 12 per cent had criminal records when young adults (aged 16 years) (Andersson et al., 1999). The presence of both alcohol use and delinquency in the young males increased the likelihood that one of these would be present at age 16 years.

Perspectives on Delinquency

There are several theoretical frameworks that guide psychological research into delinquency. These include the role of personality factors, heredity and environment, biological theory, and social factors. Each of these will be briefly described.

Delinquency and personality

A large body of research evidence supports the view that delinquency is related to personality dispositions. In particular, much research evidence pertaining to the influence of the factors extraversion–introversion, emotional stability and emotional independence (psychoticism) on delinquency has been accumulated (for example, Eysenck and Gudjonsson, 1989; Gudjonsson, 1997). These three dimensions can be regarded as major personality types, subsuming traits such as hostility, dominance, impulsiveness, venturesomeness, risk-taking and others (Eysenck and Eysenck, 1985).

According to Eysenckian theory those high on neuroticism (N), extraversion (E) and psychoticism (P) are likely to engage in delinquent and criminal behaviours. The basis of this argument is the functioning of the ascending reticular activating system that controls levels of physiological arousal (Eysenck and Eysenck, 1985). Those high on E are said to be low in arousal and, in order to raise their levels, these individuals engage in various thrill-enhancing and venturesome activities. Of course, not all stimulus-seekers are likely to engage in delinquent behaviours; some divert their energies into more acceptable ones. The factor N is linked to anxiety which acts as a drive ensuring that delinquent behaviours are amplified especially among high N scorers. Eysenckian P has been found to distinguish criminals from non-criminals, with high P individuals being described as anti-social, aggressive, cold and unempathic (H. Eysenck and M. Eysenck, 1985; H. Eysenck and S. Eysenck, 1975).

Several studies have found support for the important role of psychoticism (or toughmindedness). One study among a sample of Australian 14-year-olds found that P had important mediating and additive functions as far as the other attitudinal and personality factors are concerned (Heaven, 1994). It was also found that P exacerbates the effect of venturesomeness among males and females in that it increased the likelihood that venturesome individuals engage in delinquent acts. Among females, high P was found to mediate the effect of perceptions of negative family communication. In other words, negative communication was important, but its effect was through P. In a similar vein, a British study examined the relationships of self-reported delinquency among a sample of 19-year-olds (Furnham and Thompson, 1991). Only P was found to correlate significantly with delinquency.

Very little research has examined the relationships between the Big Five personality factors and self-reported delinquency. The results of one such study conducted among school students are shown in

TABLE 9.2   *Self-reported delinquency and five personality dimensions among school students*

Males		Females	
Interpersonal Violence	*Vandalism*	*Interpersonal Violence*	*Vandalism*
low A**	low A**	low A*	low C*
	low C**	high N*	
	high N*		

Note: A = Agreeableness; N = Neuroticism; C = Conscientiousness
    *p < 0.05. ** p < 0.01.
Source: Heaven, 1996a

Table 9.2. Agreeableness and, to a lesser extent, conscientiousness and neuroticism were significant correlates for this sample (Heaven, 1996a).

Some researchers have studied delinquency outside the Eysenckian paradigm and used measures such as the MMPI (for example, Weaver and Wootton, 1992). It was found that delinquents scored at the pathological end of the following subscales: social responsibility, alcoholism, family discord, persecutory ideas, psychomotor acceleration, depression, and apathy. According to Weaver and Wootton (1992, 551) delinquents can be described as follows:

> Such persons are socially extroverted and exhibitionistic, have difficulty concentrating, and may have a history of behaviour problems in school. They describe their home and family situations as being unpleasant, lacking in love, understanding, and support. Family members are seen as being critical, quarrelsome, and as refusing to permit adequate freedom and independence.

Adolescents in the Russian juvenile justice system were compared with a control group of school students (Ruchkin et al., 1998). The convicted youth were being detained for a variety of offences including robbery, rape and murder. Compared to the control group the detained youth were described as ranging in personality from passive–aggressive to explosive. They were observed to be 'easily distressed, conflicted, wavering, and uncertain' and as 'immature, fragile, blaming, unreliable' These individuals were also able to 'enjoy their activities without having to know the outcome and without feeling the urge to control it' (228–9).

Several noteworthy longitudinal studies have been conducted examining the relationship between various individual difference variables and delinquency (see Binder, 1988 for a review). The Gluecks, who followed up over 500 juvenile offenders, conducted an early study in this area. A sample of non-delinquent boys, matched for intelligence as well as ethnic and socio-economic background, formed the control group. Delinquent boys were more likely to be less conventional, more assertive and extraverted, and less goal-oriented. They were also more likely to display hostility and destructiveness, but to be low in anxiety and insecurity.

In Britain, a longitudinal study of over 400 boys from different primary schools was conducted (West and Farrington, 1973). It concluded that, besides some important social factors, the personality disposition of the child is an important predictor of delinquency. They argued as follows (189):

> it was the unpopular boys rather than the popular ones, those with high 'neuroticism' scores rather than those with low, those from broken homes rather than those from intact homes, those with nervous mothers rather than those with stable mothers, those born illegitimate rather than those born to married parents, who in each instance were the ones more likely to become delinquents.

One researcher tested H. Eysenck's theory by tracking adolescents for two years (Heaven, 1996b). The aim was to examine the extent to which personality factors at Time 1 (psychoticism, extraversion and self-esteem) predict self-reported delinquency at Time 2. The respondents were 14-years-old at Time 1 and 16 at Time 2. The strongest predictor of delinquency at both times was psychoticism, while the effects of extraversion and self-esteem were found to be insignificant. Moreover, whereas the combined personality factors explained 16 per cent of the variance of delinquency at Time 1, this was reduced to 6 per cent of the variance by the time the respondents were 16 years old. Thus, other factors appear to become more important in predicting delinquency as children get older.

Tremblay and colleagues (Tremblay et al., 1992) assessed, over several years, the impact of early disruptive behaviours and poor school achievement on delinquent behaviour at age 14 years. Early disruptive behaviour was a significant predictor for boys, but not for girls. Another study used the Child Behaviour Checklist as a predictor together with parents' and teachers' ratings of children (Bank et al., 1993). Teachers' ratings of behaviour were found to be accurate predictors of later delinquency.

Biological explanations of delinquency

In the previous section, the importance of cortical arousal as a link between personality types such as extraversion and delinquency was mentioned. This section will review some of the main principles that are involved. More detailed accounts are available elsewhere (for example, Eysenck and Eysenck, 1985; Eysenck and Gudjonsson, 1989; Strelau and Eysenck, 1987).

Individual differences in extraversion–introversion can be traced to differences in the reticular system, such that extraverts are typically under-aroused. Experimental studies have demonstrated differences in these personality types on tasks such as continuous serial reaction, the orienting reaction, EEG recordings, and conditioning (Eysenck and Eysenck, 1985). This theory has also been extended to the area of delinquency and criminality (Eysenck and Gudjonsson, 1989).

This Eysenckian approach to understanding delinquency implicates arousal and conditioning, with the latter being facilitated by high arousal levels. In brief, delinquents who are usually low on arousal do not condition easily, that is, parents, teachers and others find it difficult (if not impossible) to teach such adolescents acceptable behaviour through reward and punishment. Moreover, there is evidence to suggest that introverts and extraverts condition differently to different sorts of stimuli (Eysenck and Gudjonsson, 1989): introverts respond better to negative stimuli such as pain or harmful punishment, while extraverts respond better to pleasant stimuli. Extraverts also have much higher pain thresholds than introverts, which is crucial to understanding the association between extraversion and delinquency. Eysenck and Gudjonsson (1989) explain as follows:

> There is no doubt that pain thresholds and pain tolerance are higher for extraverts than for the average person and lower for introverts ... This would be directly relevant to criminal behavior, which often involves physical danger and pain ... Hence, if the intensity of physical punishment is felt less strongly by extraverts, then clearly they should respond less to such types of conditioning.

Eysenckian theory links arousability to conditionability suggesting that those who are low in arousability will not condition as easily. Those who condition easily are more likely to develop a conscience, as Raine (1997, 123) explains: 'The greater the individual's ability to develop and form classically-conditioned emotional responses, the greater the conscience development, and the less likely will be the probability of becoming anti-social. Conversely, poor conditionability will result in poor conscience development and undersocialized, antisocial behavior.'

A review of many studies in this area found support for the view that anti-social types have poorer conditionability. Thus, for instance, studies of psychopathic gamblers have shown that they display poorer differential conditioning. In addition, and somewhat surprisingly, there is also evidence that anti-socials from 'good' homes are more likely than anti-socials from less benign homes to condition poorly. In other words, if children from good homes become anti-social this is probably due to very strong biological effects (Raine, 1997).

Males are more likely to be involved in serious crime than are females with quite specific age and sex effects for violent and property offences. According to some (for example, Ellis, cited in Eysenck and Gudjonsson, 1989), androgens are finally responsible for differences in certain physiological processes which mediate the effects of the reticular formation system. Indeed, there are several studies that have documented the complex interrelationships between testosterone levels, aggression and arousal.

Other biological factors have also been implicated in the development of delinquency. One such factor is pubertal timing. Off-timers, that is, those maturing either early or later, were found on average to score higher on delinquency measures and to engage in more crime and problem behaviours at school. These include being sent out of class, quarrelling with the teacher, being sent to the head teacher and so forth (Williams and Dunlop, 1999). In conclusion, biological processes incorporating arousal, androgenic influences, conditionability and pain tolerance have been shown to have a significant impact on delinquent behaviour.

Heredity and environment

According to this perspective, some families have a greater propensity than others for delinquency and criminal behaviour (for example, Eysenck and Gudjonsson, 1989; West, 1967). In order to test such predictions, researchers have resorted to twin and adoption studies. Identical twins share the same genetic material, while non-identical or fraternal twins are no more alike than other sibling pairs. Thus, it is generally assumed that any differences in behaviour between identical twins must be due to environmental influences.

In adoption studies, researchers have checked for similarities between adoptive parents and adopted children. The assumption here is that parents and children share environmental factors, and that similarities in behaviour must be due to the effects of the environment. When studying biological parents and their children who have been adopted out, similarities are thought to be due to genetic factors, since the parents and children in these instances share genetic material.

Space does not allow us to do full justice to what is a very complex debate, characterised by the fact that environmental and genetic influences can be broken down into various sub-components. The following have been listed (Eysenck and Gudjonsson, 1989, 92):

- total genetic variance: this refers to all additive genetic variance – that is, all one's genes contributing to delinquency;
- non-additive genetic variance due to dominance at same gene loci;
- non-additive genetic variance due to interaction between different gene loci;
- assortative mating: refers to an increment in total variance due to genetic resemblance between mates.

Several studies are listed in support of both the heredity and environmental views. For instance, studies conducted from the 1930s to the 1960s show clearly that identical twins have much higher concordance rates for criminal behaviour than do fraternal twins. For all the studies cited in this regard, the average concordances are 66.7 and 30.4 per cent respectively. This is suggestive of a significant heredity effect. However, there is also an impressive *interaction* effect between heredity and environment (Eysenck and Gudjonsson, 1989).

One research team contacted 662 adoptive sons. In cases where both the biological and adoptive fathers had a criminal record, 36 per cent of the sons acquired a criminal record. Where neither father had a criminal record, only 10 per cent of sons acquired one. Of those sons whose biological, but not adoptive, father had a criminal record, 22 per cent acquired one. Of those whose biological father was not a criminal, but the adoptive father was, only 12 per cent of sons eventually acquired a criminal record. These findings suggest a complex relationship between heredity and environment.

It would seem that being reared by a criminal father does not necessarily lead to a son acquiring a record, if the biological parents are not criminal. Secondly, a genetic predisposition to engage in criminal behaviour is accentuated in those sons who are raised in an environment with a criminal father (Hutchings and Mednick, cited in Eysenck and Gudjonsson, 1989).

It is therefore quite clear that both genetic and environmental factors are important in explaining behaviours such as delinquent ones. Neither factor is capable on its own of fully explaining delinquent and anti-social behaviour. One must conclude that both factors have the ability to *mediate* the effect of the other on behaviour. Thus there is a move toward a more balanced view regarding the significance of each factor (Nigg and Hinshaw, 1998; Plomin, 1989; 1995).

In conclusion, one must bear in mind that genetic effects on behaviour are polygenic in nature. In other words, behaviour is not determined by single genes but rather reflects the effects of many. This fact in itself would undermine a simple reductionist view of delinquency (Plomin, 1989).

Family factors and delinquency

Several social factors have been identified as contributing to adolescents' delinquent behaviour. Researchers have listed school and family influences, peer influences, socio-economic deprivation, ethnic origin, parental criminality, child's poor academic performance and socialised aggressive disorder, to name just a few. This discussion will concentrate on the importance of the family.

On the basis of an earlier longitudinal study (West and Farrington, 1973), much information was generated about the importance of family life in the development of delinquency. Many, but not all, of these early findings have since been corroborated. For instance, whereas it was

---

RESEARCH HIGHLIGHT 9.2
The effects of family disruption on later delinquency
Pagani et al., 1998

These authors were interested in the effects of divorce and remarriage on reported delinquency among Canadian males. Boys were grouped as follows: as experiencing divorce between 6–11 years, or divorce between 12–15 years, or divorce and remarriage between 6–11 years, or divorce after 6 years and remarriage between 12–15 years. Results showed that boys in the last group were most vulnerable to higher delinquency, fighting, and theft, but that these behaviours had reduced to a level comparable to the other groups. The authors concluded that:

- the ages 12–14 years were most vulnerable for these boys;
- parents' parenting strategies were least effective for these boys, probably because parents were highly involved in the relationship with their new partner and less involved with their children/stepchildren.

first believed that family size might be a significant correlate of delinquency, *family process* is now regarded as important (Loeber and Dishion,
1983). Specifically, criminal activity by one or more parents or siblings,
increases the risk of delinquency. Criminal parents, it is argued, are less
likely to exercise necessary discipline, and are likely to lack the appropriate parenting skills. As Loeber and Dishion (1983, 82) explain: 'It can
be assumed that some parents, including those diagnosed as antisocial,
are less skilled in rearing children than others. Thus, in some households, parents maintain few rules, do not exercise discipline when
needed, or do not supervise youngsters.'

Family process has been investigated in a number of different ways,
one of which is to focus on the nature of parental discipline styles. Shaw
and Scott (1991) developed an instrument that measures punitive, love
withdrawal and inductive discipline styles. An inductive style reflects
a democratic, warm and communicative approach whereby parents
explain to children the consequences of the child's behaviour. Not surprisingly this style is related to lower levels of delinquency. On the
other hand punitiveness and love withdrawal are related to higher
levels of delinquency (Peiser and Heaven, 1996; Shaw and Scott, 1991).
Likewise, research using slightly different measures found that poor
discipline styles predicted conduct disorders among high or secondary
school students (Ge et al., 1996).

A well-known measure of family process is the Parental Bonding
Instrument (PBI; Parker, Tupling and Brown, 1979). It measures perceived maternal and paternal care and protectiveness throughout childhood and adolescence. In many different studies across a variety of
samples, the PBI has consistently been shown to be predictive of adolescent emotional and behavioural adjustment. Thus, for example, Mak
(1994) has demonstrated that high delinquency scores in youth are
significantly related to lower maternal and paternal care as well as to
higher maternal and paternal overprotectiveness. She also found that
teenagers who rated their parents as showing optimal bonding tended
to score lowest on the delinquency measure, while those showing weak
bonding and affectionless control tended to score highest.

Parental psychopathology has been strongly linked to maladjustment
and delinquency (West and Farrington, 1973). Important factors that
one must consider in this regard are parental neuroticism, parental
instability and psychopathic traits in parents. Some authors have also
commented on the importance of *social learning* within the context of
the family (Neapolitan, 1981). Indeed, some children learn aggressive
behaviour (a form of delinquency) as a result of family experiences.

In particular, there is evidence to suggest that sons who closely identify with a father who uses excessive physical force are more likely than other sons to engage in aggressive behaviour. It also appears that, when aggressive sons are physically punished by their mother, they are likely to commit aggressive acts against others in an attempt to reassert their masculinity.

According to the *social-interactional* perspective, parents of delinquent children very often unwittingly, although directly, train them to engage in anti-social behaviour. According to this view, parents tend to use positive reinforcement and punishment in a rather ad hoc fashion, thus reacting to deviant and prosocial behaviour inconsistently (Patterson et al., 1989). The final outcome is that children lack appropriate social skills, and are trained to be coercive and anti-social. This view is supported by numerous research studies (Patterson et al., 1989).

There are certain contextual factors operating within the home which are likely to make parental styles less effective. For example, not only is there stability of delinquent behaviour within individuals, but also across generations. Thus, anti-social parents tend to raise anti-social teenagers. Homes with mothers showing little support and emotional warmth towards teenagers, and who have low levels of mother-son affection, are more likely to produce sons who are delinquent. A likely consequence of such a parenting style is that adolescents seek an emotional anchor in the peer group, therefore often engaging in negative behaviours (Patterson et al., 1989).

The importance of delinquent groups

Although many studies of delinquency have made reference to the importance of considering the role of the peer group in such behaviour, it is only recently that these ideas have been incorporated into a coherent psychological theoretical framework. Emler and Reicher (1995) suggest that social identity theory is a useful framework for studying delinquent behaviours and note that young people are more likely to engage in delinquent behaviours when in a group than when alone. It is therefore feasible that the delinquent group fulfills an important function in the life of the delinquent.

According to social identity theory (Hogg and Abrams, 1988) delinquent groups comprise individuals who share a range of behaviours, attitudes, beliefs and values. The individuals define who they are in terms of their group membership. Being part of the delinquent group is important for the individual's sense of identity. The group (and individual

RESEARCH HIGHLIGHT 9.3
Why do some delinquents become career delinquents?
Born, Chevalier and Humblet, 1997; Scholte, 1999

Born and colleagues set out to assess why some youth who engage in delinquent and anti-social behaviours eventually cease this sort of behaviour while others do not. What psychological factors distinguish those who are resilient against further delinquency from those who persist? The study was conducted among 365 Belgian teenagers of different ages in five institutions.

Firstly, girls were found to be more resilient than boys. Resilient youth were also described as more mature, less aggressive and more easily able to adapt to a number of social constraints. They also found it easier than those who persisted with delinquency to establish 'steady' relationships with adults. Although there were some age differences, the best prognosis for not continuing with unacceptable behaviours was found to be certain personal resources and self-control. Thus, they were not labelled as psychopathological, and tended to have fewer family and personal problems than those who persisted with delinquency.

Scholte found among Dutch respondents that many delinquent adolescents ceased their unacceptable behaviour as adults. Of those who continued with delinquent behaviour into adulthood, the best predictors were the seriousness of delinquent acts performed as a teenager. Additional predictors were a combination of 'restrictive and cool' parenting styles, that is, the perception that parents were too controlling as well as perceptions of low levels of parental support during the adolescent years.

members) is defined in terms of their delinquent acts such that the members of the group act in ways that fit with their collective self-esteem (Emler and Reicher, 1995).

Delinquent groups fulfill several important functions for the individual. From Table 9.3 it is clear that these functions vary widely, and that some (for instance, behavioural norms) encompass what is referred to as 'peer pressure'. According to Emler and Reicher (1995) these functions are the driving force behind delinquent acts. This view, therefore, is a direct challenge to the view that delinquency is shaped by personality. The authors explain their position as follows (Emler and Reicher, 1995, 219):

TABLE 9.3   *The functions of delinquent groups*

Function	Description
Companionship	Members share activities; do things together.
Anonymity	Inter-member variation in the group is reduced; personal identity merges with group identity; members can lose themselves within the group and avoid detection by authorities.
Reputation management	Individuals behave in such a way that their particular reputation is maintained.
Behavioural norms	Certain behaviours only are acceptable. The behaviours reflect the values and beliefs of the group.
Security	The group provides a safe base for the individual.

Source: Emler and Reicher, 1995

this approach stands in stark contrast to traditional psychological explanations of individual differences. For us, such approaches – based on the notion that delinquent action is the reflection of some chronic internal deficit – suffer both from errors of omission and commission . . . we have challenged the notion that only internal psychological control stands between order and anarchy'.

There is empirical support for the views of Emler and Reicher (1995). In a recent investigation, Heaven and his colleagues constructed measures of delinquent companionship and behavioural norms. These have demonstrated validity and are clearly distinguishable from delinquency items (Heaven et al., 2000). Of the personality factors P, E, and N, P was the only significant predictor of delinquency among a sample of school students. However, companionship and behavioural norms explained significant amounts of additional variance beyond that explained by P.

THEORETICAL CONSIDERATIONS

It is clear that several theories contribute to an understanding of orientation to authority and delinquency: social learning, biological and Erikson's psychoanalytic view.

In the first instance, there is evidence that children who engage in anti-social, aggressive and delinquent behaviours learn to do so by observing others. This may occur through the medium of television, or by watching and experiencing particular behaviour patterns in the home. According to this view, some children are socialised to be aggressive and are taught by family members to respond to others in a coercive manner. Very often in such homes, violent and anti-social behaviour is a prerequisite for survival.

Finally, it is probably true that biological and heredity factors mediate the effects of learning and identity formation as just mentioned. These mediating effects vary, of course, from individual to individual, reflecting different social experiences, individual differences, polygenic influences and concentrations of hormones.

SUMMARY

It is possible to distinguish between general orientation to authority and delinquency among adolescents. In the former, researchers have studied general attitudes and behavioural orientation. In the latter, most studies have focused on self-reported delinquency.

This chapter noted several major theoretical perspectives on juvenile delinquency. These range from genetic/biological approaches, to social learning. As noted in the previous section, each of these approaches appears intuitively sensible, and is supported by empirical findings. The challenge for future researchers is to illustrate the links that exist between these approaches, and the extent to which some factors mediate the effects of others in explaining delinquency.

Of concern to community leaders, parents and educators must be the fact that young people under the age of twenty make up a disproportionate number of arrests for serious offences such as vehicle theft, burglary, robbery and forcible rape. What is to be done? Is it sufficient to argue, for example, that hormonal influences are causative and that there is not much one can do about it? Clearly not. Although such biological factors are important, there are policy implications here which governments and community leaders must address. There can be no doubt that social factors such as high youth unemployment, the availability of drugs, and family disruption and violence must be considered and also acted upon.

ADDITIONAL READING

Emler, N. and Reicher, S. (1995) *Adolescence and Delinquency*. Oxford: Blackwell.
Eysenck, H. and Gudjonsson, G. (1989) *The Causes and Cures of Criminality*. New York: Plenum.
West, D. (1967) *The Young Offender*. Harmondsworth: Penguin.

EXERCISE

1 Most research to date on the correlates of delinquency has been cross-sectional in nature. Devise a longitudinal study of the psychosocial predict-ors of self-reported delinquency. Find a suitable measure of the dependent variable. Include the following independent measures: family-related attitudes and personality factors. Select several measures and explain the rationale for their inclusion. Provide details of a sampling frame and time lapse between Testing 1 and Testing 2. What statistical analyses would need to be conducted?

10

The Working Adolescent

INTRODUCTION

An important developmental task during adolescence is identity achievement. Although this is a process that extends beyond the bounds of that period of the life span referred to as 'adolescence', it is during the teenage years that the individual should develop a sense of personal identity as opposed to role confusion and identity diffusion (see Chapter 2). It is conceivable that this important process is facilitated, particularly in late adolescence, by the development of a vocational identity. Selecting a vocation, or embarking on a course of study with a particular career in mind is an important part of a developing sense of self. Having a job that is perceived to be worthwhile and valued by society, and doing that job well, enhances personal self-esteem (Feather, 1990; Prause and Dooley, 1997).

There has been a remarkable change in the employment opportunities of youth over recent decades. It is no longer reasonable to assume that a teenager, upon leaving school, will automatically find employment to match his or her ability and interests. Economic circumstances and with that, job prospects, are constantly changing. There is talk of 'restructuring', of becoming more efficient and effective, of 'old' and 'new' economies. Some, but not all countries, have relatively high youth unemployment rates. In 1993 the youth unemployment rates in Ireland and Spain were over 19 per cent, 10.8 per cent in the UK, but only 5.9 per cent in the Netherlands (Winefield, 1997). Some governments face budgetary crises, with the result that they are unable (or unwilling) to spend vast sums of money on job creation and retraining schemes for youth.

At the same time, new employment prospects for youth have appeared. Think for a moment of the many new job prospects in information technology, financial services, the hospitality industry, human services, and management. Occupations are less sex-stereotyped than they were a few decades ago. At school, girls are being encouraged to study mathematics and science which has led more females to embark on careers that were once regarded as 'male'. More females are graduating as medical doctors, engineers and lawyers, while it is no longer uncommon to find male nurses and social workers. More females are now involved in local and national government. These changes in societal attitudes and expectations have therefore opened up new employment and career opportunities for teenagers.

Important questions that intrigue psychologists include how individuals come to hold certain attitudes and beliefs about work and money, what their attitudes are to work, and how they go about looking for work. Other questions include how adolescents cope with unemployment and how they spend their leisure time. These and other issues will be dealt with in this chapter.

LEARNING ABOUT WORK AND MONEY

Developmental Changes

Individuals go through various stages of vocational identity formation (Ginzberg, 1972; Holland, 1976). Beginning in childhood, vocational preference passes from the *fantasy period* to the *tentative period* during pre-adolescence, and on to the *realistic period* with late adolescence. During the fantasy period vocational preference is characterised by the exciting aspects of a job. Appearing on the cover of a glossy magazine or walking on the moon may appeal to some. During preadolescence the individual is discovering new interests, values and personal capacities, resulting in changed vocational preferences.

Individual beliefs and values are constantly being reformulated so that by the time the teenager is in late adolescence, much clearer ideas have been formed. Around this time, the late adolescent has specific and crystallised ideas about his or her interests and capabilities and will attempt to integrate these into a self-concept. In other words, ideas about a future vocation are very much a reflection of the adolescent's interests and personal values. Late adolescents looking for a job or embarking on post-school study usually select vocations or courses of study consistent with their self-esteem and world view (Holland, 1976; see also pp. 239–40).

As with the development of a vocational identity, children go through developmental stages as they learn about money. Various studies with different groups of children have found that, when quite young (around 4–6 years), children have very little understanding of monetary affairs.

By the time they enter adolescence (about 11 years), however, children come to understand that one needs money to buy goods. Soon after (about 12 years), young adolescents realise that financial dishonesty and cheating are possible (Stacey, 1982).

It would seem that most research into how ideas about economic matters develop, suggest that children's beliefs proceed through various stages. Although stage approaches are useful, they ignore the following important influences (Furnham and Argyle, 1998):

* social class – according to this view economic knowledge is not separate from our social world;
* the existence of social class differences brings about ensuing differences in our work beliefs.

We shall return to the role of social class later.

Acquiring Beliefs about Work and Money

The career a teenager will ultimately decide upon, as well as personal attitudes toward work and money, are shaped by many factors, including intelligence, personal values and beliefs, and social class (Holland, 1976; Little, 1967). In addition, factors like attitudes, values and class are closely bound up with one's experiences *within* the family. Not surprisingly, therefore, many writers are united in their view that the family is an important socialising force determining how adolescents learn about work and money. Like so many other attitudes and values, it is within the family context that adolescents acquire the work ethic and various other work-related beliefs. As Barling and his colleagues put it (1991, 725): 'There are now empirical data available to support the notion that family socialization plays a significant role in the formation of children and adolescents' occupational aspirations and expectations.'

By and large, children (especially males) tend to adopt similar careers to their fathers, while occupationally successful parents tend to have children who also achieve occupational success (Barling, Kelloway and Bremermann, 1991). Children are influenced by their parents' perceptions of employment and they assign similar importance to job rewards as do their parents. This supports the view that the family is an important context in which socialisation occurs and in which children learn about the world (see also Galambos and Sears, 1998).

Others echo this line of thought. In a review of work ethic beliefs, Furnham (1990) discusses the important role that parenting style and attitudes play in shaping the personality and work attitudes of their children. As discussed in Chapter 3, one's personality is, in part, a product of parenting style as well as the nature of communication between parent and child. Furnham proposes that a warm, caring and nurturing family environment is likely to result in children who are internally controlled: that is, those who believe that what happens to them is largely due to their own efforts. By contrast, inconsistent parental discipline is likely to result in children with an external locus of control who view the world as an unpredictable place. Research evidence demonstrates a link between personality and one's level of achievement, motivation and beliefs regarding the work ethic. Indeed, those with an internal locus of control are likely to work harder at both intellectual and performance tasks. So-called internals are also likely to endorse work ethic beliefs to a greater degree than so-called externals. They are also likely to score higher than externals on measures of job satisfaction and motivation (Feather, 1983; Furnham, Sadka and Brewin, 1992).

Several other studies have documented the important role that parents play in a child's early encounters with economic principles. It is clear from such studies that the influence of adults is varied and far-reaching. Research in Britain has examined the perceptions that adults have of pocket money or allowances received by children (Furnham, 1999a; Furnham and Thomas, 1984). It has been found that mothers are more inclined to believe that children should work for their pocket money or allowance. They are also quite willing to negotiate with children about appropriate 'rates of pay'. Some interesting class differences are also evident: Furnham found that more middle-class than working-class adults were in favour of giving children pocket money by eight years of age, while some working-class adults disapproved of the idea completely (Furnham and Thomas, 1984).

Subsequent research found that older, middle-class adults supported the idea that pocket money should be given for chores completed, while younger working-class parents were in favour of children saving a fixed portion of their allowance (Furnham, 1999a). It was also found that parents from high social class backgrounds were in favour of 'forward planning', while older parents were not in favour of children being autonomous in spending their money. Finally, females and high social class parents favoured budgeting.

These results point to the important and different ways by which children learn about money within the family context. Some may learn that pocket money is a right that should be received automatically, while others may be taught that money is received for work done around the house. Either way, parents appear to be an important agent in this learning process, transmitting their beliefs and values to the child. As Furnham (1990, 117) noted: 'This research shows...how adults teach their children about money, the virtues of thrift and saving... There seems to be sufficient evidence that parents with PWE (Protestant work ethic) beliefs stress the importance of postponement of gratification and saving; the planning of the use of money; and that money has to be earned.'

It is not unreasonable to assume that family socialisation predicts adolescent attitudes towards a wide variety of work-related beliefs. Canadian researchers were interested in whether one could predict adolescent attitudes towards trade unions on the basis of two family-related matters: adolescents' perceptions of the union activities of their parents and their perceptions of parental attitudes towards unions (Barling et al., 1991).

The results showed that adolescent perceptions of parental attitudes to unions were closely linked to their own union attitudes, although there was no significant link between adolescent perceptions of parental union *activity*, and their own attitudes. The authors concluded that parents are important in transmitting work-related beliefs to their children. As they found, the perceptions that adolescents have of their family vis-à-vis the world of work and employment are important in shaping their *own* views about such matters. The family is therefore a strong socialising agent transmitting a range of attitudes and beliefs, including economic ones, to the adolescent.

Family Transitions and Adolescent Work Values

As we noted in Chapter 3, the break-up of the original family unit has become reasonably wide-spread. Not surprisingly, many studies have examined the effects of family disruption and single parenthood on the work goals and values of adolescents in such families. Rather than adopt a *crisis* perspective (see also Chapter 3), Barber and Eccles (1992) recommend that researchers focus instead on the *processes* of functioning in new (blended as well as single-parent) families.

Adolescents in single-mother households can have their work goals and aspirations shaped in a variety of different ways. Although most single mothers *have* to work, evidence suggests that maternal employment per se is not detrimental to adolescent identity formation or their emotional adjustment (Duckett and Richards, 1995). Rather, a wide range of factors such as income, mother's attitude to work, family stress, age and sex of

RESEARCH HIGHLIGHT 10.1
What are the characteristics of a good job?
Hagstrom and Gamberale, 1995

Teenagers have quite clearly developed ideas of what makes a job worthwhile. Swedish school students were asked to rate how important different features of a job would be to them. Those factors deemed important were:

- interesting work;
- friendly workmates;
- work recognition and appreciation;
- good physical environment.

Factors thought to be less important for these respondents were:

- good relationship with immediate supervisor;
- independent work;
- flexible working hours;
- no stress or rush.

adolescent need to be considered. For example, there is now abundant evidence showing a great similarity between the occupational plans and values of males and females in late adolescence, with many more females entering high-status occupations. Yet many males and females still make gender-typed occupational decisions (Barber and Eccles, 1992). It would seem, however, that adolescent males and females in single-mother households are *less* likely to consider traditional occupations. Studies have found that in many instances, girls in single-mother households are unlikely to find investing time and energy in the family sphere attractive preferring, instead, the investment of time in the occupational sphere. Those who do consider marital roles are much more likely to ensure that they are not financially dependent on their husbands.

Single mothers are often over-committed in the workplace, and this has important effects on adolescent adjustment and work aspirations (Barber and Eccles, 1992). Although the effects of such over-commitment may sometimes be negative, evidence shows it is possible that financial rewards may offset some of the negative aspects of being in full-time work. Of importance, too, is the role model that the mother presents as an employed woman. Women in non-traditional jobs are more likely to have daughters who aspire to similar careers. In addition, if the single mother has a positive attitude to her work and successfully integrates her occupational and family commitments, this is likely to have positive effects on her daughter's occupational identity formation. Thus, in homes where family disruption has occurred, adolescent work values and aspirations are closely linked to maternal employment, and expectations, gender role values pertaining to work and the family and the adolescent's self-concept (Barber and Eccles, 1992). Work values are therefore determined by a complex web of family influences.

ATTITUDES TO WORK AND MONEY MATTERS

Cross-cultural Studies

Not only does the family help shape work-related attitudes, there are also important cultural differences (for example, Lau et al., 2000; Lynn, Yamauchi and Tachibana, 1991; Vondracek et al., 1990). For instance, there are striking differences in this regard between British and American adolescents, such that the Americans, more than the British, are in favour of hard work and competitiveness (Furnham, 1987).

Lynn and his colleagues (1991) compared attitudes to work among British and Japanese students in late adolescence. They argued that there are different cultural motivations for work effort, and that such differences may be linked to national differences in economic growth. In order to examine these questions, adolescents completed measures of work and family orientation, achievement motivation, savings, money beliefs and career preferences. Noticeable differences were observed between the groups. In the first instance, males in both samples scored higher on the competitiveness and money beliefs measure than did females. Secondly, among the British sample, there was a significant link between achievement motivation, academic achievement, occupational preference and actual achievement. Among the Japanese students, however, high competitiveness motivation was significantly related to money beliefs. The authors suggested that this higher competitive spirit among Japanese youth may be a reflection of higher economic growth rates for that country.

Do Hong Kong and American students differ in their explanations for work success? It would seem so, based on the views of a rather small

TABLE 10.1   *British adolescents' perceptions of a satisfying job*

Criterion	Respondents agreeing
Job security	72
Satisfying work	62
Good working conditions	61
Pleasant work colleagues	56
Opportunities for career development	53
High starting salary	39
A lot of responsibility	25
Short working hours	22

Source: Furnham and Gunter, 1989

sample of school students who were recently assessed (Lau et al., 2000). Hong Kong students attributed success to increased work effort and interest, a desire to 'defeat and con' others, better intelligence, as well as luck and wealth. Although Americans were found to score lower on 'defeating' others, they were much more likely to view school as a place where one acquires critical and independent thinking.

Within-cultural Differences

Not only are there cross-cultural differences regarding work beliefs, but there are also demonstrable *within* cultural differences. In an extensive report of the general social attitudes of almost 2000 British adolescents, Furnham and Gunter (1989) found important *age differences* in adolescents' views about the characteristics of a satisfying job. Older adolescents (who were much more likely to be employed) were more in favour of the intrinsic features of work than were younger ones. For instance, only 23 per cent of 17-year-olds rated a 'high starting salary' as very important, compared with 44 per cent of those aged 10–14 years. By contrast, 64 per cent of 17-year-olds thought having pleasant people to work with was very important, compared with only 47 per cent of 10–14 year-olds (see also Research Highlight 10.1). As adolescents mature cognitively and socially and have experience of being in the workforce, they learn to appreciate the intrinsic rather than extrinsic features of work.

Adolescents of different political persuasion hold different views about economic matters, such as public expenditure. Differences have been observed between adolescent supporters of the British Labour and Conservative parties (Furnham, 1987). It was found that Labour voters were much more in favour of government involvement in social welfare than were Conservative ones. Adolescents also have a clear idea of the differences *between* political groups. In the cited British study, teenagers judged the British Labour Party to spend more on housing, health and welfare and education, while the Conservative Party was judged to spend more on trade and industry and defence.

In conclusion, it is clear that, at a relatively young age, individuals are able to make judgements about the value of work and the conditions necessary to promote job satisfaction. They are also able to judge the public expenditure policies of political parties, no doubt reflecting their personal ideology, political allegiances and general social beliefs.

ADOLESCENTS AT WORK

Job Search Strategies

Given the pressures on young people to find a job and become more independent of family, one can assume that they have a clear idea of the job options available to them, as well as the strategies that might assist them in getting their first full-time job. For example, some might believe that a university education would enhance their chances of gaining long-term employment, while others might consider an apprenticeship more beneficial. Still more might believe that it is best to leave school early if and when a job becomes available.

Furnham (1984) assessed the job-search strategies of over 200 students from different schools in London. It was found that males placed more emphasis on their written applications, while females seemed to prefer a more personal approach, such as visiting companies, gaining experience and so on. Some strategies were preferred by middle-class rather than working-class youth: middle-class youth were more inclined than working-class youth to place a job advertisement in the newspaper, to study information trends and to register with a private employment service.

A similar study was conducted among Australian school students (Heaven, 1995). Teenagers discriminated among 'self-effort' and 'external' job-search strategies. Whereas the former relate to such behaviours as going for job interview training, external strategies refer to such behaviours as registering with unemployment agencies. It was also found that endorsement of self-effort strategies was strongly negatively associated with external attributions for unemployment and positively associated with perceived job value (see also Table 10.2).

TABLE 10.2   *Job-search strategies of Australian school students*

Job-search strategies fall into two groups:
1   Self-effort strategies
     (for example, 'writing a letter of enquiry'; 'taking job interview training').
2   External strategies
     (for example, 'registering with the state employment service'; 'taking a public service exam').

Source: Heaven, 1995

What strategies do unemployed youth use to find work? This question was studied from the perspective of *expectancy-valence theory* (Feather and O'Brien, 1987). It was argued that the actions we perform result in positive or negative outcomes, and that we are more motivated to perform actions we believe would have a favourable outcome. Thus, if an unemployed person *strongly desires* employment, he or she will engage in all sorts of job search strategies in order to secure it. More work-shy individuals, on the other hand, are less likely to be motivated to find work.

The authors found partial support for this view. Although they did not find job-seeking behaviour to be positively related to feelings of optimism and personal control, they did find search strategies to be significantly related to dissatisfaction with unemployment and a desire to find work. Another study found that the stronger the desire for work among youth, the greater the depressive affect among those who could not find employment (Feather and Davenport, 1981). Thus it would seem that job search strategies are partly guided by one's personal motivations and expectations about finding a job, as well as one's beliefs about the value of work. Job search behaviours therefore take on a unique quality, depending on the individual's desire and motivation to find work.

Saving and Spending Patterns

It is well known that the purchasing power of adolescents has increased dramatically over recent years. Magazines, dance music, concerts and clothes for teenagers are big business. Beyond this, however, little is known about the personal characteristics associated with adolescent spending and saving.

One research project involved a large-scale survey of over 1500 school students in part-time employment in the USA (Pritchard, Myers and Cassidy, 1989). The research team was interested in the saving and spending habits of adolescents, as well as the extent to which such behaviours were associated with individual and family factors. It was found that many adolescents spent their money on discretionary items, such as clothes or entertainment. Most of those who were heavy savers tended to be white females who usually worked hard at school, planned further study, and were internally controlled. Those who spent their money on necessities (for instance, school books) tended to be female black state school students. Perhaps surprisingly, they also tended to be externally controlled and do less well at school, while working longer hours each week for less money. Not surprisingly, those who spent their money on necessities usually came from families with fewer economic resources.

Furnham (1999b) conducted a similar, but smaller study among British youth. More than 80 per cent of respondents reported receiving a regular source of income. There were several sex and age differences:

- males reported receiving more weekly pocket money,
- males earned more from odd-jobs,
- males received more money than females at Christmas.

Older children received more money

- than younger children each week,
- at Christmas and birthdays,
- than younger children for odd jobs.

Social Relations in the Workplace

What do working adolescents learn *about* work? Some scientists have studied what working adolescents learn about authority in the workplace, how work is organised and whether adolescents' work-related attitudes are a function of certain personal factors, such as social class. It has been suggested that work accelerates adolescents' development of social sensitivity (perspective-taking), social insightfulness (understanding interpersonal processes) and social communication (manipulating others to achieve a goal).

It has been found that girls from different social backgrounds differ in their attitudes towards management, and that they have different strategies for dealing with work-related problems (Haaken and Korschgen, 1988). Table 10.3 shows in one study that, when interacting with managers, female teenagers adopted a variety of possible strategies depending on their social background. Working-class females tended to focus on

TABLE 10.3   *Perceptions of social relations in the workplace among female teenagers*

Interactions with managers
- Positive or idealised: for example, forming positive attachments to manager[1]
- Functionally congenial: for example, forming good working relationship with manager[1]
- Avoidant or critical: for example, trying to maintain distance, focusing on conflictual relations with managers[2]

Coping with workplace problems
- Resistance: individual or group defiance[2]
- Communicate with management: communicating directly with management[1]
- Endure: passive resignation in dealing with workplace conflict[2]

Note: 1 generally characteristic of middle-class workers
2 generally characteristic of working-class workers
Source: Haaken and Korschgen, 1988

maintaining their *distance* from management as well as on *conflictual relations* with it. In coping with workplace problems middle-class girls were much more likely to *communicate* with management about their problems.

These findings suggest that working teenage girls from different social class backgrounds perceive management differently, as reflected in their relations with those in authority. Working-class girls, it seems, perceive greater social distance between themselves and management than do middle-class ones. Moreover, this greater social distance also has implications for conflict resolution. Finally, one must bear in mind that it is not clear to what extent these results can be generalised to teenagers of both sexes in a variety of occupational settings, or to teenagers in other cultures. Further research is necessary to examine these effects.

Work and Stress

More and more school students are working part time. According to one report about 80 per cent of graduating high-school students in North America at some stage have had a part-time job (Barling, Rogers and Kelloway, 1995). Concern has been expressed as to what the outcomes may be for teenagers' well being (Frone, 1998; Haaken and Korschgen, 1988). One line of thought, for instance, argues that adolescents need experience of the adult world and that work in general accelerates the developmental process towards adulthood (for example, Heyneman,

RESEARCH HIGHLIGHT 10.2
Predicting when teenagers will experience work injuries
Frone, 1998

How likely is it that teenagers will experience a work injury? This is an important question especially in light of the increasing numbers of young people who are now employed. Frone conducted such a study among a sample of over 3000 16- to 19-year-olds in the USA. The following factors showed significant associations ($p < .01$) with work injuries:

- male gender

- no. of hours worked per wk
- workload
- co-worker conflict
- job dissatisfaction
- somatic symptoms (for example, headaches)

- negative affect (for example, negative moods)
- physical hazards
- conflict with supervisors
- work–school conflict
- depression
- on-the-job substance use

1976). Other writers have voiced concerns about youth employment, pointing to low wages, stressful jobs and poor working conditions (for example, Steinberg, 1982). Some have noted a link between work stress and increased use of alcohol and cigarettes among youth (Manzi, 1986). Yet others have assessed the impact of poor quality employment (for example, Barling et al., 1995). Another line of thought is that working facilitates the development of teenagers' personal responsibility but not their social responsibility. It has been suggested that working may impede family, peer, and school commitments, and increase the development of cynical work-related attitudes among youth (Steinberg et al., 1982).

In Table 10.4 are summarised some of the perceived effects on adolescents of part-time work. The proposed negative effects, it should be stressed, are particularly salient for those teenagers who work quite long hours every week (15–20 hours or more).

Most teenagers in part-time work are generally in lower-status jobs, in which employees are allowed little autonomy and initiative (Greenberger, Steinberg and Vaux, 1981). As the link between low status work, stress and adverse health outcomes among adults is well established (for example, Dohrenwend and Dohrenwend, 1974), it could be argued that

TABLE 10.4   *Hypothesised effects on adolescents of part-time work*

Positive outcomes
Enhance education
Facilitate socialisation
Ease entry into full-time employment
Learn about job finding
Learn about yourself
Learn about the world of work
Help prepare for adult roles
Learn about survival in the real world

Negative outcomes
Low wages
Stressful job
Poor working conditions
Possible alcohol and drug use
Impedes school commitment and performance
Impedes extracurricular activities
Little formal instruction by supervisors
Much time devoted to low-level types of jobs
Develop cynical attitudes towards work
No long-term impact on educational and vocational plans

Source: Manzi, 1986; Steinberg, 1982; Steinberg et al., 1982

a similar association exists among teenage workers. There are two possible reasons for this. In the first place, the work itself may be dull and boring, which could lead to frustration and increased general stress. Secondly, it is possible that part-time work may interfere with family and school commitments, may be a major constraint on an adolescent's freedom, and might possibly exacerbate the usual crises of development faced by most adolescents. These sentiments have been echoed by Greenberger and colleagues (1981, 693) who suggested that:

> we would expect that work that permits little autonomy, allows little initiative, provides no sense of purpose ... would be especially stressful for adolescents ... [and] they may have special salience for individuals at a developmental stage in which crises over autonomy, identity, intimacy, and achievement are normative.

Barling and colleagues (1995) have warned against focusing only on the number of hours worked per week. They suggested (and found) that the quality of work performed moderated the negative effects of number of hours worked per week. Indeed, the number of hours worked predicted positive self-esteem when job autonomy and role clarity were high.

TABLE 10.5   *Examples of adolescents' coping strategies in the workplace*

Problem-focused
Take things one step at a time
Concentrate on what you have to do (the next step)
Knowing what has to be done and doubling your efforts
Talking to someone to find out more about the problem
Coming up with a couple of different solutions

Emotion-focused
Maintaining pride and keeping a stiff upper lip
Wishing you could change what happened
Wishing the situation could go away or somehow be over with
Do not let it get to you; don't think about it too much
Try to look on the bright side of things; try to find good in the situation

---

Source: Manzi, 1986

They concluded as follows (Barling et al., 1995, 153): 'Our findings show that the importance of employment quality extends to teenagers employed on a part-time basis . . . the findings suggest the importance of providing teenagers with jobs that have clearly defined and non-conflicting roles, and that provide opportunities for autonomy and skill variety.'

Future research needs to address the question of just what intervention strategies can be employed to assist adolescents at school, who *have* to work part-time, cope with the pressures of employment. Future studies should also examine the long-term effects of heightened parental-adolescent disagreements in those families where teenagers are employed.

Coping with work stress

Teenagers develop a variety of coping mechanisms to deal with work-induced stress. Some use problem-focused strategies, such as coming up with solutions to the problem. Others use emotion-focused ones, such as trying to maintain pride, while some use a combination of the two (Manzi, 1986). Examples of some of these mechanisms, which were found in a small sample of adolescents in part-time employment, are shown in Table 10.5.

THE EFFECTS OF UNEMPLOYMENT

The psychological effect of unemployment on the adjustment of youth is an area that has generated considerable research. Perhaps this is due to the fact that unemployment is firmly on the political agenda in many countries. It might also be due to the fact that increases in unemployment have fallen disproportionately on those in late adolescence (Banks and Ullah, 1988). As Winefield (1997) has suggested, high youth unemployment is a serious social problem for the following reasons:

- the youth unemployment rate is much higher than that for other age groups,
- youth unemployment will have a negative impact on the psychosocial development of young people,
- widespread youth unemployment may have other serious side effects such as heightened criminality and drug use,
- widespread youth unemployment may be linked to heightened youth suicide.

Psychological Effects

How likely is it that the experience of unemployment will lead to poor psychological adjustment among youth? It has been argued that finding one's first job is an important developmental task, and therefore highly valued in our society. Thus, it is not unreasonable to expect negative psychological consequences following unemployment, even among teenagers (Feather, 1990). Indeed, this appears to be the case.

Based on their interviews with unemployed youth, Hammarstrom and Janlert (1997) found the following consequences on unemployment:

- low self confidence and feelings of worthlessness,
- depression, passivity and lethargy,
- irritableness, quarrelsomeness and impatience,
- weight gain,
- self-blame.

The results of longitudinal research over relatively short periods of up to twelve months suggest that not being able to find a job after school has a detrimental effect on perceptions of the family by the adolescent and parents (Patton and Noller, 1991). As well, there are negative effects on the unemployed's self-esteem, work ethic, mood, locus of control, stress symptoms, depressive affect, life satisfaction, attributions for unemployment and self-competence (for example, Feather, 1990; Patton and Noller, 1984; Tiggemann and Winefield, 1984). It has also been found that reductions in levels of psychological health are due to the *experience* of unemployment (Patton and Noller, 1984). It is as though not being able to find a job, irrespective of length of unemployment, indicates to youth that society regards them as less than worthy. This may lead to a lowering of self-esteem.

Longitudinal studies conducted over longer periods endorse the view that the employed become better adjusted, while the unemployed actually show little deterioration in mental health. In one study, for example, adolescents were surveyed in school and again after intervals of two and three years (Winefield and Tiggemann, 1990a). Although those who had never been employed had lower self-esteem than the group who had never been unemployed, the unemployed's level of self-esteem had not actually deteriorated. Indeed, other groups (those who had never been unemployed and those who found employment *after* a period of unemployment), showed quite large increases in their levels of self-esteem. Thus the employed seem to become psychologically 'healthier'. Winefield and colleagues (1993) concluded as follows (70):

> Our results suggest that young people who are employed in jobs that they regard as satisfactory are better off in terms of their psychological well-being than other members of the workforce because they gain a positive advantage through their employment status. By contrast, those young people who are either employed in jobs they regard as unsatisfactory, or who are unemployed, are relatively disadvantaged by comparison. Their relative disadvantage, however, comes about not because they suffer a deterioration in well-being on leaving school and entering the workforce, but because they are denied the benefits of satisfactory employment.

Not only are there changes in personality functioning among the employed, but changes have also been observed in their attitudes and perceptions. For example, those who are employed are less likely to blame unemployment on external factors such as economic recession. Those who become unemployed, however, are more likely to see such external factors as important causes of their own unemployment. Research findings suggest that becoming employed is likely to increase the likelihood that those in work will see the unemployed as lacking in important individual characteristics, such as personal motivation (Feather, 1990). In summary, therefore, it would appear that the experience of being in employment, or not, is associated with shifts in personality functioning and attitude.

Length of Unemployment

Length of unemployment influences youth in a number of ways. It is now clear, for instance, that as the frequency of unsuccessful job appli-

RESEARCH HIGHLIGHT 10.3
The psychological consequences of unemployment
Hannan, Oriain and Whelan, 1997

This study was conducted in Northern Ireland among school leavers five years after graduating from school. As was expected, more unemployed than employed school leavers were found to suffer psychological distress as measured by the General Health Questionnaire (GHQ) as were those from manual compared with non-manual backgrounds. The unemployed were more likely to attribute their current situation to external structural factors, while the employed viewed their situation as being due to personal factors. Of those unemployed youth making structural attributions, just over one in three suffered psychological distress. By contrast, the rate of psychological distress was less than one in ten among the employed who made structural attributions. The authors therefore concluded that (318) 'Feelings of loss of control and decline in feelings of personal efficacy increase significantly with unemployment, and, when present, significantly increase levels of distress.'

cations increases, so the unemployed person's expectation of finding a job decreases. There is also reduced motivation to find a job, as well as evidence of apathy and resignation as the period of unemployment increases. For some unemployed, prolonged unemployment may also see a shift in attributions. Whereas they might previously have considered external factors to be important causes of their being unemployed, they may later, after lengthy unemployment, endorse negative internal causes ('I'm just not good enough to find a job'; Feather and Davenport, 1981).

Following research with adult British samples, a curvilinear hypothesis was proposed with respect to mental health and duration of unemployment (Warr and Jackson, 1987). It was suggested that psychological distress increases for some months after job loss, before declining. Not all evidence supports this view, however. One longitudinal study (Winefield and Tiggemann, 1990b) followed a group of unemployed adolescents (aged 16–20 years) in Australia into young adulthood (19–24 years) and examined their self-esteem, negative mood, depressive affect and locus of control. The groups did not differ on self-esteem at Time 2, although results showed that depressive affect, negative mood and external locus of control increased as length of unemployment did. As the results differ from those obtained on adult samples, it could be that the psychological effects of unemployment are different for individuals in adolescence and adulthood. One explanation might be that there is greater pressure on young adults than on teenagers to find a job. Hence, the longer the period of unemployment, the greater the psychological distress (Winefield et al., 1993).

Unemployment vs. Poor Quality Employment

Do all forms of employment promote mental health among adolescents? Is poor quality work a suitable substitute for unemployment? Several research studies have examined the effects of poor quality employment on psychological adjustment among youth. These suggest that jobs which do not utilise an adolescent's skills and talents and which do not provide variety and opportunity, will lead to a reduction in job satisfaction and increased stress (Prause and Dooley, 1997; see also previous section on work stress).

Several longitudinal studies have been conducted to examine this issue (for example, O'Brien and Feather, 1990; Prause and Dooley, 1997; Winefield, Tiggemann and Winefield, 1991; Winefield et al., 1991). For instance, Winefield and his associates first interviewed respondents who were at school (Time 1) and then again seven and eight years later (Time 2). The respondents were divided into four separate groups, namely, satisfied employed, dissatisfied employed, unemployed and university students. Four psychological measures were administered at Time 1 and,Time 2: self-esteem, depressive affect, locus of control and negative mood.

As no significant differences were observed between the groups on the psychological measures at Time 1, the authors concluded that differences observed at Time 2 were due to the effects of employment status. The authors detected some important trends at Time 2. In the first instance, self-esteem among all groups showed an increase over the period, while externality in locus of control showed some decline. It was also found that the unemployed and dissatisfied employed groups performed less well than other groups on the remaining personality measures. Unemployed males exhibited higher negative mood and depressive affect than did males who were dissatisfied with their employment. Just the reverse was true for females, however. Thus one may conclude that being unemployed or in unsatisfactory employment has different effects on morale for males and females. This might be due to different pressures placed by society on men and women to find employment (Winefield et al., 1991).

Similar results were obtained by Prause and Dooley (1997) in the USA. They tracked over 3000 adolescents for seven years and found that the underemployed had lower self-esteem than the employed, after controlling for such factors as job satisfaction, age, and socio-economic status. Not surprisingly, the under-employed also expressed less job satisfaction than did the employed. What, then, are some of the broader implications of poor quality employment and under-employment? Prause and Dooley (1997, 257) concluded as follows: 'increased underemployment resulting from this ongoing economic restructuring is harmful to young workers' self-esteem and may, by extrapolation, threaten harm to older workers as well ... these findings signal a need for societal attention to the levels of underemployment on a par with the attention given to monitoring traditional unemployment levels'.

PERSONALITY AND WORK

Is it possible that certain personality types are best suited for a particular job? Is there a personality–job fit? Holland (1973) proposed the following personality–job links:

- realistic – practical career requiring few social skills (for example, farming);
- intellectual – career requiring abstract thinking (for example, a scientist);
- social – career using verbal and interpersonal relations (for example, teaching);
- conventional – career consisting of structured activities (for example, a bank teller);
- enterprising – career using verbal persuasion and leadership (for example, politics);
- artistic – career that is self-expressive (for example, writing).

Not only is personality related to certain occupational types, but has also been found to be associated with various aspects of work motivation, productivity, satisfaction, and work-related problems such as absenteeism and stress. Since it is beyond the scope of this chapter to discuss these aspects in detail, interested readers should consult more in-depth sources, like Furnham (1992). It is perhaps useful to note the following examples:

One personality trait that has important implications for job-related attitudes is locus of control. Differences in attitude and behaviour have been observed between those who are internally and externally controlled. 'Internals' have been shown to be more flexible in their career planning. They also work much harder, and are more motivated than 'externals' to get better jobs.

A British study (Bonnett and Furnham 1991) examined the personality correlates of adolescent entrepreneurs who were aged 16–19 years. As predicted, those who made the effort to get involved in an entrepreneurial venture scored higher than a control group on internal locus of control and belief in the Protestant work ethic. These results support the view that a link exists between effort (work ethic and internality) and outcome (entrepreneurial venture).

LEISURE

The study of leisure activities during the adolescent years is important for several reasons. In the first place, the number of youth in full-time or part-time employment has grown quite substantially over the last twenty to thirty years. Thus, it is important that these young people balance their working life with quality leisure time. Secondly, it has also been suggested that adolescence is a period of abundant 'free time' and a time of few responsibilities (Hendry et al., 1993). Thus, adolescents are free to explore a range of different leisure activities of either good quality or activities with little apparent personal or social value. Thirdly, adolescents may choose to participate in leisure activities for personal or social gain, something of direct interest to research psychologists. By studying the leisure activities of young people, we are able to learn something of their social world, whether their interests are being met, and their pace of psychological growth (Garton and Pratt, 1987). As Hendry and colleagues (1993, 35) have explained, 'It is therefore necessary to stress the variability among adolescents in aspiration, motivations, attitudes and in the values they place in their leisure interests and pursuits . . . leisure can be seen as an interaction of underlying influences from within the individual and from the social environment'.

FIGURE 10.1   *Changes in the leisure activities of male respondents aged 13–20 years*

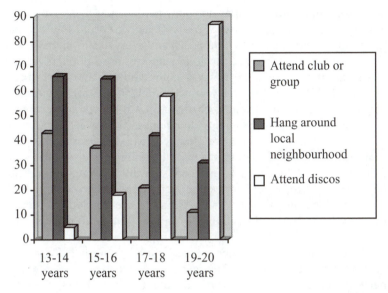

Source: Derived from Hendry et al. (1993)

Not surprisingly, leisure is age-bound (Hendry et al., 1993). It would appear that younger adolescents are much more likely to seek leisure by joining clubs and societies that have been organised by adults. For example, Girl Guides, Cubs, church groups, and soon, are more popular among 10–13 year olds than they are among older teenagers. The picture is more fluid among those in their mid-teens where the emphasis is more on forging heterosexual relations, developing peer relationships, and engaging in what has been referred to as 'casual' activities. By the late teens (about 16 years and older), individuals are more likely to seek their leisure through organised commercial activities such as attending discos, school dances, music activities, watching sports matches, and so on.

Hendry and colleagues (1993) have demonstrated the extent to which the pursuit of various leisure activities changes across the adolescent years. For example, Figure 10.1 shows that, whereas 43 per cent of males aged 13–14 years in one study attended a youth club or group, this figure has dropped to 11 per cent among 19 to 20-year-olds. By contrast, older males are much more likely to attend discos than younger males.

Leisure activities

What sorts of leisure activities do young people engage in? Undoubt-edly, teenagers pursue a wide variety of activities and it is beyond the scope of this chapter to detail each and every one of them. None-theless, it would seem that the following are more popular among a large number of teenagers today (Adams, Gullotta and Markstrom-Adams, 1994): watching television, reading books or magazines, getting together with friends, participating in sports and exercise, listening to music, and playing video games. Moreover, it has been shown that leisure habits have changed over the years. Thus, for example, the proportion of young people reading for leisure declined from 1976 to 1990 (59 to 47 per cent), as did working around the house/yard (41 to 28 per cent). Other activities such as watching tele-vision and getting together with friends have tended to remain constant over this time (about 70 and 50 per cent respectively) (Adams et al., 1994).

The activities that adolescents engage in are important for several reasons. On the one hand, they may be related to very specific and particular behaviours. Those who join reading clubs and chess clubs, for instance, are likely to be different in nature and enjoy other interests than those who join football clubs. Thus, it is possible to predict personality and behaviour on the basis of someone's leisure activities. The following has been suggested regarding two contemporary leisure activities (Adams et al., 1994, 107–11).

Rock music:

- contemporary rock music tells outsiders about what it means to be young,
- listening to too much music has a detrimental effect on school work,
- many music videos generate violent and /or sexual images,
- some music may glorify counter-culture.

Video games:

- video games are played by a large proportion of Westernised youth (up to 90 per cent in the USA and Canada),
- video games are played mainly by males,
- many of these games have a hostile nature.

The Psychological Value of Leisure Pursuits

Leisure activities result in a 'pleasurable state of mind' and give rise to feelings of self-determination and freedom (Gordon and Caltabiano, 1996, 884). Leisure pursuits, therefore, have important implications for one's psychological well-being. Although it is possible to identify different types of leisure activities, they all serve important functions for young people (Gordon and Caltabiano, 1996; Larson, Gillman and Richards, 1991). These include opportunities:

- to explore and seek out their own identity,
- to develop a sense of autonomy,
- to achieve a set of desired end-goals,
- for excitement and alleviation of boredom,
- to develop social interactions and form attachments to peers.

As has been made clear, the adolescent years are a time of changing relationships, beliefs and behaviours and leisure activities provide the avenue to widen one's horizons, explore new options, and develop new friendships. As Gordon and Caltabiano (1996, 884) have put it: 'Via leisure participation, adolescents acquire additional knowledge of the sociocultural environment, practice social and cooperative skills, experience intellectual or physical attainments, and explore a variety of peer, family, and community roles'.

It is possible to distinguish between socially acceptable leisure activities and 'leisure boredom' which is generally associated with deviant activities. The latter arises from the perception of having too much free time and not enough activities to fill that time. Not surprisingly, those adolescents tend to turn to unacceptable behaviours to relieve their boredom. Such behaviours may include smoking, alcohol use, delinquency, and the use of other prohibited substances (Gordon and Caltabiano, 1996). It is noteworthy that many adolescents who feel driven to experiment with deviant behaviours due to boredom, also tend to score higher on measures of sensation-seeking (for example, Stacy, Newcomb and Bentler, 1991). In other words, it is possible that particular personality traits may underpin this sense of 'too much time with nothing to do' which, ultimately, drives the descent into the cycle of deviant behaviours.

The types of leisure activities that adolescents are attracted to have been found to be predictive of other behaviours. Thus, for instance, one study among German adolescents showed that particular leisure pastimes predicted early onset of sexual intercourse (Meschke and Silbereisen, 1997). Early sexual intercourse was more likely to be predicted by social-romantic leisure (e.g. time spent with members of the opposite sex) and risky leisure (for example, engaging in shoplifting, scaring other people). These results suggest that certain leisure activities attract a particular type of individual with particular values and beliefs. Those attracted to risky leisure behaviours are therefore more likely to engage in a wider range of risky behaviours, including early sexual intercourse.

THEORETICAL CONSIDERATIONS

As was noted, finding a worthwhile and satisfying job is one of the most important developmental tasks of adolescence. The outcome of vocational identity formation is shaped by several factors, intrinsic as well as extrinsic. Particular personality traits and personal values are related not only to job motivation and satisfaction, but also to career choice. In addition, there are several extrinsic factors that help shape vocational identity formation. These include the family, and work experiences such as stress and social relations. The formation of a vocational identity is therefore a complex process, and adolescents need as much help as possible in selecting the career that matches their personal beliefs and values.

Finally, it is important that all adolescents pursue leisure activities that are likely to enhance, rather than limit, their psychological growth, autonomy and identity. Leisure is useful for the development of a range of important skills during adolescence (for instance, interpersonal skills, athletic skills), and the challenge for parents and professionals is to assist in channeling that energy into 'socially acceptable' behaviours.

SUMMARY

This chapter has reviewed the processes by which adolescents come to learn about the world of work and money, the effects of unemployment, and the importance of leisure. From the review, it is clear that ideas about work are formed in the child's mind at a relatively young age. No doubt there are many important factors (such as ethnicity or social class) which are important in shaping an individual's beliefs about work and money. In this chapter we have emphasised the family as an important socialising force, and noticed the extent to which parents' and adolescents' attitudes and beliefs correspond on matters relating to work attitudes and beliefs. It is quite clear that parents are important in helping their children acquire certain beliefs, attitudes and values connected with work and money.

More recent reviews of the literature have hinted at important changes occurring in 'new' or 'non-traditional' families. In terms of vocational identity, single-mother families have a profound effect on the vocational choices of sons and daughters and evidence suggests that occupational choices for these teenagers are less sex-stereotyped. These findings need to be pursued in further research. Are the same trends found in children of single-father families, for instance?

Researchers have shed light on the job search strategies of youth and the psychological consequences of unemployment. Some have suggested that too much part-time work during adolescence may not be as beneficial as previously thought. Important longitudinal work has been done on the effects of unemployment as well as unsatisfactory employment, and their links to psychological distress. Since relatively high levels of youth unemployment are likely in the foreseeable future, the challenge facing mental health professionals is how to maintain pride and motivation in those who have little chance of finding full-time employment.

The final section dealt with the importance of leisure activities. Leisure pursuits are an important part of the search for self-knowledge and identity. As researchers have noted, leisure pursuits can have many beneficial effects on one's psychological well-being, although this is not the case across the board.

ADDITIONAL READING

Feather, N. (1990) *The Psychological Impact of Unemployment*. New York: Springer-Verlag.

Furnham, A. (1992) *Personality at Work: The Role of Individual Differences in the Workplace*. London: Routledge.

Winefield, A. H., Tiggeman, M., Winefield, H. and Goldney, R. D. (1993) *Growing up with Unemployment: A Longitudinal Study of its Psychological Impact*. London: Routledge.

EXERCISE

1 Visit a business in your community that employs teenagers on a part-time casual basis. Interview some of them, noting details about their

backgrounds; how many hours per week they work; how old they are; what they tend to spend their money on; what their grades are like at school; and so on. Are there different spending patterns for different groups of youth? What reasons do they give for working part-time? What else are you able to deduce from your data? What does this suggest about the nature of part-time work among adolescents?

11

Concluding Comments

INTRODUCTION

This book has reviewed some of the most important psychological determinants of adolescent well-being and development. The focus has been on the development of social and interpersonal behaviours, rather than on the development of cognitive and physical abilities. This has been a deliberate choice, as the areas selected for inclusion in this book have generated considerable interest from professionals and lay people alike (Stefanko, 1984). This book has demonstrated the very different ways by which development can be affected and how each domain of adolescent experience is important for psychological health. Our sweep has been a broad one, covering the development of adolescent identity, the role of the family, the role of peers, sexual behaviour, and mental health. We have also considered the importance of delinquent and criminal behaviours as well as the important issues of employment and leisure.

When reviewing the research evidence summarised in this book it is possible to detect several themes. One such factor is personality, crucial for determining whether individuals will engage in delinquent behaviours, select a particular vocation, or whether or not they are likely to strive to achieve at school. A second theme to emerge is family life: Delinquent behaviours, mental health, sexual behaviours, whether students decide to complete school or not are, in part, determined by one's family climate. What is abundantly clear from the research literature is the extent to which children's behaviour is shaped by parental discipline styles, parenting styles, family communication and general quality of family life. This is not to suggest that other factors such as one's socio-economic status or life opportunities are irrelevant, but it would appear as though personality factors and family climate have the potential to play a quite substantial role in adolescent adjustment. We shall briefly discuss the significance of these factors below.

THE IMPORTANCE OF PERSONALITY

It has been well established that personality factors are implicated in the psychological well-being of teenagers (for example, Eysenck and Eysenck, 1985; Furnham and Greaves, 1994; Goldstein and Heaven, 2000; Heaven, 1996c; Heaven et al., 2000; Kirkcaldy and Siefen, 1998). Thus, it is possible to make predictions about an adolescent's level of suicide ideation or the likelihood of their participation in delinquent and criminal activities based, in part, on their particular personality traits.

The study of personality traits is now well advanced and there seems to be general agreement among many personality theorists as to their structure and, with respect to some traits, their origin (for example, Costa and McCrae, 1985; Furnham and Heaven, 1999; Matthews and Deary, 1998; Mervielde et al., 1999). Trait theorists appear unanimous in suggesting that traits are important in predicting a wide range of social behaviours. But, just what are personality traits? McCrae and Costa (1995) have suggested the following:

- Traits are not merely summaries of behaviour. In fact, they are able to predict and do account for one's thoughts, feelings and actions.
- Personality traits are not explained by such factors as cultural norms or learned responses. Indeed, the pattern of personality traits appears to be reliably present across cultures and may even have a genetic basis, as evidenced in twin studies.
- We can use personality traits to predict unseen or unobservable behaviours.
- Some personality traits have an identifiable and discernible biological basis.
- Traits can interact with the environment so as to produce unique adaptations to effect attitudes, relationships, and so on.
- These unique adaptations interact with the situation and have an indirect effect on behaviours.

'How do young people acquire their personality traits?' and 'Can I teach my child acceptable traits?', are reasonable questions to ask. It now seems to be generally accepted that the heritability rates of some of the basic personality traits are quite high (for example, Brody and Ehrlichman, 1998). In other words, researchers have concluded that the basic personality traits such as extraversion have a substantial genetic basis to them, while other traits like psychoticism may be linked to hormonal influences (Matthews and Deary, 1998). Note that traits are not totally due to genetic and hormonal influences, but the effect does appear to be significant. Thus, for example, it has been estimated that the heritabilities for extraversion range between 0.60 and 0.70 (Brody and Ehrlichman, 1998). Interestingly, the heritability estimates of aggressive behaviours in young people tend to be higher (0.60) than that of delinquent behaviours (0.35) (Edelbrock et al., 1995).

Considerable scientific research has been conducted into the biological bases of personality (see, for example, Eysenck, 1967; Gray, 1970; Stelmack, 1981). Space does not allow a detailed discussion of this body of work, suffice to say that the evidence is quite compelling. For example, Eysenck (1967) has argued that a distinguishing feature of introversion-extraversion can be found in the functioning of the ascending reticular activating system, a structure in the brain that determines cortical arousal. Typically, extraverts are under-aroused such that they tend to be stimulus-hungry. Thus, they seek out 'arousal jags' and tend to score higher on measures of sensation-seeking (see Chapter 9). Because introverts are over-aroused, they are stimulus-shy. One consequence of this difference is that extraverted teenagers are more likely to study successfully while distracted (for example, while having the television on), than are introverts who are much more easily distracted (Furnham and Bradley, 1997).

Personality has also been shown to have hormonal and psychophysio-logical bases. For example, both extraversion and Eysenckian psychoticism (both predicted to be related to high delinquency levels in adolescents), are said to have links with gonadal hormones (testosterone) and dopa-mine (see Matthews and Deary, 1998 for a review). It therefore seems to be highly likely that anti-social and delinquent teenage behaviours, while no doubt influenced by family and socio-economic circumstances, may also be due to biological factors beyond one's control. This would have important implications for policy development, which would have to shift from a strongly economic perspective (for instance, alleviating poverty) to how best to manage innate behaviour.

In conclusion, there can be no question that the role of personality factors in shaping adolescent behaviours is important. As our review has made clear, it is not the only influence. This brings us to the role of the family.

THE IMPORTANCE OF FAMILY LIFE

As has already been made clear, the family is an important socialising influence on young people. There can be no doubt that the psychological well-being of young people is, in part, determined by the quality of family communication, parental personalities, parental styles, family cohesion and friction, and parental discipline styles. Each of these factors has been shown to be related to a wide range of behavioural outcomes including, for example, delinquency, whether a young teenage mother decides to keep her baby or not, whether a young person is likely to complete school and attend university, and so forth. It is clear that the family sets the 'tone' for how teenagers will interact with others and how they will accommodate and deal with their many varied experiences. The individual's first experience of others occurs within the family home. This suggests that one's family experiences have a crucial impact on the behaviours, perceptions, and expectations of the child, an experience that the child carries into adolescence.

Earlier sections of this book discussed the evidence that shows strong links between parental psychopathology and the behaviours of their teenage children. Of considerable interest and importance is the fact that there is a common genetic influence that accounts for many parent-children linkages (Plomin, 1995). In a noteworthy study, Pike and colleagues showed that there is a sizeable and common genetic thread that predicts levels of negativity in mothers and depression in their children (Pike et al., 1996). In addition, these genetic threads have been traced and found to be influential in the lives of children who have been adopted out. Thus, Ge and colleagues noted that it is possible to predict the behaviour of adoptees as well as of adoptive parents based on the behaviour of biological parents. For instance, adoptive parents' behaviours toward their adopted children was a function of whether the children's biological parents had a psychiatric disorder or not (Ge et al., 1996).

In summary, the influence of the family is not simply limited to environmental influences. Indeed, the impact of the family appears to be far-reaching and complete. The evidence suggests that there are also strong cross-generational genetic threads that help shape adolescent well-being.

SUMMARY

The influence of family life and personality traits on adolescent behaviours is complex indeed and much has yet to be learned about the intricate ways that these factors co-determine behaviour. Much research needs to be done to understand how personality factors interact with unique environmental and common genetic influences in determining adolescent adjustment. It is doubtful that the last word has been written on this topic. One way to better understand these issues would be to use longitudinal research designs incorporating twins and other siblings.

In conclusion, there are many different factors that have an impact on adolescent behaviours, but two pervading and consistent ones appear to be individual differences and family life, factors that permeate nearly every aspect of adolescent life. Notwithstanding the importance of these two broad factors, one must not lose sight of the fact that others such as one's cultural background and specific life experiences will also be implicated in determining adolescent well-being.

Bibliography

Abramson, L. Y., Alloy, L. B., Hogan, M. E., Whitehouse, W. G. et al. 'Suicidality and Cognitive Vulnerability to Depression among College Students: A Prospective Study', *Journal of Adolescence, 21* (1998) 473–87.

Abramson, L., Seligman, M. and Teasdale, J. 'Learned Helplessness in Humans: Critique and Reformulation', *Journal of Abnormal Psychology, 87* (1978) 49–74.

Adams, G. R, Abraham, K. and Markstrom, C. 'The Relations among Identity Development, Self-consciousness, and Self-focusing during Middle and Late Adolescence', *Developmental Psychology, 23* (1987) 292–7.

Adams, G. R., Gullotta, T. P. and Markstrom-Adams, C. *Adolescent Life Experiences*, 3rd edn. (Pacific Grove, California: Brooks/Cole Publishing Company, 1994).

Addeo, R. R., Greene, A. F. and Geisser, M. E. 'Construct Validity of the Robson Self-esteem Questionnaire in a College Sample', *Educational and Psychological Measurement, 54* (1994) 439–46.

Adelson, J. 'The Mystique of Adolescence', *Psychiatry, 27* (1964) 1–5.

Ainley, J., Foreman, J. and Sheret, M. 'High School Factors that Influence Students to Remain at School', *Journal of Educational Research, 85* (1991) 69–80.

Ajdukovic, M. 'Displaced Adolescents in Croatia: Sources of Stress and Posttraumatic Stress Reaction', *Adolescence, 33* (1998) 209–17.

Amann-Gainotti, M. 'Sexual Socialization during Early Adolescence: The Menarche', *Adolescence, 21* (1986) 703–10.

Amato, P. 'Dimensions of the Family Environment as Perceived by Children: A Multidimensional Scaling Analysis', *Journal of Marriage and the Family, 52* (1990) 613–20.

Amato, P. and Booth, A. 'A Prospective Study of Divorce and Parent-child Relationships', *Journal of Marriage and the Family, 58* (1996) 356–65.

Amato, P and Keith, B. 'Parental Divorce and the Well-being of Children: A Meta-analysis', *Psychological Bulletin, 110* (1991) 26–46.

Amato, P., Loomis, L. S. and Booth, A. 'Parental Divorce, Marital Conflict, and Offspring Well-being during Early Adulthood', *Social Forces, 73* (1995) 895–915.

American Psychiatric Association *Diagnostic and Statistical Manual of Mental Disorders*, 4th edn. (Washington, DC: American Psychiatric Association, 1994).

Andersson, T., Mahoney, J. L., Wennberg, P., Kuehlhorn, E. and Magnusson, D. 'The Co-occurrence of Alcohol Problems and Criminality in the Transition from Adolescence to Young Adulthood: A Prospective Longitudinal Study on Young Men', *Studies in Crime and Crime Prevention, 8* (1999) 169–88.

Angold, A. 'Childhood and Adolescent Depression 1: Epidemiological and Aetiological Aspects', *British Journal of Psychiatry, 152* (1988) 601–17.

Archer, S. 'Gender Role Learning', in J. Coleman (ed.), *The School Years: Current Issues in the Socialization of Young People*, 2nd edn. (London: Routledge, 1992).

Arnett, J. J. 'Adolescent Storm and Stress, Reconsidered', *American Psychologist 54* (1999) 317–26.

Arrindell, W. A., Gerlsma, C., Vandereycken, W., Hageman, W. J. and Daeseleire, T. 'Convergent Validity of the Dimensions underlying the Parental Bonding Instrument (PBI) and the EMBU'. *Personality and Individual Differences, 2,* (1998) 341–50.

Ary, D. V., Duncan, T. E., Duncan, S. C. and Hops, H. 'Adolescent Problem Behavior: The Influence of Parents and Peers', *Behaviour Research and Therapy, 37* (1999) 217–30.

Asarnow, J., Carlson, G. and Guthrie, D. 'Coping Strategies, Self-perceptions, Hopelessness, and Perceived Family Environments in Depressed and Suicidal Children', *Journal of Consulting and Clinical Psychology, 55* (1987) 361–6.

Asher, S. and Dodge, K. 'Identifying Children who are Rejected by their Peers', *Developmental Psychology, 22* (1986) 444–9.

Australian Bureau of Statistics *Causes of Death: Australia 1990*, Catalogue No. 3303.0. (Canberra: Government Printer, 1991).

Australian Bureau of Statistics, *Australian Social Trends*, Catalogue No. 4102.0 (Canberra: Government Printer, 1998).

Australian Bureau of Statistics, *Children, Australia: A Social Report*, Catalogue No. 4119.0 (Canberra: Government Printer, 1999).

Ausubel, D., Montemayor, R. and Svajian, P. *Theory and Problems of Adolescent Development.* (New York: Grune and Stratton, 1977).

Avison, W. and McAlpine, D. 'Gender Differences in Symptoms of Depression among Adolescents', *Journal of Health and Social Behavior, 33* (1992) 77–96.

Bahr, J. *Family Research: A Sixty-year Review, 1930–1990*, vol. 1. (New York: Lexington Books, 1991).

Baker, S., Thalberg, S. and Morrison, D. 'Parents' Behavioral Norms as Predictors of Adolescent Sexual Activity and Contraceptive Use', *Adolescence, 23* (1988) 265–82.

Balassone, M. 'A Social Learning Model of Adolescent Contraceptive Behaviour', *Journal of Youth and Adolescence, 20* (1991) 593–616.

Baldwin, W. and Cain, V. 'The Children of Teenage Parents', *Family Planning Perspectives, 12* (1980) 34–43.

Bandura, A. *Aggression: A Social Learning Analysis*. (Englewood Cliffs, NJ: Prentice-Hall, 1973).

Bank, L., Duncan, T., Patterson, G. and Reid, J. 'Parent and Teacher Ratings in the Assessment and Prediction of Antisocial and Delinquent Behaviors', *Journal of Personality, 61* (1993) 693–709.

Banks, M. and Ullah, P. *Youth Unemployment in the 1980s: Its Psychological Effects.* (London: Croom Helm, 1988).

Barber, B. and Eccles, J. 'Long-term Influence of Divorce and Single Parenting on Adolescent Family- and Work-related Values, Behaviors, and Aspirations', *Psychological Bulletin, 111* (1992) 108–26.

Barling, J., Kelloway, E. K. and Bremermann, E. H. 'Preemployment Predictors of Union Attitudes: The Role of Family Socialization and Work Beliefs', *Journal of Applied Psychology, 76* (1991) 725–31.

Barling, J., Rogers, K. and Kelloway, E. K. 'Some Effects of Teenagers' Part-time Employment: The Quantity and Quality of Work Make the Difference', *Journal of Organizational Behavior, 16* (1995) 143–54.

Barling, N. and Moore, S. 'Adolescents' Attitudes towards AIDS Precautions and Intention to Use Condoms', *Psychological Reports, 67* (1990) 883–90.

Barnes, H. and Olson, D. 'Parent–adolescent Communication and the Circumplex Model', *Child Development, 56* (1985) 438–47.

Barrera, M. and Garrison-Jones, C. 'Family and Peer Social Support as Specific Correlates of Adolescent Depressive Symptoms', *Journal of Abnormal Child Psychology, 20* (1992) 1–16.

Bartle-Haring, S. 'The Relationships among Parent-adolescent Differentiation, Sex-role Orientation and Identity Development in Late Adolescence and Early Adulthood', *Journal of Adolescence, 20* (1997) 553–65.

Beautrais, A., Joyce, P. R. and Mulder, R. T. 'Precipitating Factors and Life Events in Serious Suicide Attempts among Youths aged 13 through 24 years', *Journal of the American Academy of Child and Adolescent Psychiatry, 36* (1997) 1543–51.

Beautrais, A. L., Joyce, P. R. and Mulder, R. T. 'Unemployment and Serious Suicide Attempts', *Psychological Medicine, 28* (1998) 209–18.

Beck, A., Weissman, A., Lester, D. and Trexler, L. 'The Measurement of Pessimism: The Hopelessness Scale', *Journal of Consulting and Clinical Psychology, 42* (1975) 861–5.

Ben-Ari, A. T. and Gil, S. 'Perceptions of Life and Death among Suicidal Gay Adolescents', *Omega – Journal of Death and Dying, 37* (1998) 107–19.

Ben-Zur, H., Breznitz, S., Wardi, N. and Berzon, Y. 'Denial of HIV/AIDS and Preventive Behaviour among Israeli Adolescents', *Journal of Adolescence, 23* (2000) 157–74.

Berk, L. *Child Development*. (Boston: Allyn and Bacon, 1989).

Biederman, J., Milberger, S., Faraone, S. V., Kiely, K. et al. 'Impact of Adversity on Functioning and Comorbidity in Children with Attention-deficit Hyperactivity Disorder', *Journal of the American Academy of Child and Adolescent Psychiatry, 34* (1995) 1495–1503.

Biggam, F. H. and Power, K. G. 'The Quality of Perceived Parenting Experienced by a Group of Scottish Incarcerated Young Offenders and its Relation to Psychological Distress', *Journal of Adolescence, 21* (1998) 161–76.

Binder, A. 'Juvenile Delinquency', *Annual Review of Psychology, 39* (1988) 253–82.

Bisnaire, L., Firestone, P. and Rynard, D. 'Factors Associated with Academic Achievement in Children following Parental Separation', *American Journal of Orthopsychiatry, 60* (1990) 67–76.

Blakers, C. *Youth and Society: The Two Transitions*. (Melbourne: ACER Research, 1990) Monograph No. 38.

Blaske, D., Borduin, C., Henggeler, S. and Mann, B. 'Individual, Family, and Peer Characteristics of Adolescent Sex Offenders and Assaultive Offenders', *Developmental Psychology, 25* (1989) 846–55.

Bonnet, C. and Furnham, A. 'Who Wants to be an Entrepreneur? A Study of Adolescents Interested in a Young Enterprise Scheme', *Journal of Economic Psychology, 12* (1991) 465–78.

Bootzin, R. and Acocella, J. *Abnormal Psychology: Current Perspectives*, 5th edn. (New York: Random House, 1988).

Born, N., Chevalier, V. and Humblet, I. 'Resilience, Desistance and Delinquent Career of Adolescent Offenders', *Journal of Adolescence, 20* (1997) 679–94.

Bornholt, L. J., Goodnow, J. J. and Cooney, G. H. 'Influences of Gender Stereotypes on Adolescents' Perceptions of their own Achievement', *American Educational Research Journal, 31* (1994) 675–92.

Boyle, D. *A Student's Guide to Piaget.* (Oxford: Pergamon Press, 1969).

Brody, N. and Ehrlichman, H. *Personality Psychology: The Science of Individuality.* (Upper Saddle River, NJ: Prentice Hall, 1998).

Brooks-Gunn, J. and Furstenberg, F. 'The Children of Adolescent Mothers: Physical, Academic and Psychological Outcomes', *Developmental Review, 6* (1986) 224–51.

Brooks-Gunn, J. and Furstenberg, F. 'Adolescent Sexual Behavior', *American Psychologist, 44* (1989) 249–57.

Brooks-Gunn, J. and Lewis, M. 'The Development of Early Visual Self-recognition', *Developmental Review, 4* (1984) 215–39.

Brown, B., Clasen, D. and Eicher, S. 'Perceptions of Peer Pressure, Peer Conformity Dispositions, and Self-reported Behavior among Adolescents', *Developmental Psychology, 22* (1986) 521–30.

Bruner, J. and Tagiuri, R. 'The Perception of People'. In G. Lindzey (ed.), *Handbook of Social Psychology* (Reading, MS: Addison-Wesley, 1954).

Buchanan, C., Eccles, J. and Becker, J. 'Are Adolescents the Victims of Raging Hormones: Evidence for Activational Effects of Hormones on Moods and Behavior at Adolescence', *Psychological Bulletin, 111* (1992) 62–107.

Buchanan, C., Maccoby, E. and Dornbusch, S. 'Caught between Parents: Adolescents' Experience in Divorced Homes', *Child Development, 62* (1991) 1008–29.

Buhrmester, D. 'Intimacy of Friendship, Interpersonal Competence, and Adjustment during Preadolescence and Adolescence', *Child Development, 61* (1990) 1101–11.

Burns, A. and Dunlop, R. 'Parental Divorce, Parent-child Relations, and Early Adult Relationships: A Longitudinal Australian Study', *Personal Relationships, 5* (1998) 393–407.

Burns, R. *The Self-concept in Theory, Measurement, Development and Behaviour.* (Longman: London, 1979).

Bush, R. 'Rural Youth Suicide', *Rural Welfare Research Bulletin 6*: 25–7 (Wagga Wagga, NSW: Charles Sturt University, 1990).

Buzi, R. S., Weinman, M. L. and Smith, P. B. 'Ethnic Differences in STD Rates among Female Adolescents', *Adolescence, 33* (1998) 313–18.

Byrne, A. and Byrne, D. 'Adolescent Personality, School Type and Educational Outcomes: An Examination of Sex Differences', in P. Heaven and V. Callan (eds), *Adolescence: An Australian Perspective.* (Sydney: Harcourt Brace Jovanovich, 1990).

Callan, V. and Noller, P. *Marriage and the Family.* (Sydney: Methuen, 1987).

Campbell, E., Adams, G. and Dobson, W. 'Familial Correlates of Identity Formation in Late Adolescence: A Study of the Predictive Utility of Connectedness and Individuality in Family Matters', *Journal of Youth and Adolescence, 13* (1984) 509–25.

Cantor, C. H. and Baume, P. J. M. 'Changing Methods of Suicide by Young Australians 1974–1994', *Archives of Suicide Research, 4* (1998) 41–50.

Cantwell D. and Baker, L. 'Manifestations of Depressive Affect in Adolescence', *Journal of Youth and Adolescence, 20* (1991) 121–33.

Caprara, G. V., Barbaranelli, C., Pastorelli, C., Bandura, A. and Zimbardo, P. 'Prosocial Foundations of Children's Academic Achievement', *Psychological Science, 11* (2000) 302–6.

Carlson, G. and Kashani, J. 'Phenomenology of Major Depression from Childhood through Adulthood: Analysis of Three Studies', *American Journal of Psychiatry, 145* (1988) 1222–5.

Chan, D. W. 'Depressive Symptoms and Perceived Competence among Chinese Secondary School Students in Hong Kong', *Journal of Youth and Adolescence, 26* (1997) 303–19.

Chapman, J. and Lawes, M. 'Consistency of Causal Attributions for Expected and Actual Examination Outcome: A Study of the Expectancy Confirmation and Egotism Models', *British Journal of Educational Psychology, 54* (1984) 177–88.

Cherian, V. Parental Aspiration and Academic Achievement of Xhosa Children', *Psychological Reports, 68* (1991) 547–53.

Chiariello, M. A. and Orvaschel, H. 'Patterns of Parent–child Communication: Relationship to Depression', *Clinical Psychology Review, 15* (1995) 395–407.

Christ, M., Lahey, B., Frick, P., Russo, M., McBurnett, K., Loeber, R., Stouthamer-Loeber, M and Green, S. 'Serious Conduct Problems in the Children of Adolescent Mothers: Disentangling Confounded Correlations', *Journal of Consulting and Clinical Psychology, 58* (1990) 840–4.

Cloninger, S. C. *Theories of Personality: Understanding Persons*. (Upper Saddle River, NJ: Prentice Hall, 1996).

Cohen, D. A. and Rice, J. 'Parenting Styles, Adolescent Substance Use, and Academic Achievement', *Journal of Drug Education, 27* (1997) 199–211.

Cole, D. and Rehm, L. 'Family Interaction Patterns and Childhood Depression', *Journal of Abnormal Child Psychology, 14* (1986) 297–314.

Cole, M. and Cole, S. *The Development of Children*. (Scientific American Books, 1989).

Coleman, J. 'Current Views of the Adolescent Process', in J. Coleman (ed.) *The School Years: Current Issues in the Socialization of Young People*, 2nd edn. (London: Routledge, 1992).

Coleman, M. and Ganong, L. 'Remarriage and Stepfamily Research in the 1980s: Increased Interest in an Old Family Form', *Journal of Marriage and the Family, 52* (1990) 925–40.

Coleman, M. and Ganong, L. 'Stepfamilies from the Stepfamily's Perspective', *Marriage and Family Review, 26* (1997) 107–121.

Coleman, J. and Hendry, L. *The Nature of Adolescence*, 2nd edn. (London: Routledge, 1990).

Collins, W. 'Parent–child Relationships in the Transition to Adolescence: Continuity and Change in Interaction, Affect, and Cognition', in R. Montemayor, G. Adams and T. Gullotta (eds), *From Childhood to Adolescence: A Transition Period?* (Newbury Park, California: Sage, 1990).

Compas, B. E., Oppedisano, G., Connor, J. K., Gerhardt, C. A. et al. 'Gender Differences in Depressive Symptoms in Adolescence: Comparison of National Samples of Clinically Referred and Nonreferred Youths', *Journal of Consulting and Clinical Psychology, 65* (1997) 617–26.

Compas, B., Orosan, P. and Grant, K. 'Adolescent Stress and Coping: Implications for Psychopathology during Adolescence', *Journal of Adolescence, 16* (1993) 331–49.

Conger, J. and Petersen, A. *Adolescence and Youth: Psychological Development in a Changing World*, 3rd edn. (New York: Harper and Row, 1984).

Connel, R., Ashenden, D., Kessler, S. and Dowsett, G. *Making the Difference: Schools, Families and Social Divisions*. (Sydney: Allen and Unwin, 1982).

Cooper, M. L., Shapiro, C. M. and Powers, A. M. 'Motivations for Sex and Risky Sexual Behavior among Adolescents and Young Adults: A Functional Perspective' *Journal of Personality and Social Psychology, 75* (1998) 1528–58.

Correy, J., Kwok, P., Newman, N. and Curran, J. 'Adolescent Pregnancy in Tasmania', *Medical Journal of Australia, 141* (1984) 150–4.

Costa, P. and McCrae, R. '*The NEO Personality Inventory*', (Odessa, FL: Psychological Assessment Resources, 1985).

Costanzo, P. and Shaw, M. 'Conformity as a Function of Age Level', *Child Development, 37* (1966) 967–75.

Craig, W. M. 'The Relationship among Bullying, Victimization, Depression, Anxiety, and Aggression in Elementary School Children', *Personality and Individual Differences, 24* (1998) 123–30.

Crain, W. *Theories of Development: Concepts and Applications*. (Englewood Cliffs, NJ: Prentice-Hall, 1985).

Cramer, P. 'Identity, Personality, and Defense Mechanisms: An Observer-based Study', *Journal of Research in Personality, 31* (1997) 58–77.

Crawford, J., Turtle, A. and Kippax, S. 'Student-favoured Strategies for AIDS Avoidance', *Australian Journal of Psychology, 42* (1990) 123–37.

Cullen, A. and Connolly, J. F. 'Aspects of Suicide in Rural Ireland 1978–1994', *Archives of Suicide Research, 3* (1997) 43–52.

Culp, R., Culp, A., Osofsky, J. and Osofsky, H. 'Adolescent and Older Mothers' Interaction Patterns with their Six-month-old Infants', *Adolescence, 14* (1991) 195–200.

Custer, M. 'Adoption as an Option for Unmarried Pregnant Teens', *Adolescence, 28* (1993) 891–902.

Daly, K. J. 'Adolescent Perceptions of Adoption: Implications for Resolving an Unplanned Pregnancy', *Youth and Society, 25* (1994) 330–50.

Damon, W. 'Self-concept, Adolescent'. In R. M. Lerner and J. Brooks-Gunn (eds), *The Encyclopaedia of Adolescence*, vol. 2. (New York: Garland, 1990).

Damon, W. and Hart, D. 'The Development of Self-Understanding from Infancy through Adolescence', *Child Development, 53* (1982) 841–64.

Darom, E. and Rich, Y. 'Sex Differences in Attitudes Toward School: Student Self-reports and Teacher Perceptions', *British Journal of Educational Psychology, 58* (1988) 350–5.

Davis, C., Noel, M. B., Chan, S. F. and Wing, L. S. 'Knowledge, Attitudes and Behaviors Related to HIV and AIDS among Chinese Adolescents in Hong Kong', *Journal of Adolescence, 21* (1998) 657–65.

Davis, G. and Leitenberg, H. 'Adolescent Sex Offenders', *Psychological Bulletin, 101* (1987) 417–27.

Davis, R. 'Adolescent Pregnancy and Infant Mortality: Isolating the Effects of Race', *Adolescence, 23* (1988) 899–908.

Dayton, C. 'The Young Person's Job Search: Insights from a Study', *Journal of Counselling Psychology, 28* (1981) 321–33.

Deaux, K. and Emswiller, T. 'Explanations of Successful Performance on Sex-linked Tasks: What is Skill for the Male is Luck for the Female', *Journal of Personality and Social Psychology, 29* (1974) 80–5.

De Fruyt, F. and Mervielde, I. 'Personality and Interests as Predictors of Educational Streaming and Achievement, *European Journal of Personality, 10* (1996) 405–25.

Deisher, R., Litchfield, C. and Hope, K. 'Birth Outcomes of Prostituting Adolescents', *Journal of Adolescent Health, 12* (1991) 528–33.

Dekovic, M., Noom, M. J. and Meeus, W. 'Expectations Regarding Development during Adolescence: Parental and Adolescent Perceptions', *Journal of Youth & Adolescence, 26* (1997) 253–72.

Demb, J. 'Abortion in Inner-city Adolescents: What the Girls Say', *Family, Systems Medicine, 9* (1991) 93–102.

Demo, D. 'Parent–child Relations: Assessing Recent Changes', *Journal of Marriage and the Family, 54* (1992) 104–17.

De Raad, B. and Schouwenburg, H. 'Personality in Learning and Education: A Review', *European Journal of Personality, 10* (1996) 303–36.

De Wilde, E., Kienhorst, L, Diekstra, R. and Wolters, W. 'The Relationship between Adolescent Suicidal Behavior and Life Events in Childhood and Adolescence', *American Journal of Psychiatry, 149* (1992) 45–51.

Diekstra, R. and Moritz, B. 'Suicidal Behaviour among Adolescents: An Overview', in R. Diekstra and K. Hawton (eds), *Suicide in Adolescence.* (Dordrecht: Martinus Nijhoff Publishers, 1987).

Dishion, T., Patterson, G., Stoolmiller, M. and Skinner, M. 'Family, School, and Behavioral Antecedents to Early Adolescent Involvement with Antisocial Peers', *Developmental Psychology, 27* (1991) 172–80.

Dohrenwend, B. and Dohrenwend, B. (eds), *Stressful Life Events.* (New York: Wiley, 1974).

Dollard, J and Miller, N. E. *Personality and Psychotherapy: An Analysis in Terms of Learning, Thinking and Culture.* (New York: McGraw-Hill, 1950).

Donnelly, M. 'Depression among Adolescents in Northern Ireland', *Adolescence, 30* (1995) 339–50.

Donovan, J. and Jessor, R. 'Structure of Problem Behavior in Adolescence and Young Adulthood', *Journal of Consulting and Clinical Psychology, 53* (1985) 890–904.

Donovan, J., Jessor, R. and Costa, F. 'Syndrome of Problem Behavior in Adolescence: A Replication', *Journal of Consulting and Clinical Psychology, 56* (1988) 762–5.

Dornbusch, S., Ritter, P., Liederman, P., Roberts, D. and Fraleigh, M. 'The Relation of Parenting Style to Adolescent School Performance', *Child Development, 58* (1987) 1244–57.

Douvan, E. and Adelson, J. *The Adolescent Experience.* (New York: John Wiley, 1966).

Dowling, J. 'Adjustment from Primary to Secondary School: A One Year Follow-up', *British Journal of Educational Psychology, 50* (1980) 26–32.

Downey, G. and Coyne, J. 'Children of Depressed Parents: An Integrative Review', *Psychological Bulletin, 108* (1990) 50–76.

Dubow, E. and Luster, T. 'Adjustment of Children Born to Teenage Mothers: The Contribution of Risk and Protective Factors', *Journal of Marriage and the Family, 52* (1990) 393–404.

Duckett, E. and Richards, M. 'Maternal Employment and the Quality of Daily Experience for Young Adolescents of Single Mothers', *Journal of Family Psychology, 9* (1995) 418–32.

Dunne, M., Donald, M., Lucke, J. and Raphael, B. 'The Sexual Behaviour of Young People in Rural Australia', in K. Malko (ed.), *A Fair Go for Rural Health – Forward Together: 2nd National Rural Health Conference*, (Canberra: Australian Government Publishing Service, 1993).

Dunphy, D. 'The Social Structure of Urban Adolescent Peer Groups', *Sociometry, 26* (1963) 230–76.

Dunphy, D. 'Peer Group Socialisation', in R. Muuss (ed.), *Adolescent Behavior and Society: A Book of Readings*. (New York: McGraw-Hill, 1990).

Dusek, J. *Adolescent Development and Behavior*, 2nd edn. (Englewood Cliffs, NJ: Prentice-Hall, 1991)

East, P. L., Matthews, K. L. and Felice, M. E. 'Qualities of Adolescent Mothers' Parenting', *Journal of Adolescent Health, 15* (1994) 163–8.

Edelbrock, C., Rende, R., Plomin, R. and Thompson, A. 'A Twin Study of Competence and Problem Behavior in Childhood and Early Adolescence', *Journal of Child Psychology and Psychiatry, 36* (1995) 775–85.

Eisen, M. and Zellman, G. 'Factors Predicting Pregnancy Resolution Decision Satisfaction of Unmarried Adolescents', *Journal of Genetic Psychology, 145* (1984) 231–9.

Eisen, M., Zellman, G., Leibowitz, A., Chow, W. and Evans, J. 'Factors Discriminating Pregnancy Resolution Decisions of Unmarried Adolescents', *Genetic Psychology Monographs, 108* (1983) 69–95.

Elkind, D. 'Egocentrism in Adolescence', *Child Development, 38* (1967) 1025–34.

Elster, A. and Hendricks, L. 'Stresses and Coping Strategies of Adolescent Fathers' in A. Elster and M. Lamb (eds), *Adolescent Fatherhood*. (Hillsdale, NJ: Lawrence Erlbaum, 1986).

Emler, N. and Reicher, S. *Adolescence and Delinquency: The Collective Management of Reputation* (Oxford: Blackwell, 1995).

Entwistle, N. 'Personality and Academic Attainment', *British Journal of Educational Psychology, 42* (1972) 137–51.

Erikson, E. *Identity: Youth and Crisis*. (New York: W.W. Norton and Company, 1968).

Erlanger, D. M. 'Identity Status and Empathic Response Patterns: A Multi-dimensional Investigation', *Journal of Adolescence, 21* (1998) 323–35.

Espelage, D. L., Bosworth, K. and Simon, T. R. 'Examining the Social Context of Bullying Behaviors in Early Adolescence', *Journal of Counseling and Development, 78* (2000) 326–33.

Eysenck, H. *The Biological Basis of Personality*. (Springfield, IL: Charles C. Thomas, 1967).

Eysenck, H. *The Decline and Fall of the Freudian Empire*. (Harmondsworth: Viking, 1985).

Eysenck, H. and Eysenck, M. *Personality and Individual Differences: A Natural Science Approach*. (New York: Plenum, 1985).

Eysenck, H. J. and Eysenck, S. *Manual of the Eysenck Personality Questionnaire* (London: Hodder & Stoughton, 1975).

Eysenck, H. and Gudjonsson, G. *The Causes and Cures of Criminality.* (New York: Plenum, 1989).

Fagot, B. I., Pears, K. C., Capaldi, D. M., Crosby, L. and Leve, C. S. 'Becoming an Adolescent Father: Precursors and Parenting', *Developmental Psychology, 34* (1998) 1209–19.

Farber, N. 'The Process of Pregnancy Resolution among Adolescent Mothers', *Adolescence, 26* (1991) 697–716.

Fasick, F. 'Parents, Peers, Youth Culture and Autonomy in Adolescence', *Adolescence, 19* (1984) 143–57.

Faulkner, A. H. and Cranston, K. 'Correlates of Same-sex Behavior in a Random Sample of Massachusetts High School Students', *American Journal of Public Health, 88* (1998) 262–6.

Feather, N. 'Human Values and the Prediction of Action: An Expectancy-valence Analysis', in N. Feather (ed.), *Expectations and Actions: Expectancy-value Models in Psychology.* (Hillsdale, NJ: Lawrence Erlbaum, 1982).

Feather, N. 'Some Correlates of Attributional Style: Depressive Symptoms, Self-esteem, and Protestant Ethic Values', *Personality and Social Psychology Bulletin, 9* (1983) 125–35.

Feather, N. *The Psychological Impact of Unemployment.* (New York: Springer-Verlag, 1990).

Feather, N. and Davenport, P. 'Unemployment and Depressive Affect: A Motivational and Attributional Analysis', *Journal of Personality and Social Psychology, 41* (1981) 422–36.

Feather, N. and O'Brien, G. 'Looking for Employment: An Expectancy-valence Analysis of Job-seeking Behaviour among Young People', *British Journal of Psychology, 78* (1987) 251–72.

Fehrenbach, P. and Monastersky, C. 'Characteristics of Female Adolescent Sexual Offenders', *American Journal of Orthopsychiatry, 58* (1988) 148–51.

Fergusson, D. M. and Woodward, L. J. 'Educational, Psychosocial, and Sexual Outcomes of Girls with Conduct Problems in Early Adolescence', *Journal of Child Psychology and Psychiatry, 41* (2000) 779–92.

Fine, M., Moreland, J. and Schwebel, A. 'Long-term Effects of Divorce on Parent–child Relationships', *Developmental Psychology, 19* (1983) 703–13.

Fleming, J., Offord, D. and Boyle, M. 'Prevalence of Childhood and Adolescent Depression in the Community: Ontario Child Health Study', *British Journal of Psychiatry, 155* (1989) 647–54.

Foon, A. 'The Relationship between School Type and Adolescent Self-esteem, Attribution Styles, and Affiliation Needs: Implications for Educational Outcome', *British Journal of Educational Psychology, 58* (1988) 44–54.

Forrest, S. 'Suicide and the Rural Adolescent', *Adolescence, 23* (1988) 341–7.

Foster-Clark, F. and Blyth, D. 'Peer Relations and Influences', in R. Lerner, A. Petersen and J. Brooks-Gunn (eds), *Encyclopedia of Adolescence*, vol. 2. (New York: Garland Publishing, 1991).

Franklin, C. W. *Theoretical Perspectives in Social Psychology.* (Boston: Little Brown & Co., 1982).

French, D. C., Conrad, J. and Turner, T. M. 'Adjustment of Antisocial and Nonantisocial Rejected Adolescents', *Development and Psychopathology, 7* (1995) 857–74.

Freud, S. *An Outline of Psycho-analysis.* (New York: Norton, 1949).

Frone, M. R. 'Predictors of Work Injuries among Employed Adolescents', *Journal of Applied Psychology, 83* (1998) 565–76.

Frost, A. and Pakiz, B. 'The Effects of Marital Disruption on Adolescents: Time as a Dynamic', *American Journal of Orthopsychiatry, 60* (1990) 544–55.

Fry, P. and Coe, K. 'Achievement Performance of Internally and Externally Oriented Black and White High School Students under Conditions of Competition and Co-operation Expectancies', *British Journal of Educational Psychology, 50* (1980) 162–7.

Furnham, A. 'Getting a Job: School-leavers' Perceptions of Employment Prospects', *British Journal of Educational Psychology, 54* (1984) 293–305.

Furnham, A. 'Predicting Protestant Work Ethic Beliefs', *European Journal of Personality, 1* (1987) 93–106.

Furnham, A. *The Protestant Work Ethic: The Psychology of Work-related Beliefs and Behaviours.* (London: Routledge, 1990).

Furnham, A. *Personality at Work: The Role of Individual Differences in the Workplace.* (London: Routledge, 1992).

Furnham, A. 'Economic Socialization: A Study of Adults' Perceptions and Uses of Allowances (Pocket Money) to Educate Children', *British Journal of Developmental Psychology, 17* (1999a) 585–604.

Furnham, A. 'The Saving and Spending Habits of Young People', *Journal of Economic Psychology, 20* (1999b) 677–97.

Furnham, A. and Argyle, M. *'The Psychology of Money'.* (London: Routledge, 1998).

Furnham, A. and Bradley, A. 'Music While you Work: the Differential Distraction of Background Music on the Cognitive Test Performance of Introverts and Extraverts', *Applied Cognitive Psychology, 8* (1997) 705–11.

Furnham, A. and Greaves, N. 'Gender and Locus of Control Correlates of Body Image Dissatisfaction', *European Journal of Personality, 8* (1994) 183–200.

Furnham, A. and Gunter, B. *The Anatomy of Adolescence: Young People's Social Attitudes in Britain.* (London: Routledge, 1989).

Furnham, A. and Heaven, P. C. L. *Personality and Social Behaviour.* (London: Arnold, 1999).

Furnham, A. and Medhurst, S. 'Personality Correlates of Academic Seminar Behaviour: A Study of Four Instruments', *Personality and Individual Differences, 19* (1995) 197–208.

Furnham, A. and Rawles, R. 'Job Search Strategies, Attitudes to School and Attributions about Employment', *Journal of Adolescence, 19* (1996) 355–69.

Furnham, A., Sadka, V. and Brewin, C. 'The Development of an Occupational Attributional Style Questionnaire', *Journal of Organizational Behaviour, 13* (1992) 27–39.

Furnham, A. and Stacey, B. *Young People's Understanding of Society.* (London: Routledge, 1991).

Furnham, A. and Thomas, P. 'Adults' Perceptions of the Economic Socialization of Children', *Journal of Adolescence, 7* (1984) 217–31.

Furnham, A. and Thompson, J. 'Personality and Self-reported Delinquency', *Personality and Individual Differences, 12* (1991) 585–93.

Furstenberg, F, Brooks-Gunn, J. and Chase-Lansdale, L. 'Teenaged Pregnancy and Childbearing', *American Psychologist*, 44 (1989) 313–20.

Furstenberg, F., Brooks-Gunn, J. and Morgan, S. *Adolescent Mothers in Later Life*. (Cambridge: Cambridge University Press, 1987).

Galambos, N. L. and Sears, H. A. 'Adolescents' Perceptions of Parents' Work and Adolescents' Work Values in Two-earner Families', *Journal of Early Adolescence, 18* (1998) 397–420.

Gallois, C. and Callan, V. 'Sexuality in Adolescence', in P. Heaven and V. Callan (eds), *Adolescence: An Australian Perspective*. (Sydney: Harcourt Brace Jovanovich, 1990).

Garland, A. and Zigler, E. 'Adolescent Suicide Prevention: Current Research and Social Policy Implications', *American Psychologist, 48* (1993) 169–82.

Garnefski, N. and Arends, E. 'Sexual Abuse and Adolescent Maladjustment: Differences between Male and Female Victims', *Journal of Adolescence, 21* (1998) 99–107.

Garnets, L. and Kimmel, D. 'Lesbian and Gay Male Dimensions in the Psychological Study of Human Diversity', in J. Goodchilds (ed.), *Psychological Perspectives on Human Diversity, in America: Master Lectures*. (Washington, DC: American Psychological Association, 1991).

Garrett, S. C. and Tidwell, R. 'Differences between Adolescent Mothers and Nonmothers: An Interview Study', *Adolescence, 34* (1999) 91–105.

Garrison, C. Z., Waller, J. L., Cuffe, S., McKeown, R. E. et al. 'Incidence of Major Depressive Disorder and Dysthymia in young adolescents', *Journal of the American Academy of Child and Adolescent Psychiatry, 36* (1997) 458–65.

Garton, A. and Pratt, C. 'Participation and Interest in Leisure Activities by Adolescent Schoolchildren', *Journal of Adolescence, 10* (1987) 341–51.

Gavin, L. and Furman, W. 'Age Differences in Adolescents' Perceptions of their Peer Groups', *Developmental Psychology, 25* (1989) 827–34.

Ge, X., Best, K. M., Conger, R. and Simons, R. 'Parenting Behaviors and the Occurrence and Co-occurrence of Adolescent Depressive Symptoms and Conduct Problems', *Developmental Psychology, 32* (1996) 717–31.

Ge, X., Conger, R., Cadoret, R., Neiderhiser, J., Yates, W., Troughton, E. and Stewart, M. 'The Developmental Interface between Nature and Nurture: A Mutual Influence Model of Child Antisocial Behavior and Parent Behaviors', *Developmental Psychology, 32* (1996) 574–89.

Geber, G. and Resnick, M. 'Family Functioning of Adolescents who Parent and Place for Adoption', *Adolescence, 23* (1988) 417–28.

Gecas, V. and Seff, M. 'Families and Adolescents: A Review of the 1980s', *Journal of Marriage and the Family 52* (1990) 941–58.

Gesell, A. *Infancy and Human Growth* (New York: Macmillan, 1928).

Ginzberg, E. 'Toward a Theory of Occupational Choice: A Restatement', *Vocational Guidance Quarterly, 20* (1972) 169–76.

Giordano, P. C., Cernkovich, S. A., Groat, H. T., Pugh, M. D. and Swinford, S. 'The Quality of Adolescent Friendships: Long-Term Effects?', *Journal of Health and Social Behavior, 39* (1998) 55–71.

Gladstone, T. R., Kaslow, N. J., Seeley, J. R. and Lewinsohn, P. M. 'Sex Differences, Attributional Style, and Depressive Symptoms among Adolescents', *Journal of Abnormal Child Psychology, 25* (1997) 297–305.

Glasgow, K. L., Dornbusch, S. M., Troyer, L., Steinberg, L. et al. 'Parenting Styles, Adolescents' Attributions and Educational Outcomes in Nine Heterogeneous High Schools', *Child Development, 68* (1997) 507–29.

Glasser, M. 'Homosexuality in Adolescence', *British Journal of Medical Psychology, 50* (1977) 217–25.

Goldsmith, J. 'The Postdivorce Family System', in F. Walsh (ed.), *Normal Family Processes*. (New York: The Guilford Press, 1982).

Goldstein, M. 'The Family and Psychopathology', *Annual Review of Psychology, 39* (1988) 283–99.

Goldstein, M. and Heaven, P. C. L. 'Perceptions of the Family, Delinquency, and Emotional Adjustment among Youth', *Personality and Individual Differences, 29* (2000) 1169–78.

Goodyer, I. M., Cooper, P. J., Vize, C. M. and Ashby, L. 'Depression in 11–16-year old girls: The Role of Past Parental Psychopathology and Exposure to Recent Life Events', *Journal of Child Psychology and Psychiatry, 34* (1993) 1103–15.

Gordon, W. and Caltabiano, M. 'Urban-rural Differences in Adolescent Self-esteem, Leisure Boredom, and Sensation-seeking as Predictors of Leisure-time Usage and Satisfaction', *Adolescence, 31* (1996) 883–901.

Gordon, D. 'Formal Operational Thinking: The Role of Cognitive-developmental Processes in Adolescent Decision-making about Pregnancy and Contraception', *American Journal of Orthopsychiatry, 60* (1990) 346–56.

Gore, S., Aseltine, R. and Colton, M. 'Social Structure, Life Stress and Depressive Symptoms in a High School-aged Population', *Journal of Health and Social Behavior, 33* (1992) 97–113.

Graetz, B. 'Private Schools and Educational Attainment: Cohort and Generational Effects', *Australian Journal of Education, 34* (1990) 174–91.

Graham, M. 'Reported Family Dynamics, Sexual Abuse, and Suicidal Behaviors in Community Adolescents'. *Archives of Suicide Research, 2* (1996) 183–95.

Gray, J. A. 'The Psychophysiological Nature of Introversion-extraversion', *Behaviour Research and Therapy, 8* (1970) 249–66.

Gray, P. *Psychology*. (New York: Worth, 1991).

Greenberger, E., Chen, C., Tally, S. R. and Dong, Q. 'Family, Peer, and Individual Correlates of Depressive Symptomatology among U.S. and Chinese Adolescents', *Journal of Consulting and Clinical Psychology, 68* 7(2000) 209–19.

Greenberger, E., Steinberg, L. and Vaux, A. 'Adolescents Who Work: Health and Behavioral Consequences of Job Stress', *Developmental Psychology, 17* (1981) 691–703.

Griffin, C. *Representations of Youth: The Study of Youth and Adolescence in Britain and America* (Cambridge, UK: Polity Press, 1993).

Griffin, C. 'Representations of the Young'. In J. Roche and S. Tucker (eds), *Youth in Society* (London: Sage, 1997).

Grindstaff, C. 'Adolescent Marriage and Childbearing: The Long-term Economic Outcome, Canada in the 1980s', *Adolescence, 23* (1988) 45–58.

Grinder, R. 'The Promise of Critical Literacy for Irrelevant Adolescents'. In R. Muuss (ed.), *Adolescent Behaviour and Society: A book of Readings*, 4th edn. (New York: McGraw-Hill, 1990).

Gudjonsson, G. 'Crime and Personality', In H. Nyborg (ed.), *The Scientific Study of Human Nature: Tribute to Hans J. Eysenck at Eighty*. (Oxford and New York: Pergamon, 1997).

Haaken, J. and Korschgen, J. 'Adolescents and Conceptions of Social Relations in the Workplace', *Adolescence, 23* (1988) 1–14.

Hagstrom, T. and Gamberale, F. 'Young People's Work Motivation and Value Orientation', *Journal of Adolescence, 18*, (1995) 475–90.

Hamburg, D. 'Preparing for life: The critical transition of adolescence', In R. Muuss (ed.), *Adolescent Behaviour and Society: A Book of Readings*, 4th edn. (New York: McGraw-Hill, 1990).

Hamer, R. J. and Bruch, M. A. 'The Role of Shyness and Private Self-consciousness in Identity Development', *Journal of Research in Personality, 28* (1994) 436–52.

Hammarstrom, A. and Janlert, U. 'Nervous and Depressive Symptoms in a Longitudinal Study of Youth Unemployment – Selection or Exposure?', *Journal of Adolescence, 20* (1997) 293–305.

Hannan, D. F., O'Riain, S. and Whelan, C. T. 'Youth Unemployment and Psychological Distress in the Republic of Ireland', *Journal of Adolescence, 20* (1997) 307–20.

Hanson, R. A. 'Initial Parenting Attitudes of Pregnant Adolescents and a Comparison with the Decision about Adoption', *Adolescence, 25* (1990) 629–43.

Harper, J. and Ryder, J. 'Parental Bonding, Self-esteem and Peer Acceptance in Father-absent Male Adolescents', *Australian Journal of Sex, Marriage and Family, 7* (1986) 17–26.

Harris, J. and Liebert, R. *The Child*, 2nd edn. (Englewood Cliffs, NJ: Prentice-Hall, 1987).

Harris, J. L. J. 'Urban African American Adolescent Parents: Their Perceptions of Sex, Love, Intimacy, Pregnancy, and Parenting', *Adolescence, 33* (1998) 833–44.

Hart, G., MacHarper, T., Moore, D. and Roder, D. 'Aboriginal Pregnancies and Births in South Australia 1981–1982', *Medical Journal of Australia, 143*, (special supplement) (1985) S54–S56.

Harter, S. 'Developmental Perspectives on the Self-system', in P. Mussen (ed.), *Handbook of Child Psychology, vol. 4: Socialization, Personality, and Social Development*. (New York: John Wiley, 1983).

Harter, S. 'Processes Underlying Adolescent Self-concept Formation'. In R. Montemayor, G. Adams and T. Gullotta (eds), *From Childhood to Adolescence: A Transitional Period?* (Newbury Park, California: Sage, 1990).

Harter, S. Developmental Changes in Self-understanding across the 5 to 7 Shift. In A. J. Sameroff and M. M. Haith (eds), *The Five to Seven Year Shift*. (Chicago: University of Chicago Press, 1996).

Harter, S. The Development of Self-representations. In N. Eisenberg (ed.), *Handbook of Child Psychology: (vol. 3) Social, emotional, and personality development*, 5th edn. (New York: Wiley, 1998).

Hartup, W. 'Peer Relations', in P. Mussen (ed.), *Handbook of Child Psychology*, vol. 4. (New York: Wiley, 1983).

Hartup, W. 'Social Relationships and their Developmental Significance', *American Psychologist, 44* (1989) 120–6.

Hartup, W. and Stevens, N. 'Friendships and Adaptation across the Life span', *Current Directions in Psychological Science, 8* (1999) 76–9.

Havighurst, R. *Developmental Tasks and Education*, 3rd edn. (New York: David McKay, 1972)

Hayden, M. and Carpenter, P. 'From School to Higher Education in Australia', *Higher Education, 20* (1990) 175–96.

Hays, R. 'A Longitudinal Study of Friendship Development', *Journal of Personality and Social Psychology, 48* (1985) 909–24.

Hays, R. 'Friendship', in S. Duck (ed.), *Handbook of Personal Relationships: Theory, Research and Interventions*. (Chichester: John Wiley and Sons, 1988).

Heaven, P. 'Locus of Control and Attitudes to Authority among Adolescents', *Personality and Individual Differences, 9* (1988) 181–3.

Heaven, P. 'Adolescent Smoking, Toughmindedness, and Attitudes to Authority', *Australian Psychologist, 24* (1989) 27–35.

Heaven, P. 'Affitudinal and Personality Correlates of Achievement Motivation among High School Students', *Personality and Individual Differences, 11* (1990) 705–10.

Heaven, P. 'Personality Predictors of Self-reported Delinquency', *Personality and Individual Differences, 14* (1993) 67–76.

Heaven, P. 'Family of Origin, Personality, and Self-reported Delinquency', *Journal of Adolescence, 17* (1994) 445–59.

Heaven, P. 'Job-search Strategies among Teenagers: Attributions, Work Beliefs, and Gender', *Journal of Adolescence, 18* (1995) 217–28.

Heaven, P. 'Personality and Self-reported Delinquency: Analysis of the 'Big Five' Personality Dimensions', *Personality and Individual Differences, 20* (1996a) 47–54.

Heaven, P. 'Personality and Self-reported Delinquency: A Longitudinal Analysis', *Journal of Child Psychology and Psychiatry, 37* (1996b) 747–51.

Heaven, P. *Adolescent Health: The Role of Individual Differences*. (London: Routledge, 1996c).

Heaven, P. C. L. 'Perceptions of Family Influences, Self-esteem and Psychoticism: A Two-year Longitudinal Analysis', *Personality and Individual Differences, 23* (1997) 569–74.

Heaven, P. C. L., Caputi, P., Trivellion-Scott, D., and Swinton, T. 'Personality and Group Influences on Self-reported Delinquent Behaviour', *Personality and Individual Differences, 28* (2000) 1143–58.

Heaven, P., Connors, J. and Kellehear, A. 'Health Locus of Control Beliefs and Attitudes toward People with AIDS', *Australian Psychologist, 27* (1992) 172–5.

Heaven, P. and Furnham, A. 'Orientation to Authority Among Adolescents: Relationships with Personality and Human Values', *Personality and Individual Differences*, 12 (1991) 977–82.

Heffernan, R., Chiasson, M. A. and Sackoff, J. E. 'HIV Risk Behaviors among Adolescents at a Sexually Transmitted Disease Clinic in New York City", *Journal of Adolescent Health, 18* (1996) 429–34.

Hendry, L., Shucksmith, J., Love, J. and Glendinning, A. *Young People's Leisure and Lifestyles*. (London: Routledge, 1993).

266   *Bibliography*

Herr, K. 'Adoption vs. Parenting Decisions among Pregnant Adolescents', *Adolescence, 24* (1989) 795–9.

Hetherington, E., Stanley-Hagan, M. and Anderson, E. 'Marital Transitions: A Child's Perspective', *American Psychologist, 44* (1989) 303–12.

Heyneman, S. 'Continuing Issues in Adolescence: A Summary of Current Transitions to Adulthood Debates', *Journal of Youth and Adolescence, 5* (1976) 309–23.

Hill, M. E. and Augoustinos, M. 'Re-examining Gender Bias in Achievement Attributions', *Australian Journal of Psychology, 49* (1997) 85–90.

Ho, T. P., Hung, S. F., Lee, C. C., Chung, K. F. et al. 'Characteristics of Youth Suicide in Hong Kong', *Social Psychiatry and Psychiatric Epidemiology, 30* (1995) 107–12.

Hoffman, L. 'Childrearing Practices and Moral Development: Generalisations from Empirical Research', *Child Development, 34* (1963) 295–318.

Hogg, M. A. and Abrams, D. *Social Identifications: A Social Psychology of Intergroup Relations and Group Processes* (London: Routledge, 1988).

Holden, G. W., Nelson, P. B., Velasquez, J. and Ritchie, K. L. 'Cognitive, Psychosocial, and Reported Sexual Behavior Differences between Pregnant and Nonpregnant Adolescents', *Adolescence, 28* (1993) 557–72.

Holland, J. *Making Vocational Choices: A Theory of Careers.* (New York: Prentice-Hall, 1973).

Holland, J. 'Vocational Preferences', in M. Dunnette (ed.), *Handbook of Industrial and Organizational Psychology.* (Chicago: Rand McNally, 1976).

Hollander, E. *Principles and Methods of Social Psychology.* (New York: Oxford University Press, 1967).

Holsen, I., Kraft, P. and Vitterso, J. 'Stability in Depressed Mood in Adolescence: Results from a 6-year Longitudinal Panel Study', *Journal of Youth and Adolescence, 29* (2000) 61–78.

Hooker, K. 'Developmental Tasks', in R. Lerner, A. Petersen and J. Brooks-Gunn (eds) *Encyclopedia of Adolescence* vol. 1. (New York: Garland Publishing, 1991).

Hopkins, N 'Peer Group Processes and Adolescent Health-related Behaviour: More than "Peer Group Pressure"?, *Journal of Community and Applied Social Psychology, 4* (1994) 329–45.

Hughes, F. and Noppe, L. *Human Development across the Life Span.* (St Paul: West Publishing Company, 1985).

Huston, A. 'Sex-typing', in P. Mussen (ed.) *Handbook of Child Psychology (vol. 4): Socialization, Personality, and Social Development.* (New York: Wiley, 1983).

Imbimbo, P. V. 'Sex Differences in the Identity Formation of College Students from Divorced Families', *Journal of Youth and Adolescence, 24* (1995) 745–61.

Irion, J., Coon, R. and Blanchard-Fields, F. 'The Influence of Divorce on Coping in Adolescence', *Journal of Youth and Adolescence, 17* (1988) 135–45.

Jaccard, J. and Dittus, P. *Parent-teen Communication: Toward the Prevention of Unintended Pregnancies.* (New York: Springer-Verlag, 1991).

Jekielek, S. M. 'Parental Conflict, Marital Disruption and Children's Emotional Well-being', *Social Forces, 76* (1998) 905–35.

Jessor, R., Donovan, J. and Costa, F. *Beyond Adolescence: Problem Behaviour and Young Adult Development* (Cambridge: Cambridge University Press, 1991).

Joesoef, M. R., Linnan, M., Barakbah, Y., Idajadi, A., Kambodji, A. and Schulz, K. 'Patterns of Sexually Transmitted Diseases in Female Sex Workers in Surabaya, Indonesia', *International Journal of STD and AIDS, 8* (1997) 576–80.

Joffe, A. and Radius, S. 'Self-efficacy and Intent to Use Condoms among Entering College Freshmen', *Journal of Adolescent Health, 14* (1993) 262–8.

Johnson, A. E., Wadsworth, J., Wellings, K. and Field, J. *Sexual Attitudes and Lifestyles*. (Oxford: Blackwell Scientific Publications, 1994).

Jones, J. 'Outcomes of Girls' Schooling: Unravelling Some Social Differences', *Australian Journal of Education, 34* (1990) 153–67.

Kalmuss, D. 'Adoption and Black Teenagers: The Validity of a Pregnancy Resolution Strategy', *Journal of Marriage and the Family, 54* (1992) 485–95.

Kaltiala, H. R., Rimpelae, M. and Rantanen, P. 'School Performance and Self-reported Depressive Symptoms in Middle Adolescence', *Psychiatrica Fennica, 29* (1998) 40–9.

Kandel, D. 'On Processes of Peer Influences in Adolescent Drug Use: A Developmental Perspective', in R. Muuss (ed.), *Adolescent Behavior and Society: A Book of Readings*. (New York: McGraw-Hill, 1990).

Kashani, J., Carlson, G., Beck, N., Hoeper, E., Corcoran, C., McAllister, J., Fallahi, C., Rosenberg, T., Reid, J. 'Depression, Depressive Symptoms, and Depressed Mood among a Community Sample of Adolescents', *American Journal of Psychiatry, 144* (1987) 931–4.

Kashani, J., Rosenberg, T. and Reid, J. 'Developmental Perspectives in Child and Adolescent Depressive Symptoms in a Community Sample', *American Journal of Psychiatry, 146* (1989) 871–5.

Kaufman, G., Poston, D. L. Hirschl, T. A. and Stycos, J. M. 'Teenage Sexual Attitudes in China', *Social Biology, 43* (1996) 141–54.

Kazdin, A., French, N., Unis, A., Esveldt-Dawson, K. and Sherick, R. 'Hopelessness, Depression, and Suicidal Intent among Psychiatrically Disturbed Inpatient Children', *Journal of Consulting and Clinical Psychology, 51* (1983) 504–10.

Kerpelman, J., Pittman, J. F. and Lamke, L. K. 'Toward a Microprocess Perspective on Adolescent Identity Development: An Identity Control Theory Approach', *Journal of Adolescent Research, 12* (1997) 325–46.

Kidwell, J. S., Dunham, R., Bacho, R. A., Pastorino, E. and Portes, P. R. 'Adolescent Identity Exploration: A Test of Erikson's Theory of Transitional Crisis', *Adolescence, 30* (1995) 785–93.

Kiernan, K. 'Teenage Motherhood – Associated Factors and Consequences: The Experiences of a British Birth Cohort', *Journal of Biosocial Science, 12* (1980) 393–405.

Kinard, E. and Reinherz, H. 'Behavioral and Emotional Functioning in Children of Adolescent Mothers', *American Journal of Orthopsychiatry, 54* (1984) 578–94.

Kirkcaldy, B. and Siefen, G. 'Depression, Anxiety and Self-image among Children and Adolescents', *School Psychology International, 19* (1998) 135–49.

Kohlberg, L. 'A Cognitive Developmental Analysis of Children's Sex-role Concepts and Attitudes' in E. E. Maccoby (ed.), *The Development of Sex Differences* (Stanford, CA: Stanford University Press, 1966).

Kovacs, M. 'Affective Disorders in Children and Adolescents', *American Psychologist, 44* (1989) 209–15.

Kovacs, M., Beck, A. and Weissman, A. 'Hopelessness: An Indicator of Suicidal Risk', *Suicide, 5* (1975) 98–103.

Lackovic-Grgin, K. and Dekovic, M. 'The Contribution of Significant Others to Adolescents' Self-esteem', *Adolescence, 25* (1990) 839–46.

Lamb, M. and Elster, A. 'Adolescent Mother-infant-father Relationships', *Developmental Psychology, 21* (1985) 768–73.

Lamborn, S., Mounts, N., Steinberg, L. and Dornbusch, S. 'Patterns of Competence and Adjustment among Adolescents from Authoritative, Authoritarian, Indulgent, and Neglectful Families', *Child Development, 62* (1991) 1049–65.

Langlois, J. and Downs, A. 'Mothers, Fathers, and Peers as Socialization Agents of Sex-typed Play Behaviors in Young Children', *Child Development, 51* (1980) 1237–47.

Larson, R., Gillman, S. and Richards, M. 'Divergent Experiences of Family Leisure: Fathers, Mothers, and Young Adolescents', *Journal of Leisure Research, 29* (1997) 78–97.

Larson, R. and Richards, M. 'Daily Companionship in Late Childhood and Early Adolescence: Changing Developmental Contexts', *Child Development, 62* (1991) 284–300.

Lau, S., Nicholls, J. G., Thorkildsen, T. A. and Patashnick, M. 'Chinese and American Adolescents' Perceptions of the Purposes of Education and Beliefs about the World of Work', *Social Behavior and Personality, 28*, (2000) 73–90.

Lee, P. and Walters, W. 'Adolescent Primigravidae and their Obstetric Performance' *Australian and New Zealand Journal of Obstetrics and Gynaecology, 23* (1983) 3–7.

Leenaars, A. 'Psychological Perspectives on Suicide', in D. Lester (ed.), *Current Concepts of Suicide*. (Philadelphia: The Charles Press, 1990).

Lefkowitz, M. and Tesiny, E. 'Depression in Children: Prevalence and Correlates', *Journal of Consulting and Clinical Psychology, 53* (1985) 647–56.

Lester, D. 'Youth Suicide: A Cross-cultural Perspective', *Adolescence, 23* (1988) 953–8.

Lester, D. *Current Concepts of Suicide*. (Philadelphia: The Charles Press, 1990).

Levy, S. R., Jurkovic, G. L. and Spirito, A. 'A Multisystems Analysis of Adolescent Suicide Attempters', *Journal of Abnormal Child Psychology, 23* (1995) 221–34.

Liebert, R. and Spiegler, M. *Personality: Strategies and Issues*. (Pacific Grove, California: Brooks/Cole, 1990).

Lindsay, J., Smith, A. and Rosenthal, D. *Secondary Students, HIV/AIDS and Sexual Health* (Monograph Series No. 3) (Melbourne: Centre for the Study of Transmissable Diseases, La Trobe University, 1997).

Little, J. 'The Occupations of Non-college Youth', *American Educational Research Journal, 4* (1967) 147–53.

Llabre, M. M. and Hadi, F. 'Social Support and Psychological Distress in Kuwaiti Boys and Girls Exposed to the Gulf crisis', *Journal of Clinical Child Psychology, 26* (1997) 247–55.

Lobel, T. E., Slone, M. and Winch, G. 'Masculinity, Popularity, and Self-esteem among Israeli Preadolescent Girls', *Sex Roles, 36* (1997), 395–408.

Loeber, R. 'The Stability of Antisocial and Delinquent Child Behavior: A Review', *Child Development, 53* (1982) 1431–46.

Loeber, R. and Dishion, T. 'Early Predictors of Male Delinquency: A Review', *Psychological Bulletin, 94* (1983) 68–99.

Long, B. 'Parental Discord vs. Family Structure: Effects of Divorce on the Self-esteem of Daughters', *Journal of Youth and Adolescence, 15* (1986) 19–27.

Lynn, R., Yamauchi, H. and Tachibana, Y. 'Attitudes Related to Work of Adolescents in the United Kingdom and Japan', *Psychological Reports, 68* (1991) 403–10.

Maccoby, E. and Jacklin, C. *The Psychology of Sex Differences.* (Stanford: Stanford University Press, 1974).

Maccoby, E. and Martin, J. 'Socialization in the Context of the Family: Parent-child Interaction', in P. Mussen (ed.), *Handbook of Child Psychology (vol. 4): Socialization, Personality, and Social Development.* (New York: Wiley, 1983).

Mak, A. 'A Self-report Delinquency Scale for Australian Adolescents', *Australian Journal of Psychology, 45* (1993) 75–9.

Mak, A. 'Parental Neglect and Overprotection as Risk Factors in Delinquency', *Australian Journal of Psychology, 46* (1994) 107–11.

Manaster, G. *'Adolescent Development: A Psychological Interpretation.* (Itasca, IL: Peacock, 1989).

Mannarino, A. 'Friendship Patterns and Self-concept Development in Pre-adolescent Males', *Journal of Genetic Psychology, 133* (1978) 105–10.

Manzi, P. 'Cognitive Appraisal, Stress, and Coping in Teenage Employment', *Vocational Guidance Quarterly*, March (1986) 160–70.

Marcia, J. 'Development and Validation of Ego-identity Status', *Journal of Personality and Social Psychology, 3* (1966) 551–8.

Marcia, J. 'Identity in Adolescence', in J. Adelson (ed.), *Handbook of Adolescent Psychology.* (New York: Wiley, 1980).

Marsh, H. 'Effects of Attending Single-sex and Coeducational High Schools on Achievement, Attitudes, Behaviors, and Sex Differences', *Journal of Educational Psychology, 81* (1989) 70–85.

Marsh, H., Relich, J. and Smith, I. 'Self-concept: The Construct Validity of Interpretations based upon the SDQ', *Journal of Personality and Social Psychology, 45* (1983) 173–87.

Marsh, H. and Rowe, K. 'The Effects of Single-sex and Mixed-sex Mathematics Classes within a Coeducational School: A Reanalysis and Comment', *Australian Journal of Education, 40* (1996) 147–62.

Marsiglio, W. 'Teenage Fatherhood: High School Completion and Educational Attainment', in A. Elster and M. Lamb (eds), *Adolescent Fatherhood.* (Hillsdale, NJ: Lawrence Erlbaum, 1986).

Martin, G. 'Reported Family Dynamics, Sexual Abuse, and Suicidal Behaviors in Community Adolescents', *Archives of Suicide Research, 2* (1996) 183–195.

Martin, J. I. and Knox, J. 'Loneliness and Sexual Risk Behavior in Gay Men', *Psychological Reports, 81* (1997) 815–25.

Marttunen, M., Aro, H. and Lonnqvist, J. 'Adolescent Suicide: Endpoint of Long-term Difficulties', *Journal of the American Academy of Child and Adolescent Psychiatry, 31* (1992) 649–54.

Mason, G. *Youth Suicide in Australia: Prevention Strategies.* (Canberra: Government Printer, 1990).

Massad, C. 'Sex Role Identity and Adjustment during Adolescence', *Child Development, 52* (1981) 1290–8.

Masselam, V., Marcus, R. and Stunkard, C. 'Parent-adolescent Communication, Family Functioning, and School Performance', *Adolescence, 25* (1990) 725–37.

Masten, A. 'Developmental Psychopathology and the Adolescent', in R. Lerner, A. Petersen and J. Brooks-Gunn (eds) *Encyclopedia of Adolescence*, vol. 1. (New York: Garland Publishing, 1991).

Matthews, G. and Deary, I. *Personality Traits*. (Cambridge: Cambridge University Press, 1998).

McCauley, E., Mitchell, J., Burke, P. and Moss, S. 'Cognitive Attributes of Depression in Children and Adolescents', *Journal of Consulting and Clinical Psychology, 56* (1988) 903–8.

McClure, G. 'Recent Changes in Suicide among Adolescents in England and Wales', *Journal of Adolescence, 9* (1986) 135–43.

McClure, G. 'Suicide in Children and Adolescents in England and Wales 1960–1990', *British Journal of Psychiatry, 165* (1994) 510–14.

McCombs, A. and Forehand, R. 'Adolescent School Performance following Parental Divorce: Are there Family Factors that can Enhance Success?' *Adolescence, 24* (1989) 871–80.

McCrae, R. R. and Costa, P. T. 'Trait Explanations in Personality Psychology', *European Journal of Personality, 9* (1995) 231–52.

McKinney, J. and Vogel, J. 'Developmental Theories', in V. Van Hasselt and M. Hersen (eds), *Handbook of Adolescent Psychology*. (New York: Pergamon Press, 1987).

McLaughlin, C. S., Chen, C., Greenberger, E. and Biermeier, C. 'Family, Peer, and Individual Correlates of Sexual Experience among Caucasian and Asian American Late Adolescents', *Journal of Research on Adolescence, 7* (1997) 33–53.

McLoughlin, D. and Whitfield, R. 'Adolescents and their Experience of Parental Divorce', *Journal of Adolescence, 7* (1984) 155–70.

McMullen, R. 'Youth Prostitution: A Balance of Power', *Journal of Adolescence, 10* (1987) 35–43.

Mechanic, D. 'Adolescents at Risk: New Directions', *Journal of Adolescent Health, 12* (1991) 638–43.

Mednick, B., Baker, R., Reznick, C. and Hocevar, D. 'Long-term Effects of Divorce on Adolescent Academic Achievement', *Journal of Divorce, 13* (1990) 69–88.

Medora, N. P., Goldstein, A. and von der Hellen, C. 'Romanticism and Self-esteem among Pregnant Adolescents, Adolescent Mothers, and Nonpregnant, Nonparenting Teens', *Journal of Social Psychology, 134* (1994) 581–91.

Meeus, W. and Dekovic, M. 'Identity Development, Parental and Peer Support in Adolescence: Results of a National Dutch Survey', *Adolescence, 30* (1995) 931–44.

Meeus, W., Iedema, J., Helsen, M. and Vollebergh, W. 'Patterns of Adolescent Identity Development: Review of Literature and Longitudinal Analysis', *Developmental Review, 19* (1999) 419–61.

Mervielde, I., Deary, I., De Fruyt, F. and Ostendorf, F. (eds). *Personality Psychology in Europe*, vol. 7. (Tilburg: Tilburg University Press, 1999).

Meschke, L. and Silbereisen, R. 'The Influence of Puberty, Family Processes, and Leisure Activities on the Timing of First Sexual Experience', *Journal of Adolescence, 20* (1997) 403–18.

Meyerowitz, J. and Malev, J. 'Pubescent Attitudinal Correlates Antecedent of Adolescent Illegitimate Pregnancy', *Journal of Youth and Adolescence, 2* (1973) 251–8.

Michael, R. T., Gagnon, J. H., Laumann, E. O. and Kolata, G. *Sex in America*. (Boston: Little, Brown, 1994).

Miller, B. and Dyk, P. 'Sexuality', In P. Tolan and B. Cohler (eds.), *Handbook of Clinical Research and Practice with Adolescents* (New York: John Wiley & Sons, 1993).

Miller, B. and Moore, K. 'Adolescent Sexual Behavior, Pregnancy, and Parenting: Research through the 1980s', *Journal of Marriage and the Family, 52* (1990) 1025–44.

Miller, C. L., Miceli, P. J., Whitman, T. L. and Borkowski, J. G. 'Cognitive Readiness to Parent and Intellectual-emotional Development in Children of Adolescent Mothers', *Developmental Psychology, 32,* (1996) 533–41.

Miller, P. H. *Theories of Developmental Psychology* (3rd edn). (New York: W. H. Freeman and Co., 1993).

Minkoff, K., Bergman, E., Beck, A. and Beck, R. 'Hopelessness, Depression, and Attempted Suicide', *American Journal of Psychiatry, 130* (1973) 455–9.

Mitchell, K. and Wellings, K. 'First Sexual Intercourse: Anticipation and Communication. Interviews with Young People in England', *Journal of Adolescence, 21* (1998) 717–26.

Mohr, S., Preisig, M., Fenton, B. T. and Ferrero, F. 'Validation of the French Version of the Parental Bonding Instrument in Adults', *Personality and Individual Differences, 26* (1999) 1065–74.

Mok, M. and Flynn, M. 'Quality of School Life and Students' Achievement in the HSC: A Multilevel Analysis', *Australian Journal of Education, 41* (1997) 169–88.

Montemayor, R. and Eisen, M. 'The Development of Self-conceptions from Childhood to Adolescence', *Developmental Psychology, 13* (1977) 314–9.

Montgomery, M. J. and Sorell, G. T. 'Love and Dating Experience in Early and Middle Adolescence: Grade and Gender Comparisons', *Journal of Adolescence, 21* (1998) 677–89.

Moore, S. and Rosenthal, D. 'Adolescent Invulnerability and Perceptions of AIDS Risk', *Journal of Adolescent Research, 6* (1991a) 164–80.

Moore, S. and Rosenthal, D. 'Condoms and Coitus: Adolescents' Attitudes to AIDS and Safe Sex Behaviour', *Journal of Adolescence, 14* (1991b) 211–27.

Moore, S. and Rosenthal, D. *Sexuality in Adolescence*. (London: Routledge, 1993).

Moore, S., Rosenthal, D. and Mitchell, A. *'Youth, AIDS and Sexually Transmitted Diseases'* (London: Routledge, 1996).

Morgan, C., Chapar, G. N. and Fisher, M. 'Psychosocial Variables Associated with Teenage Pregnancy', *Adolescence, 30* (1995) 277–89.

Mueller, K. and Powers, W. 'Parent-child Sexual Discussion: Perceived Communicator Style and Subsequent Behavior', *Adolescence, 25* (1990) 469–82.

Murphy, D. A., Rotheram-Borus, M. J. and Reid, H. M. 'Adolescent Gender Differences in HIV-related Sexual Risk Acts, Social-Cognitive Factors and Behavioral Skills', *Journal of Adolescence, 21* (1998) 197–208.

Muuss, R. *Theories of Adolescence*, 5th edn. (New York: Random House, 1988).

Mynard, H. and Joseph, S. 'Bully/Victim Problems and their Association with Eysenck's Personality Dimensions in 8 to 13-year-olds', *British Journal of Educational Psychology, 67* (1997) 51–4.

Namerow, P. B., Kalmuss, D. S. and Cushman, L. F. 'The Determinants of Young Women's Pregnancy-resolution Choices', *Journal of Research on Adolescence, 3* (1993) 193–215.

Namerow, P. B., Kalmuss, D. S. and Cushman, L. F. 'The Consequences of Placing Versus Parenting among Young Unmarried Women', *Marriage and Family Review, 25* (1997) 175–97.

Neale, J. Children's Understanding of Their Parents' Divorces', *New Directions for Child Development, 19* (1983) 3–14.

Neapolitan, J. 'Parental Influences on Aggressive Behavior: A Social Learning Approach', *Adolescence, 16* (1981) 831–40.

Neville, B. and Parke, R. 'Adolescent Fathers', in R. Lerner, A. Petersen, and J. Brooks-Gunn (eds), *Encyclopedia of Adolescence*, vol. 1. (New York: Garland Publishing, 1991).

Newcomer, S. and Udry, J. 'Parental Marital Status Effects on Adolescent Sexual Behavior', *Journal of Marriage and the Family, 49* (1987) 235–40.

Newman, B. and Newman, P. *Development through Life: A Psychological Approach*, 4th edn. (Chicago: The Dorsey Press, 1987).

Newman, B. and Newman, P. 'Differences between Childhood and Adulthood: The Identity Watershed', *Adolescence 23* (1988) 551–7.

New South Wales Bureau of Crime Statistics and Research. *New South Wales Lower Criminal Courts and Children's Courts Statistics, 1990* (Sydney: Attorney General's Department, 1991).

Nigg, J. T and Hinshaw, S. P. 'Parent Personality Traits and Psychopathology Associated with Antisocial Behaviors in Childhood Attention-deficit Hyperactivity Disorder', *Journal of Child Psychology and Psychiatry, 39* (1998) 145–59.

Noller, P. and Callan, V. 'Adolescents' Perceptions of the Nature of their Communication with Parents', *Journal of Youth and Adolescence, 19* (1990) 349–62.

Noller, P. and Callan, V. *The Adolescent in the Family*. (London: Routledge, 1991).

Noller, P. and Patton, W. 'Maintaining Family Relationships at Adolescence', in P. Heaven and V. Callan (eds), *Adolescence: An Australian Perspective*. (Sydney: Harcourt Brace Jovanovich, 1990).

Nurmi, J. E., Poole, M. E. and Kalakoski, V. 'Age Differences in Adolescent Identity Exploration and Commitment in Urban and Rural Environments', *Journal of Adolescence, 19* (1996) 443–52.

O'Brien, G. and Feather, N. 'The Relative Effects of Unemployment and Quality of Employment on the Affect, Work Values and Personal Control of Adolescents', *Journal of Occupational Psychology, 63* (1990) 151–65.

O'Brien, S. and Bierman, K. 'Conceptions and Perceived Influence of Peer Groups: Interviews with Preadolescents and Adolescents', *Child Development, 59* (1988) 1360–5.

Ochiltree, G. *Children in Stepfamilies*. (New York: Prentice-Hall, 1990).

Offer, D. and Church, R. 'Adolescent Turmoil', in R. Lerner, A. Petersen and J. Brooks-Gunn (eds) *Encyclopedia of Adolescence* (vol. 2). (New York: Garland Publishing, 1991).

O'Koon, J. 'Attachment to Parents and Peers in Late Adolescence and their Relationship with Self-image', *Adolescence, 32* (1997) 471–82.

Olweus, D. 'Bully/Victim Problems in School: Facts and Intervention', *European Journal of Psychology of Education, 12* (1997) 495–510.

O'Malley, P. and Bachman, J. 'Self-esteem: Change and Stability between Ages 13 and 23', *Developmental Psychology, 19* (1983) 257–68.

Oppel, W. and Royston, A. 'Teen-age Births: Some Social, Psychological and Physical Sequelae', *American Journal of Public Health, 61* (1971) 751–6.

Orlofsky, J. and O'Heron, C. 'Stereotypic and Nonstereotypic Sex Role Trait and Behavior Orientations: Implications for Personal Adjustment', *Journal of Personality and Social Psychology, 52* (1987) 1034–42.

Pagani, L., Boulerice, B., Tremblay, R. E. and Vitaro, F. 'Behavioural Development in Children of Divorce and Remarriage', *Journal of Child Psychology and Psychiatry, 38* (1997) 769–81.

Pagani, L., Tremblay, R. E., Vitaro, F., Kerr, M. and McDuff, P. 'The Impact of Family Transition on the Development of Delinquency in Adolescent Boys: A 9-year longitudinal study', *Journal of Child Psychology and Psychiatry, 39* (1998) 489–99.

Paikoff, R. and Brooks-Gunn, J. 'Physiological Processes: What Role Do They Play during the Transition to Adolescence?', in R. Montemayor, G. Adams and T. Gullotta (eds) *From Childhood to Adolescence: A Transitional Period?* (Newbury Park, California: Sage Publications, 1990).

Paikoff, R. and Brooks-Gunn, J. 'Do Parent-child Relationships Change during Puberty?' *Psychological Bulletin, 110* (1991) 47–66.

Papini, D., Sebby, R. and Clark, S. 'Affective Quality of Family Relations and Adolescent Identity Exploration', *Adolescence, 24* (1989) 457–66.

Parke, R. and Asher, S. 'Social and Personality Development', *Annual Review of Psychology, 34* (1983) 465–509.

Parke, R., Power, T. and Fisher, T. 'The Adolescent Father's Impact on the Mother and Child', *Journal of Social Issues, 36* (1980) 88–106.

Parke, R. and Slaby, R. 'The Development of Aggression', in P. Mussen (ed.), *Handbook of Child Psychology* (vol. 4). (New York: Wiley, 1983).

Parker, G., Tupling, H. and Brown, L. B. 'A Parental Bonding Instrument', *British Journal of Medical Psychology, 52* (1979) 1–10.

Parker, J. and Asher, S. 'Peer Relations and Later Personal Adjustment: Are Low-accepted Children at Risk?' *Psychological Bulletin, 102* (1987) 357–89.

Parkhurst, J. and Asher, S. 'Peer Rejection in Middle School: Subgroup Differences in Behavior, Loneliness, and Interpersonal Concerns', *Developmental Psychology, 28* (1992) 231–41.

Parsons, J. T., Halkitis, P. N., Bimbi, D. and Borkowski, T. 'Perceptions of the Benefits and Costs Associated with Condom Use and Unprotected Sex among Late Adolescent College Students', *Journal of Adolescence, 23* (2000) 377–92.

Patterson, G., DeBarsyshe, B. and Ramsey, E. 'A Developmental Perspective on Antisocial Behavior', *American Psychologist, 44* (1989) 329–35.

Patton, W. and Noller, P. 'Unemployment and Youth: A Longitudinal Study', *Australian Journal of Psychology, 36* (1984) 399–413.

Patton, W. and Noller, P. 'The Family and the Unemployed Adolescent', *Journal of Adolescence, 14* (1991) 343–61.

Payne, M. and Furnham, A. 'Barbadian Adolescents' Views of the "Ideal" Family', *Psychological Reports, 67* (1990) 611–8.

Peiser, N. and Heaven, P. 'Family Influences on Self-reported Delinquency among High school Students', *Journal of Adolescence, 19* (1996) 557–68.

Pellegrini, A. D., Bartini, M. and Brooks, F. 'School Bullies, Victims, and Aggressive Victims: Factors Relating to Group Affiliation and Victimization in Early Adolescence', *Journal of Educational Psychology, 91* (1999) 216–24.

Perris, C., Jacobsson, L., Lindstrom, H., Von Knorring, L. and Perris, H. 'Development of a New Inventory for Assessing Memories of Parental Rearing Behaviour', *Acta Psychiatrica Scandinavica, 61* (1980) 265–74.

Perry, D., Kusel, S. and Perry, L. 'Victims of Peer Aggression', *Developmental Psychology, 24* (1988) 807–14.

Pete, J. and DeSantis, L. 'Sexual Decision-making in Young Black Adolescent Females', *Adolescence, 25* (1990) 145–54.

Petersen, A. 'Adolescent Development', *Annual Review of Psychology, 39* (1988) 583–607.

Petersen, A., Compas, B. Brooks-Gunn, J., Stemmler, M. et al. 'Depression in Adolescents', *American Psychologist, 48* (1993) 155–68.

Petersen, A., Sarigiani, P. and Kennedy, R. 'Adolescent Depression: Why More Girls?', *Journal of Youth and Adolescence, 20* (1991) 247–71.

Peterson, C. 'Disagreement, Negotiation and Conflict Resolution in Families with Adolescents', in P. Heaven and V. Callan (eds), *Adolescence: An Australian Perspective*. (Sydney: Harcourt Brace Jovanovich, 1990).

Petti, T. and Larson, C. 'Depression and Suicide', in V. Van Hasselt and M. Hersen (eds), *Handbook of Adolescent Psychology*. (New York: Pergamon, 1987).

Pettit, G. S., Bates, J. E. and Dodge, K. A. 'Supportive Parenting, Ecological Context, and Children's Adjustment: A Seven-year Longitudinal Study', *Child Development, 68* (1997) 908–23.

Phares, E. *Introduction to Personality*, 3rd edn. (New York: Harper Collins, 1991).

Pike, A., McGuire, S., Hetherington, E. M., Reiss, D. and Plomin, R. 'Family Environment and Adolescent Depressive Symptoms and Antisocial Behavior: A Multivariate Genetic Analysis', *Developmental Psychology, 32* (1996) 590–603.

Pistella, C. L. Y. and Bonati, F. A. 'Communication about Sexual Behavior among Adolescent Women, their Family, and Peers', *Families in Society: The Journal of Contemporary Human Services, 79* (1998) 206–11.

Pittman, R. 'Social Factors, Enrolment in Vocational/Technical courses, and High School Dropout Rates', *Journal of Educational Research, 84* (1991) 288–95.

Pleck, J., Sonenstein, F. and Ku, L. 'Adolescent Males' Condom Use: Relationships between Perceived Costs-benefits and Consistency', *Journal of Marriage and the Family, 53* (1991) 733–45.

Plomin, R. 'Environment and Genes: Determinants of Behavior', *American Psychologist, 44* (1989) 105–11.

Plomin, R. 'Genetics and Children's Experiences in the Family', *Journal of Child Psychology and Psychiatry, 36* (1995) 33–68.

Poole, M. *Youth: Expectations and Transitions*. (Melbourne: Routledge and Kegan Paul, 1983).

Poole, M. 'Attitudes to School, Careers and the Future', in P. Heaven and V. Callan (eds), *Adolescence: An Australian Perspective*. (Sydney: Harcourt Brace Jovanovich, 1990).

Power, C. 'Factors Influencing Retentivity and Satisfaction with Secondary Schooling', *Australian Journal of Education, 28* (1984) 115–25.

Power, T. and Fisher, T. 'The Adolescent Father's Impact on the Mother and Child', *Journal of Social Issues, 36* (1980) 88–106.

Prause, J. and Dooley, D. 'Effect of Underemployment on School-leavers' Self-esteem', *Journal of Adolescence, 20* (1997) 243–60.

Pritchard, M., Myers, B. and Cassidy, D. 'Factors Associated with Adolescent Saving and Spending Patterns', *Adolescence, 24* (1989) 711–23.

Rabin, D. and Chrousos, G. 'Gonadal Androgens', in R. Lerner, A. Petersen, and J. Brooks-Gunn (eds) *Encyclopedia of Adolescence*, vol. 1. (New York: Garland Publishing, 1991a).

Rabin, D. and Chrousos, G. 'Adrenal Androgens', in R. Lerner, A. Petersen, and J. Brooks-Gunn (eds) *Encyclopedia of Adolescence*, vol. 1. (New York: Garland Publishing, 1991b).

Radziszewska, B., Richardson, J. L., Dent, C. W. and Flay, B. R. 'Parenting Style and Adolescent Depressive Symptoms, Smoking, and Academic Achievement: Ethnic, Gender, and SES differences', *Journal of Behavioral Medicine, 19* (1996) 289–305.

Raine, A. 'Classical Conditioning, Arousal, and Crime: A Biosocial Perspective', In H. Nyborg (ed.), *The Scientific Study of Human Nature: Tribute to Hans J. Eysenck and Eighty*. (Oxford and New York: Pergamon, 1997).

Ralph, N., Lochman, J. and Thomas, T. 'Psychosocial Characteristics of Pregnant and Nulliparous Adolescents', *Adolescence, 19* (1984) 283–94.

Rao, U., Hammen, C. and Daley, S. 'Continuity of Depression during the Transition to Adulthood: A 5-year Longitudinal Study of Young Women', *Journal of the American Academy of Child and Adolescent Psychiatry, 38* (1999) 908–915.

Reicher, S. and Emler, N. 'Delinquent Behaviour and Attitudes to Formal Authority', *British Journal of Social Psychology, 24* (1985) 161–8.

Reinherz, H., Giaconia, R., Pakiz, B., Silverman, A. et al. 'Psychosocial Risks for Major Depression in Late Adolescence: A Longitudinal Community Study', *Journal of the American Academy of Child and Adolescent Psychiatry, 32* (1993) 1155–63.

Remafedi, G. 'Homosexual Youth: A Challenge to Contemporary Society', *Journal of the American Medical Association, 258* (1987) 222–5.

Remafedi, G. 'Homosexuality, Adolescent', in R. Lerner, A. Petersen and J. Brooks-Gunn (eds), *Encyclopedia of Adolescence*, vol. 1. (New York: Garland Publishing, 1991).

Rice, F. P. *Child and Adolescent Development* (Upper Saddle River, NJ: Prentice Hall, 1992).

Rice, F. P. *The Adolescent: Development, Relationships, and Culture*, 9th edn (Boston: Allyn and Bacon, 1999).

Richey, M. and Richey, H. 'The Significance of Best-friend Relationships in Adolescence', *Psychology in the Schools, 17* (1980) 536–40.

Rigby, K. 'Youth and their Attitudes towards Institutional Authorities', in P. Heaven and V. Callan (eds), *Adolescence: An Australian Perspective*. (Sydney: Harcourt Brace Jovanovich, 1990).

Rigby, K. and Densley, T. 'Religiosity and Attitude Toward Institutional Authority among Adolescents', *Journal of Social Psychology, 125* (1985) 723–8.

Rigby, K., Mak, A. and Slee, P. 'Impulsiveness, Orientation to Authority, and Gender as Factors in Self-reported Delinquency among Australian Adolescents', *Personality and Individual Differences, 10* (1989) 689–92.

Rigby, K. and Rump, E. 'The Generality of Attitude to Authority', *Human Relations, 32* (1979) 469–87.

Rigby, K., Schofield, P. and Slee, P. 'The Similarity of Attitudes towards Personal and Impersonal Types of Authority among Adolescent Schoolchildren', *Journal of Adolescence, 10* (1987) 241–53.

Rigby, K. and Slee, P. 'Bullying among Australian School Children: Reported Behavior and Attitudes toward Victims', *Journal of Social Psychology, 131* (1991) 615–27.

Robertson, J. and Simons, R. 'Family Factors, Self-esteem, and Adolescent Depression'. *Journal of Marriage and the Family, 51* (1989) 125–38.

Robinson, B. *Teenage Fathers*. (Lexington, Massachusetts: Lexington Books, 1988a).

Robinson, B. 'Teenage Pregnancy from the Father's Perspective', *American Journal of Orthopsychiatry, 58* (1988b) 46–51.

Robinson, R. B. and Frank, D. I. 'The Relation between Self-esteem, Sexual Activity, and Pregnancy', *Adolescence, 29* (1994) 27–35.

Rodriquez, C. and Moore, N. B. 'Perceptions of Pregnant/Parenting Teens: Reframing Issues for an Integrated Approach to Pregnancy Problems', *Adolescence, 30* (1995) 685–706.

Roscoe, B. and Peterson, K. 'Older Adolescents: A Self-report of Engagement in Developmental Tasks', *Adolescence 19* (1984) 391–6.

Rosenberg, M. and Kaplan, H. (eds) *Social Psychology of the Self-concept*. (Illinois: Harlam Davidson, 1982).

Rosenthal, D., Feldman, S. S. and Edwards, D. 'Mum's the Word: Mothers' Perspectives on Communication about Sexuality with Adolescents', *Journal of Adolescence, 21* (1998) 727–43.

Rosenthal, D., Hall, C. and Moore, S. 'AIDS, Adolescents, and Sexual Risk Taking: A Test of the Health Belief Model', *Australian Psychologist, 27* (1992) 166–71.

Rosenthal, D. and Smith, A. M. A. 'Adolescent Sexual Timetables', *Journal of Youth and Adolescence, 26* (1997) 619–36.

Ross, M. and Fletcher, G. 'Attribution and Social Perception', in G. Lindzey and E. Aronson (eds), *Handbook of Social Psychology*, vol. 2. (New York: Random House, 1985).

Rotheram-Borus, M. J., Reid, H., Rosario, M. and Kasen, S. 'Determinants of Safer Sex Patterns among Gay/Bisexual Male Adolescents', *Journal of Adolescence, 18* (1995) 3–15.

Rowe, C. *Outline of Psychiatry*. (Dubuque, Iowa: W. C. Brown, 1980).

Rowe, K. 'Single-sex and Mixed-sex Classes: The Effects of Class Type on Student Achievement, Confidence and Participation in Mathematics', *Australian Journal of Education, 32* (1988) 180–201.

Ruchkin, V., Eisemann, M., Hagglof, B. and Cloninger, C. R. 'Interrelations between Temperament, Character, and Parental Rearing in Male Delinquent Adolescents in Northern Russia', *Comprehensive Psychiatry, 39* (1998) 225–30.

Rutter, M. 'The Developmental Psychopathology of Depression: Issues and Perspectives', in M. Rutter, C. Izard, and P. Read (eds), *Depression in Young People: Developmental and Clinical Perspectives*. (New York: The Guilford Press, 1986).

Ryan, G. 'The Juvenile Sex Offender's Family', in G. Ryan and S. Lane (eds), *Juvenile Sexual Offending: Causes, Consequences, and Correction*. (Lexington: Lexington Books, 1991).

Sandven, K and Resnick, M. 'Informal Adoption among Black Adolescent Mothers', *American Journal of Orthopsychiatry, 60* (1990) 210–24.

Santrock, J. *Adolescence*, 4th edn. (Dubuque, IA.: W. C. Brown Publishers, 1990).

Savin-Williams, R. 'Gay and Lesbian Youth', in R. Lerner, A. Petersen and J. Brooks-Gunn (eds), *Encyclopedia of Adolescence* (vol. 1). (New York: Garland Publishing, 1991).

Savin-Williams, R. and Demo, D. 'Developmental Change and Stability in Adolescent Self-concept'. *Developmental Psychology, 20* (1984) 1100–10.

Savin-Williams, R and Small, S. 'The Timing of Puberty and its Relationship to Adolescent and Parent Perceptions of Family Interactions', *Developmental Psychology, 22* (1986) 342–7.

Schaefer, E. 'A Circumplex Model for Maternal Behavior', *Journal of Abnormal and Social Psychology, 59* (1959) 226–35.

Schaffer, B. and DeBlassie, R. 'Adolescent Prostitution', *Adolescence, 19* (1984) 689–96.

Scheinfeld, D. 'Family Relationships and School Achievement among Boys of Lower-income Urban Black Families', *American Journal of Orthopsychiatry, 53* (1983) 127–43.

Schneewind, K. 'The Analysis of Family and Parent-child Relations in a Systems-oriented Perspective', in B. Barber and B. Rollins (eds), *Parent-adolescent Relationships*. (Lanham, Maryland: University Press of America, 1990).

Scholte, E. M. 'Factors Predicting Continued Violence into Young Adulthood', *Journal of Adolescence, 22* (1999) 3–20.

Scholte, R. H. J., Van Aken, M. A. G. and Van Lieshout, C. F. M. 'Adolescent Personality Factors in Self-ratings and Peer Nominations and their Prediction of Peer Acceptance and Peer Rejection', *Journal of Personality Assessment, 69* (1997) 534–554.

Scott, R. and Scott, W. A. *Adjustment of Adolescents: Cross-cultural Similarities and Differences*. (London: Routledge, 1998).

Scott, W. A. and Scott, R. 'Individual Pathology and Family Pathology', *Australian Journal of Psychology, 39* (1987) 183–205.

Scott, W. A. and Scott, R. 'Family Correlates of High-school Student Adjustment: A Cross-Cultural study', *Australian Journal of Psychology, 41* (1989) 269–84.

Seddon, G. 'The Effects of Chronological Age on the Relationship of Academic Achievement with Extraversion and Neuroticism: A Follow-up Study'. *British Journal of Educational Psychology, 47* (1977) 187–92.

Seeman, M. and Seeman, J. 'Alienation and Learning in a Hospital Setting', *American Sociological Review 27* (1983) 772–83.

Shams, M. and Williams, R. 'Differences in Perceived Parental Care and Protection and Related Psychological Distress between British Asian and Non-Asian Adolescents', *Journal of Adolescence, 18* (1995) 329–48.

Sharabany, R., Gershoni, R. and Hofman, J. 'Girlfriend, Boyfriend: Age and Sex Differences in Intimate Friendship', *Developmental Psychology, 17* (1981) 800–8.

Shavelson, R., Hubner, J. and Stanton, G. 'Self-concept: Validation of Construct Interpretations', *Review of Educational Research, 46* (1976) 407–41.

Shaw, J. and Scott, W. A. 'Influence of Parent Discipline Style on Delinquent Behaviour: The Mediating Role of Control Orientation', *Australian Journal of Psychology, 43* (1991) 61–7.

Shek, D. T. L. 'A Longitudinal Study of the Relations Between Parent–Adolescent Conflict and Adolescent Well-being'. *Journal of Genetic Psychology, 159* (1998) 53–67.

Shek, D. T. L. 'A Longitudinal Study of the Relations between Parent-adolescent Conflict and Adolescent Psychological Well-being', *Journal of Genetic Psychology, 159* (2000) 53–67.

Shucksmith, J., Hendry, L. and Glendinning, A. 'Models of Parenting: Implications for Adolescent Well-being within Different Types of Family Contexts'. *Journal of Adolescence, 18* (1995) 253–70.

Shulman, S., Laursen, B., Kalman, Z. and Karpovsky, S. 'Adolescent Intimacy Revisited', *Journal of Youth and Adolescence, 26* (1997) 597–617.

Sibthorpe, B., Drinkwater, J., Gardner, K. and Bammer, G. 'Drug Use, Binge Drinking and Attempted Suicide among Homeless and Potentially Homeless Youth', *Australian and New Zealand Journal of Psychiatry, 29* (1995) 248–56.

Siegel, J. and Brown, J. 'A Prospective Study of Stressful Circumstances, Illness Symptoms, and Depressed Mood among Adolescents', *Developmental Psychology, 24* (1988) 715–21.

Sieman, J. R., Warrington, C. A., Mangano, E. L. 'Comparison of the Millon Adolescent Personality Inventory and the Suicide Ideation Questionnaire – Junior with an Adolescent Inpatient Sample', *Psychological Reports, 75* (1994) 947–50.

Simon, J. and Feather, N. 'Causal Attributions for Success and Failure at University Examinations', *Journal of Personality and Social Psychology, 64* (1973) 46–56.

Simons, R. and Murphy, P. 'Sex Differences in the Causes of Adolescent Suicide Ideation', *Journal of Youth and Adolescence, 14* (1985) 423–34.

Skinner, B. F. *Science and Human Behavior* (New York: Macmillan, 1953).

Slater, E. and Haber, J. 'Adolescent Adjustment following Divorce as a Function of Familial Conflict', *Journal of Consulting and Clinical Psychology, 52* (1984) 920–1.

Slee, P. T. and Rigby, K. 'The Relationship of Eysenck's Personality Factors and Self-esteem to Bully-victim Behaviour in Australian Schoolboys', *Personality and Individual Differences, 14* (1993) 371–3.

Smith, E., Udry, J. and Morris, N. 'Pubertal Development and Friends: A Biosocial Explanation of Adolescent Sexual Behavior', *Journal of Health and Social Behavior, 26* (1985) 183–92.

Sobol, M. and Daly, K. 'The Adoption Alternative for Pregnant Adolescents: Decision Making, Consequences, and Policy Implications', *Journal of Social Issues, 48* (1992) 143–61.

Spitz, A. M., Velebil, P., Koonin, L. M., Strauss, L. T. et al. 'Pregnancy, Abortion, and Birth Rates among US Adolescents – 1980, 1985, and 1990'. *Journal of the American Medical Association, 275* (1996) 989–94.

Sprinthall, N. and Collins, W. *Adolescent Psychology: A Developmental Review.* (New York: Random House, 1988).

Stacey, B. 'Economic Socialization in the Pre-adult Years', *British Journal of Social Psychology, 21* (1982) 159–73.

Stacy, A., Newcomb, M. and Bentler, P. 'Personality Problem Drinking, and Drunk Driving: Mediating, Moderating, and Direct-effect Models', *Journal of Personality and Social Psychology, 60* (1991) 795–811.

Stefanko, M. (1984) 'Trends in Adolescent Research: A Review of Articles Published in Adolescence: 1976–1981', *Adolescence, 19* (1–14).

Steele, B. and Ryan, G. 'Deviancy: Development Gone Wrong', in G. Ryan and S. Lane (eds), *Juvenile Sexual Offending: Causes, Consequences, and Correction.* (Lexington: Lexington Books, 1991).

Steinberg, L. 'Jumping off the Work Experience Bandwagon', *Journal of Youth and Adolescence, 11* (1982) 183–205.

Steinberg, L., Elmen, J. and Mounts, N. 'Authoritative Parenting, Psychosocial maturity, and Academic Success among Adolescents', *Child Development, 60* (1989) 1424–36.

Steinberg, L., Greenberger, E., Garduque, L., Ruggiero, M. and Vaux, A. 'Effects of Working on Adolescent Development', *Developmental Psychology, 18* (1982) 385–95.

Stelmack, R. 'The Psychophysiology of Extraversion and Neuroticism', In H. J. Eysenck (ed.) *A Model for Personality.* (Berlin: Springer, 1981).

Stoelb, M. and Chiriboga, J. 'A Process Model for Assessing Adolescent Risk for Suicide', *Journal of Adolescence, 21* (1998) 359–70.

Strelau, S. and Eysenck, H. *Personality Dimensions and Arousal.* (London: Plenum, 1987).

Strunin, L. 'Adolescents' Perceptions of Risk for HIV Infection: Implications for Future Research', *Social Science and Medicine, 32* (1991) 221–8.

Suominen, K., Isometsa, E., Henriksson, M., Ostamo, A. and Loennqvist, J. 'Hopelessness, Impulsiveness and Intent among Suicide Attempters with Major Depression, Alcohol Dependence, or Both', *Acta Psychiatrica Scandinavica, 96* (1997) 142–9.

Susman, E. 'Stress and the Adolescent', in R. Lerner, A. Petersen and J. Brooks-Gunn (eds), *Encyclopedia of Adolescence*, vol. 2. (New York: Garland Publishing, 1991).

Susman, E. and Dorn, L. 'Hormones and Behavior in Adolescence', in R. Lerner, A. Petersen and J. Brooks-Gunn (eds) *Encyclopedia of Adolescence*, vol. 1. (New York: Garland Publishing, 1991).

Talwar, R. and Lerner, J. 'Theories of Adolescent Behavior', in R. Lerner, A. Petersen and J. Brooks-Gunn (eds) *Encyclopedia of Adolescence* (vol. 2). (New York: Garland Publishing, 1991).

Tanner, J. 'Adolescent Growth Spurt, V, in R. Lerner, A. Petersen and J. Brooks-Gunn (eds) *Encyclopedia of Adolescence*, vol. 1. (New York: Garland Publishing, 1991).

Tanner, J. and Davies' P. 'Clinical Longitudinal Standards for Height and Height Velocity for North American Children', *Journal of Pediatrics, 107* (1985) 317–29.

Taris, T. W. and Bok, I. A. 'Parenting Environment and Scholastic Achievement during Adolescence: A Retrospective Study', *International Journal of Adolescence and Youth, 6* (1996) 223–44.

Taylor, R. D. and Oskay, G. 'Identity Formation in Turkish and American Late Adolescents', *Journal of Cross-Cultural Psychology, 26* (1995) 8–22.

Tedesco, L. and Gaier, E. 'Friendship Bonds in Adolescence', *Adolescence, 23* (1988) 127–36.

Tiggemann, M. and Winefield, A. 'The Effects of Unemployment on the Mood, Self-esteem, Locus of Control, and Depressive Affect of School-leavers', *Journal of Occupational Psychology, 57* (1984) 33–42.

Tremblay, R., Masse, B., Perron, D. and Leblanc, M. 'Early Disruptive Behavior, Poor School Achievement, Delinquent Behavior, and Delinquent Personality: Longitudinal Analyses', *Journal of Consulting and Clinical Psychology, 60* (1992) 64–72.

Trent, L. M. Y., Cooney, G., Russell, G. and Warton, P. M. 'Significant Others' Contribution to Early Adolescents' Perceptions of their Competence', *British Journal of Educational Psychology, 66* (1996) 95–107.

Tucker, J. S., Friedman, H. S., Schwartz, J. E., Criqui, M. H. et al. 'Parental Divorce: Effects on Individual Behavior and Longevity', *Journal of Personality and Social Psychology, 73* (1997) 381–91.

Tucker, S. 'Adolescent Perceptions of Communication about Sexually Related Topics', *Adolescence, 24* (1989) 269–78.

Udry, J. 'Biological Predispositions and Social Control in Adolescent Sexual Behavior', *American Sociological Review, 53* (1988) 709–22.

Udry, J. and Billy, J. 'Initiation of Coitus in Early Adolescence', *American Sociological Review, 52* (1987) 841–55.

Udry, J., Billy, J., Morris, N., Groff, T. and Raj, M. 'Serum Androgenic Hormones Motivate Sexual Behavior in Adolescent Human Males', *Fertility and Sterility, 43* (1985) 90–4.

Valliant, P. M. and Bergeron, T. 'Personality and Criminal Profile of Adolescent Sexual Offenders, General Offenders in Comparison to Nonoffenders'. *Psychological Reports, 81* (1997) 483–9.

Verschueren, K., Marcoen, A. and Buyck, P. 'Five-year-olds' Behaviorally Presented Self-esteem: Relations to Self-perceptions and Stability across a Three-year Period', *Journal of Genetic Psychology, 159* (1998) 273–9.

Violato, C. and Wiley, A. 'Images of Adolescence in English Literature: The Middle Ages to the Modern Period', *Adolescence, 25* (1990) 253–64.

Visher, J. and Visher, E. 'Stepfamilies and Step-parenting', in F. Walsh (ed.), *Normal Family Processes*. (New York: The Guilford Press, 1982).

Vondracek, F., Shimizu, K., Schulenberg, J., Hostetler, M. and Sakayanagi, T. 'A Comparison between American and Japanese Students' Work Values', *Journal of Vocational Behavior, 36* (1990) 274–86.

Wall, W. *Constructive Education for Adolescents*. (London: Harrap, 1977).

Wallerstein, J. 'Children of Divorce: Preliminary Report of a Ten Year Follow-up of Young Children'. *American Journal of Orthopsychiatry, 54* (1984) 444–58.

Walsh, F. 'Conceptualizations of Normal Family Functioning' 'in F. Walsh (ed.), *Normal Family Processes*. (New York: The Guilford Press, 1982).

Walters, L., Walters, J. and McHenry, P. 'Differentiation of Girls at Risk of Early Pregnancy from the General Population of Adolescents', *Journal of Genetic Psychology, 148* (1986) 19–29.

Warr, P. and Jackson, P. 'Adapting to the Unemployed Role: A Longitudinal Investigation', *Social Science and Medicine, 25* (1987) 1219–24.

Warren, K. and Johnson, R. 'Family Environment, Affect, Ambivalence and Decisions about Unplanned Adolescent Pregnancy', *Adolescence, 24* (1989) 505–22.

Waterman, A. 'Identity Development from Adolescence to Adulthood: An Extension of Theory and a Review of Research', *Developmental Psychology, 18* (1982) 341–58.

Watkins, D., Adair, J., Akande, A., Cheng, C. et al. 'Cultural Dimensions, Gender, and the Nature of Self-concept: A Fourteen-country Study', *International Journal of Psychology, 33* (1998) 17–31.

Wearing, B. 'The Impact of Changing Patterns of Family Living on Identity Formation in Late Adolescence', *Australian Journal of Sex, Marriage and Family, 5* (1984) 16–24.

Weaver, G. and Wootton, R. 'The Use of the MMPI Special Scales in the Assessment of Delinquent Personality', *Adolescence, 27* (1992) 545–54.

Weiner, B. 'A Theory of Motivation for Some Classroom Experiences', *Journal of Educational Psychology, 71* (1979) 3–25.

Wentzel, K. 'Relations between Social Competence and Academic Achievement in Early Adolescence', *Child Development, 62* (1991) 1066–78.

Wentzel, K 'Social Relationships and Motivation in Middle School: The Role of Parents, Teachers, and Peers' *Journal of Educational Psychology, 90* (1998) 202–9.

West, D. *The Young Offender*. (Harmondsworth: Penguin Books, 1967).

West, D and Farrington. D. *Who Becomes Delinquent? Second Report of the Cambridge Study in Delinquent Development*. (London: Heinemann, 1973).

Westman, J. 'The Impact of Divorce on Teenagers', *Clinical Pediatrics, 22* (1983) 692–7.

Wetzel, R. 'Hopelessness, Depression, and Suicide Intent', *Archives of General Psychiatry, 33* (1976) 1069–73.

Wetzel, R., Margulies, T., Davis, R. and Karam, E. 'Hopelessness, Depression and Suicide Intent', *Journal of Clinical Psychiatry, 41* (1980) 159–60.

Whitaker, D. J. and Miller, K. S. 'Parent-adolescent Discussions about Sex and Condoms: Impact on Peer Influences of Sexual Risk Behavior', *Journal of Adolescent Research, 15* (2000) 251–73.

Whitley, B. 'Sex Role Orientation and Self-esteem: A Critical Meta-analytic Review', *Journal of Personality and Social Psychology, 44* (1983) 765–78.

Wielandt, H. and Boldsen, J. 'Age of First Intercourse', *Journal of Biosocial Science, 21* (1989) 169–77.

Wilgenbusch, T. and Merrell, K. W. 'Gender Differences in Self-concept among Children and Adolescents: A Meta-analysis of Multidimensional Studies', *School Psychology Quarterly, 14* (1999) 101–20.

Williams, J. M. and Dunlop, L. C. 'Pubertal Timing and Self-reported Delinquency among Male Adolescents', *Journal of Adolescence, 22* (1999) 157–71.

Williams, S., Kimble, D., Covell, N., Weiss, L. et al. 'College Students Use Implicit Personality Theory instead of Safer Sex', *Journal of Applied Social Psychology, 22* (1992) 921–33.

Williamson, J., Karp, D., Dalphin, J. and Gray, P. *'The Research Craft: An Introduction to Social Research Methods*, 2nd edn. (Boston: Little, Brown and Co., 1982).

Wilson, S. and Medora, N. 'Gender Comparisons of College Students' Attitudes toward Sexual Behavior', *Adolescence, 25* (1990) 615–27.

Winefield, A. H. 'Introduction to the Psychological Effects of Youth Unemployment: International Perspectives', *Journal of Adolescence, 20* (1997) 237–41.

Winefield, A. and Tiggemann, M. 'Employment Status and Psychological Well-being. A Longitudinal Study', *Journal of Applied Psychology, 75* (1990a) 455–9.

Winefield, A. and Tiggemann, M. 'Length of Unemployment and Psychological Distress: Longitudinal and Cross-sectional Data', *Social Science and Medicine, 31* (1990b) 461–5.

Winefield, A., Tiggemann, M. and Winefield, H. 'The Psychological Impact of Unemployment and Unsatisfactory Employment in Young Men and Women: Longitudinal and Cross-sectional Data', *British Journal of Psychology, 82* (1991) 473–86.

Winefield, A. H., Tiggemann, M., Winefield, H. R. and Goldney, R. D. *'Growing Up with Unemployment: A Longitudinal Study of its Psychological Impact'*, (London: Routledge, 1993).

Winefield, A. H., Tiggemann, M., Winefield, H. R. and Goldney, R. 'A Longitudinal Study of the Psychological Effects of Unemployment and Unsatisfactory Employment on Young Adults', *Journal of Applied Psychology, 76* (1991) 424–31.

Winefield, H. and Winefield, A. 'Psychological Development in Adolescence and Youth: Education, Employment, and Vocational Identity', in P. Heaven (ed.) *Life Span Development*. (Sydney: Harcourt Brace Jovanovich, 1992).

Winefield, H., Winefield, A., Tiggemann, M. and Goldney, R. 'Psychological and Demographic Predictors of Entry to Tertiary Education in Young Australian Females and Males', *British Journal of Developmental Psychology, 6* (1988) 183–90.

Wood, J., Chapin, K. and Hannah, M. 'Family Environment and its Relationship to Underachievement', *Adolescence, 23* (1988) 283–90.

World Health Organization. *World Health Statistics Annual, 1995* (Geneva: World Health Organization, 1996).

Yates, L. 'Transitions and the Year 7 Experience: A Report from the 12 to 18 Project', *Australian Journal of Education, 43* (1999) 24–41.

Zarbatany, L., Hartmann, D. and Rankin, D. 'The Psychological Functions of Preadolescent Peer Activities', *Child Development, 61* (1990) 1067–80.

Zhang, L., Welte, J. W. and Wieczorek, W. E. 'Peer and Parental Influences on Male Adolescent Drinking', *Substance Use and Misuse, 32* (1997) 2121–36.

Zimiles, H. and Lee, V. 'Adolescent Family Structure and Educational Progress', *Developmental Psychology, 27* (1991) 314–20.

Zuschlag, M. K. and Whitbourne, S. K. 'Psychosocial Development in Three Generations of College Students', *Journal of Youth and Adolescence, 23* (1994) 567–77.

Index